ART IN NORTH CAROLINA

ART IN NORTH CAROLINA

Episodes and Developments, 1585-1970

by Ola Maie Foushee

CHAPEL HILL, NORTH CAROLINA

For
my beloved family
John, John Jr., June, Sally,
and
Chad

Foreword

This is a book that could not remain unwritten. It is a book that could not be unpublished. It is the creation of a woman of tenacity and purpose, a work of love by a North Carolina artist conscious of the cultural maturity developing about her. It is a canticle of praise for many persons of special ability, restlessly preoccupied with the state's own special form of enlightenment. It is the preface to the flowering of the visual arts to an extent as yet undreamed in North Carolina.

It seems that life in North Carolina has never been a monotonous affair, full only of ugliness. Since 1585, when John White came to the new world, painters, sculptors and the congenitally sensitive folk have had their talents in battle array against the forces of darkness! Every civilization develops its own unique artistic tradition, its own distinctiveness being the result of a multitude of forces, many of which are peculiar to that particular area, people, and culture. High on a list of such forces is the strong influence of dedicated, gifted individuals, some endowed with creative leadership and others with an insistent, driving desire to improve the quality of life. Many of these person-forces are named here, some of greater moment and some of lesser. But perhaps the greatest power of all comes from those loyal culturists *not* named in this book. The broad base of our visual art development is built upon the legislators who voted "aye" for art, the ever-constant memberships of state and local art societies, and the friends of North Carolina's many museums. We marvel, and rightly so, at the Blairs, the Phifers, the Arringtons, and the Humbers for their great leadership. We should marvel even more at those who did their smaller thing year after year. Like a coral atoll, our culture is a magnificent encrustation of labor upon labor, ideal upon ideal, and dream upon dream.

North Carolina can be justly proud of the present substance of the visual arts within its borders. In the brief twenty years of its existence, the youthful North Carolina Museum of Art has become one of the major art museums in the United States. Several cities and towns now have their own developing museums. Creative artists in the state are significant both in quality and in numbers. The annual North Carolina Artists Exhibition attracts hundreds of them. With such a great body of painters and sculptors available, sales galleries have begun to proliferate in evidence of an active, widespread growing group of collectors. The arts council movement is also strong in the state. Each city is proud of its widely supported organization and cities celebrate their centennials with concerts, exhibitions, and other cultural activities instead of frontier days horseplay. The media have also become art-conscious, many newspapers devoting full pages to news of creative activity. Educational television is building large audiences during prime time with art features such as the *Civilisation* films. One of the state's largest banks now employs fulltime college-trained artists to select works of art to be hung in its banking halls. An area of great progress and significant influence in North Carolina today is to be found in the extensive art curricula of our universities and colleges. A steady output of both art historians and studio artists becomes available annually to staff museum positions and to teach in the colleges and public schools. Surely, we are approaching the time when all school children will be exposed to the arts and become involved in them.

Both the federal and the state governments have recognized the need for greater quality in our lives and have become both enlightened and generous in the encouragement of culture. North Carolinians benefit greatly from federal grants for educational programs and for the purchase of works of art. Currently, under a government grant, art historians are researching long defunct Black Mountain College (1933–1956), finding that this unappreciated North Carolina activity has been one of the great germinating influences in American art of all types: painting, weaving, sculpture, poetry, music, the dance, architecture, etc. Federal grants usually require matching funds from foundations or other donors and, so, are doubly valuable! The state's day-to-day support of the arts has made necessary the establishment of a state cabinet officer to direct the activities of art, culture, and history. Its first director is the honorable Sam Ragan of Southern Pines who has long been a person-force influencing the arts. Additionally, the state of North Carolina is currently planning a multi-million dollar new home for the North Carolina Museum of Art and rumor suggests that it may become a complex developed not only for the art museum but also for the symphony and other cultural activities. All of this is testimony that culture in North Carolina is healthy, young and vigorous, with promise of a great future!

Mrs. Foushee's exciting and interesting account of 400 years of cultural development is not an epitaph of a glorious period. One knows that this is not the prelude to decadency, not the end of it all, and "the rest is *not* silence." It seems clear that we stand, instead, on a threshold looking into an era of growth and development in the arts. The future is ours to guess at if not to see. For what purposes have we struggled? Why do we create, collect, preserve and exhibit works of art to the citizenry? Why do we educate and train our young in the arts? Is the culmination of our effort to bring design, order, and creativity into our lives to make it a part of our life styles? The answer must be that we are destined to bring as many North Carolinians as possible into a deep involvement with the arts not only as spectators but also as performers, so that we may develop a symbiotic relationship in art.

Mrs. Foushee's work is a preface to a vast, unfolding canvas. Hers is a record of the beginning; and this record challenges all North Carolinians to become involved in the arts and to do significant things for creativity in North Carolina. New leaders *will* come forth and new support *will* develop. Greater things yet undreamed *will* happen. Let us hope that Ola Maie Foushee will at some point in the future continue the story with volume two. But, if she does not, our prayer is that her crown of laurel pass to someone else in love with art, and with strong internal pressures, who will tell the world how the visual arts flowered in North Carolina!

FINLEY T. WHITE, *President*
North Carolina Art Society

Durham, N. C.
July 23, 1972

Preface

It is difficult for me to throw anything away. Consequently, by 1962 my studio was bulging with files of clippings, bulletins, catalogues, and other memorabilia on art in North Carolina. The accumulation stemmed from the early thirties before there was an art department at the University at Chapel Hill, when Margery Graves and I organized private art classes. Added to this was an accumulation of material from my weekly column, "Art in North Carolina," which for several years ran in most of the state's Sunday papers. House-cleaning was inevitable. But, "What to do with the material and yet save it?"

Reminded of the many letters and telephone calls I receive from people seeking sources of information on Tarheel art and artists, I decided to make a little book of the heap and share the information with others. "If I could write a column-a-week, why not a chapter-a-week?" I reasoned. Had I foreseen the vicissitudes ahead, I would not have announced in 1963 my intentions to write such a book.

The development of art in North Carolina has been episodal, and, consequently, difficult to record chronologically. Organizations come and go, and some reorganize under different names. Great strides have overlapped short backward steps; but each event has given impetus to further growth and at times projected us into world leadership. Philip Hanes has written of North Carolina as "a land of firsts," and some of these firsts are recorded here; notably, our North Carolina Museum of Art and its gallery for the blind.

North Carolina has many competent artists, and I meant to write more about them. The development of organizations, museums, and the teaching of art soon took precedence, however, as stepping stones to where we are today. To establish some criteria for selecting the few artists included, I chose as a measure their age, their inclusion in the Metropolitan Museum of Art, the Museum of Modern Art, or their international achievements. All had to be Tarheel-born.

Certainly there are errors and omissions, as I am neither a historian nor an enthusiastic researcher, but a Tarheel painter deeply enamored of every facet of Art in North Carolina—especially its artists—and most especially those laymen who create opportunities for artists to thrive. I hope my feeble efforts will inspire someone to continue the story.

Innumerable friends and artists have lent encouragement and given invaluable advice, among them Robert Burton House, Robert Lee Humber, Gregory D. Ivy, James Tucker, Lucy Cherry Crisp, Zoe Webster, John F. Blair, Kenneth Ness, Lynette Warren, Claire Newman, Mae Carmichael, Emma Cobb, John Allcott, Joseph C. Sloane, Beth Paschal, Claude Howell, Leonard White, Emily Pollard, William C. Fields, Lucy Hairston, Margery Daingerfield Howlett, Katheryn Kortheuer, Mrs. Harold Dwelle, Alice Steadman, Robert W. Schlageter, Le Grand Tennis, Jean Fonville, Hughes Fagge, and Arthur Collier, among others.

Dr. Louise Hall and Dr. Marianna Jenkins of Duke University and Billie Curtis of the University of North Carolina graciously supplied information on the Ackland bequest; Dr. Wellington B. Gray made available to me his study on college and university art departments, which helped me update information furnished by other art department heads around the state; to all of whom I am grateful. Dean Henry Kamphoefner of the School of Design in Raleigh was most generous with his time during interviews, and President William Friday's staff has been just a telephone away when data on colleges and universities have been needed.

For reading the entire manuscript during particularly busy schedules, I am especially indebted to Phillips Russell, Edwin Gill, Ben F. Williams, Sam Ragan, Mrs. Ray Wilder, J. O. Bailey, and Elsie Smith, all of whom did some editing and offered much encouragement. The courtesy and help extended to me by Mrs. Jane C. Bahnson and William S. Powell of the North Carolina Collection of the Louis R. Wilson Library, in person and by telephone, saved me many hours of research. And I never could have found the Governors' papers and other historical data in the Department of Archives and History, but for the kindness of Mrs. Ellen McGrew.

R. Philip Hanes has supported my writing from the time I began my art column in 1958. His faith was manifested throughout the ten years of "off and on" writing of this book by the material he continued to furnish, particularly on the Arts Councils. My bibles of reference have been the little *History of the North Carolina State Art Society*, written by Lucy Cherry Crisp in 1956, and Hugh T. Lefler's *North Carolina, the History of a Southern State*. Charles Stanford, director of the North Carolina Museum of Art, and Ben Williams, its Curator of Art, and their staff, have always been available for discussion.

For designing and editorial assistance, I am deeply grateful to Moreland Hogan of Chapel Hill, North Carolina.

My husband's enduring patience with my frustrations and worries over the manuscript is, I hope, rewarded by the enjoyment he has witnessed when I could work uninterruptedly. He has been an excellent critic. For beautiful typing I am indebted to Mrs. Mae Neville, Mrs. Shirley Johnson, and Miss Mary Coley who also did some research for me and almost cured me of dangling participles. Many others whom I should thank will probably come to mind during a sleepless night, too late to enter here.

Ola Maie Foushee

Chapel Hill, N. C.

CONTENTS

ILLUSTRATIONS

[*following page 112*]

ART IN NORTH CAROLINA

CHAPTER ONE

The Beginnings

1. JOHN WHITE'S DRAWINGS

Art came to North Carolina with its first settlers in 1585. John White, who in 1587 would become the second governor appointed by Sir Walter Raleigh (and the grandfather of Virginia Dare), was an accomplished draftsman and water-colorist. He accompanied the early expeditions to "Virginia" to record through pictures life in the new land. His finely executed illustrations of the colonists, their villages, the Indians, and the exotic flora and fauna, provide a unique visual record of the unpropitious Roanoke Island settlements.

Whether the Dares carried some of these paintings with them when they disappeared remains as much a mystery as their own destiny. But when White returned to Roanoke Island in 1590, after revisiting England, he found only some ransacked chests he had left for safekeeping "with frames of some of my pictures and Mappes rotten and spoyled."

That any of White's art works survived, to be bought by the British Museum in London in 1866, is miraculous in view of their hazardous existence described by Paul Hulton of the British Museum: "Some were lost during White's hurried departure with his fellow colonists from Roanoke Island in 1585, thrown overboard with other baggage to lighten the boat in rough seas; others seem to have been ransacked by Indians after White as Governor had left them on the Island before returning to England in 1585."

After two hundred years of unknown ownership, White's drawings briefly emerged to view in 1788 when they were advertised for sale by a London bookseller, Thomas Payne the Elder, and bought for James Caulfield, the first Earl of Charlemont. In 1865, James Molyneux, the third Earl of Charlemont, sent them to Sotheby's auction house in London. Again they narrowly escaped destruction when a fire broke out next door to Sotheby's. Their edges were charred and they were saturated with water, "remaining for three weeks under pressure." Subsequently salvaged, they were bought by the dealer Henry Stevens, who later offered them to James Lenox, an American collector, and, finally, to the British Museum.

This collection might eventually have found its way to the North Carolina Museum of Art, if Stevens had kept them, or if Lenox had not turned them down—because, "he was still in the mood of the Civil War and probably, not having seen them, did not realize their purport for his already large DeBry collection," his biographer says.

Although the John White drawings were well known to historians and a number of them had appeared as illustrations in books, the collection was not published as a whole until 1964. Fruit of an idea originating with the Institute of Early American History and Culture in Williamsburg, *American Drawings of John White 1577–1590* was co-published in two volumes by the University of North Carolina Press and the British Museum. The volumes were planned and produced by the John White Committee of the British Museum, with William S. Powell, curator of the North Carolina Collection at the University of North Carolina, as the only American representative. The text was written by Paul Hulton and David Beers Quinn. Six hundred sets were printed and divided evenly between the University Press and the British Museum. One volume is of the drawings, faithfully reproduced from the originals, many in color; the other is devoted to descriptive material.

In April, 1964, a delegation of North Carolinians attended ceremonies in Washington, D. C., celebrating the publication of the White volumes, and presented a set of the books to Mrs. Lyndon B. Johnson for the White House. Later, through the efforts of Mrs. John B. MacLeod of Chapel Hill, a set of these books was placed in the American Collection of the National Society of the Daughters of the American Revolution Museum in Washington.

Several years prior to publication of the White volumes, Ben F. Williams, curator of the North Carolina Museum of Art, visited the British Museum in an effort to borrow the original drawings for an exhibition in Raleigh, but at that time British law did not permit the loan. Later, Williams learned that the law was relaxed and that the National Gallery of Art in Washington also wanted to exhibit White's art. He reopened negotiations with the British Museum and arranged for these works of art to return to North Carolina in 1965—over three and one-half centuries after they were taken from Roanoke Island. They were exhibited in Raleigh at the North Carolina Museum of Art from February 26 to March 14.

Following White's departure, little of significance is recorded about art in North Carolina until the early eighteenth century, when an upper class composed of high officials and "those who through luck or ability were gaining wealth and influence, began to play a definitive role in America's taste for arts and crafts." These later settlers brought fine paintings with them. They also supported private academies, and, as they became more firmly established, adopted the portrait as a status symbol. Of this aristocratic element, Virgil Barker writes in his book, *American Painting*: "In the absence of banks, handsome silver on a mahogany sideboard would give its owner economic reassurance as well as visual pleasure; and freshly painted likenesses hung on the paneled walls of withdrawing rooms would speak to the families even more strongly of their own social position."

2. MORAVIAN ARTISTS

When the Moravians came down from Pennsylvania in 1753 and established Wachovia in the Piedmont area of North Carolina, they brought with them some religious paintings by John Valentine Haidt. A German artist, Haidt joined the Moravian Brethren in London in 1740 and accompanied them to Bethlehem, Pennsylvania, in 1754, where he specialized in religious paintings and portraits until his death in 1780. Old Salem, Incorporated, owns a collection of his religious paintings as well as his portraits of Christian Thomas Benzien and Mrs. Benzien, reproduced in *The North Carolina Portrait Index* (1700–1860), published for the National Society of the Colonial Dames of America in the State of North Carolina.

Another Moravian, Ludwig Gottfried Von Redeken, is recorded as having "made a drawing of Bethabara as seen from the hill on which God's Acre lies," on August 18, 1787. And in 1824, Christian Daniel Wohlfahrt (Welfare), a bachelor Moravian Brother, went to Pennsylvania "on a visit and to perfect himself in the art of painting."

Welfare, as Wohlfahrt is referred to in the *Portrait Index*, studied under Thomas Sully and exhibited at the Pennsylvania Academy in 1825. He also collected paintings, and upon his return to Wachovia opened an art gallery (20′ x 36′, with windows in the roof) to "procure himself a moderate source of income." The first private art gallery on record in the state, it became a successful venture, judging from an advertisement in the *Weekly Gleaner*, Salem, May 12, 1829: "Exhibition. D. Welfare's Gallery of Paintings will again open on Monday . . . Some new Pieces will be added to the collection. Grateful for past encouragement, he would again solicit the attention of his friends and the public, and claim a share of their patronage."

Among the subjects he painted were John Gottlieb Herman, Bishop of the Moravian Church, and Mrs. Herman; Isaac Boner and his wife, Elizabeth; Matthew Rights, and Mrs. Rights with baby son Zacharias. Mrs. A. Shelbourne Johnson of Winston-Salem now owns the Herman portraits. Several others, including a handsome self-portrait and a portrait of Sully, are in the Wachovia Historical Society collection in Winston-Salem.

3. ITINERANT PAINTERS

Accessibility by water established New Bern as a waystop for itinerant painters, whose advance newspaper notices usually warned that their stay would be short. Mostly, they came from Philadelphia via Washington, as did F. Rabineau, who arrived in New Bern in March of 1797 "from Philadelphia but last from Washington." But M. E. Mynarts, in 1822, advertised himself simply as "Cast Away on the Hammock near Cape Look Out."

Mynarts not only did "striking likenesses," but "altered and retouched portraits to former lustre," and advertised in April, 1822, that he was "determined to reduce the price of his portraits, during the short time he will remain in Newbern." Then, on May 4, 1822, he set his departure date as of "the 21st instant."

Occasionally these itinerant painters extended their visits. Cornelius Schroeder remained in Halifax for two years, and in 1806 announced that he would, if desired, "attend families in the country," and that "a deduction in the price will be made to those who will have the Likenesses of their families taken." His price for a "correct likeness" was $15.00.

It was not uncommon for itinerant painters to subsidize their income by teaching, or doing miniatures. Occasionally a new method of painting was introduced. When John Crawley, portrait painter, arrived in New Bern in 1824, "having returned from the North," he solicited students. He moved to Raleigh in 1835 to open a school there "as soon as a class can be formed," and his advertisement in the *Raleigh Register*, December 1, 1835, established him as a "Portrait Painter and Professor of Drawing" who "for many years past, turned his attention to the Water Colour Department, and has taught in several of the Northern Cities. . . Oriental Tinting taught in eight Lessons."

A "New Style of Painting—Fancy, Bird, Fruit and Flower Painting, Taught in Six Lessons" was introduced by J. Herbert to the ladies and gentlemen of Milton, July 31, 1830. He promised that "those who have never taken brush in hand, can, at the expiration of the six lessons, paint with the same facility as those who have been practicing for years."

Among those who pushed inland were Charles Weindel who was painting miniatures in New Bern in 1825, in Raleigh January 13, 1826, and in Fayetteville in May of 1826; and B. Gardner, portrait painter, "in town for a few weeks," who was working in Fayetteville in 1828, in Salisbury in 1830, and in Wilmington in 1833.

Numerous other short-term itinerant painters roamed the Eastern Seaboard, as noted by James H. Craig in his book, *The Arts and Crafts in North Carolina, 1699–1840.*

Of more permanent residence was William Joseph Williams, originally from New York City, who painted portraits and miniatures in New Bern from 1804 to 1807. He went back to New York for ten years but returned to New Bern in 1817 and lived there the rest of his life. His portraits of Charles Pettigrew (Rector of St. Paul's Church at Edenton) and of Mrs. Pettigrew (Mary Blount) were owned by Charles W. Pettigrew of Asheville and are reproduced in the *North Carolina Portrait Index.*

A scholarly article in the 1967 *North Carolina Historical Review* establishes Williams as the nephew of John Mare, a portrait painter of Albany, New York, and of New York City. Entitled "John Mare: A Composite Portrait," it brings together as authors Helen Burr Smith of New York City and Elizabeth V. Moore of Edenton, who believe the Northern painter, John Mare, to be the John Mare who moved to Edenton in 1782, to become a business tycoon and a respected politician. John Mare of New York, however, began painting portraits around 1759 (his "Portrait of a Man," owned by the Metropolitan Museum of Art, was used for a cover illustration of the February, 1958, issue of the Book-of-the-Month-Club News), whereas the John Mare of Edenton, so far as is known, never painted a stroke after moving there. Also, the Colonial Dames failed in their search for portraits to find a single one by Edenton's John Mare. So, as the article concedes, "there are important questions still unanswered."

Jacob Marling and Other Artists in Raleigh

Soon after the completion of the first State House at Raleigh in 1796, Jacob Marling (portraitist, landscapist, teacher, and businessman) arrived there. By 1813 the first museum was established in the capital city with Marling as director, and, although he referred to it as the North Carolina Museum, old records indicate that he owned it. He probably leased the property at first, for it stood on a plot on Fayetteville Street which he bought from John Marshall and Joel Brown on January 4, 1819. An important feature of the museum was the Reading Room, "where most of the principal newspapers, literary works, reviews, etc., are filed." A notice he ran for some time in the *Raleigh Register,* beginning October 2, 1818, promised that "Natural and artificial curiosities, sketches, maps, drawings and paintings, rare coins and books will be thankfully received and added to the collection, with the name of the liberal donor appended to them. . . ."

The museum was short-lived, and Marling was soon free to devote himself to his painting and his hobby—cardplaying. His engraving of the first State House has special historical significance as a record of changes in its architecture before and after it was destroyed by fire in 1831.

The North Carolina Museum of Art exhibited Marling's paintings in March, 1964, and in the catalogue Ben F. Williams, curator, throws considerable light on this artist:

> The presentation of an artist such as Jacob Marling, who has gone unnoticed and unrecorded for more than a century and a half, has provided those of us who have worked on this exhibition with much pleasure as well as many problems. Marling never signed his paintings, or at least we have not found signatures on the works we have located; thus his work has to be attributed stylistically. Often works which in photographs seem to be by Marling, upon inspection of certain details in the originals indicate another hand. For instance, some of the works executed by James McGibbon have been attributed to Marling, since McGibbon was in Raleigh about 1825 and was obviously influenced by the work of Marling during that period.

In Jacob Marling's day, Raleigh became an important center in which to practice art. Marling's wife, Louisa, not only taught art in the Raleigh Academy but held private classes. She taught drawing and painting on velvet, paper, and satin and gave what was probably the first exhibition of art held in the state, for in June of 1820 the following announcement appeared in the *Raleigh Register*:

> The following young ladies, pupils of Mrs. Marling, to-wit— Catherine Clark, Mary Ann Clark, Adeline Allison, Margaret Allison, Eliza Lane, Martha Branch, Ann Fort, Rebecca Branch, and Julie Sanders, exhibited a great variety of flowers in pots and grapes, executed with a great deal of taste and beauty. . . . A landscape by Miss Ann Fort is entitled to particular distinction. Miss Sanders is a promising young artist.

Other painters and art teachers in Raleigh during this period were Mr. and Mrs. T. Sambourne from Philadelphia, who also taught in the Raleigh Academy, and the aforementioned James McGibbon, who "takes the liberty to inform the ladies and gentlemen of Raleigh and its vicinity, that his painting room is at Miss Susanah Schaub's, Fayetteville St., where specimens of his execution may be seen and orders executed on the most reasonable terms."

Raleigh attracted itinerant painters, too, and in 1837 William Garl Browne, Jr., from Leicester, England, found his way there. He produced so many portraits in North Carolina and Virginia that a century later he was to be characterized as "the Sully of the South." A later chapter tells of his portraits discovered on the University of North Carolina campus in Chapel Hill in 1942. Apparently he delivered his portraits in person, for Mrs. Lucy Phillips Russell, in her book, *A Rare Pattern*, quotes her father as saying, "I met on the train William Garl Brown who had with him an excellent portrait of Governor Morehead which he has just finished, and which was destined for the Dialectic Society."

Browne went to Mexico in 1847 to paint portraits of Zachary Taylor and other war heroes, later exhibiting them in Richmond and Philadelphia. He tarried for some time in Richmond, for the Valentine Museum of Richmond compiled a book entitled *Notes on Richmond Artists* that reproduces a letter from Browne's daughter, Mrs. Carolina Browne Harveycutter of Salem, Virginia, stating that her father came to this country with his parents when he was eighteen years old; that his father was also an artist and a member of the Royal Academy in London.

Browne sent paintings back to his native land, and was represented in an exhibition at the National Academy in 1840. He is alleged to have painted over two thousand portraits before he died at Buffalo, New York, in 1894.

While living in Raleigh, Browne designed North Carolina's first flag, adopted by the Constitutional Convention on June 22, 1861. Commissioned by Colonel John D. Whitford, a member of the Convention, this flag was official until 1885, when the Legislature adopted a new one.

J. F. G. Mittag also painted a number of portraits in North Carolina, one of which is of Dr. Samuel Williamson, president of Davidson College from 1841–1854. Commissioned by the Philanthropic Literary Society, whose minutes date the portrait as of 1842, it is owned by Davidson College. Mittag is listed in the *North Carolina Portrait Index* as "portrait painter, lawyer, physician." His multiple professions suggest that portrait painting was an avocation. A native of Hagerstown, Maryland, he died in Lancaster, South Carolina, in 1890.

Affluent Tarheels often went afield for their portraits, commissioning painters such as John Singleton Copley, Thomas Sully, Chester Harding, Henry Inman, William Dunlap, and all six of the Peales—Charles, Wilson, James, Raphaelle, Rembrandt, and Sarah. Doubtless, study of the works of these artists produced amateurs at home, and it is not too far-fetched to attribute some of the many portraits in North Carolina by "unidentified artists" as products of Tarheel painters.

4. EARLY ART INSTRUCTION

North Carolina was slow in establishing public schools, but private schools and academies were widespread, one having been established as early as 1705. Predominantly for boys, the academies taught reading, writing, arithmetic, astronomy, map-making, and trades. The "ornamental" branches—painting, drawing, and music—were chiefly the responsibility of schools for young ladies. A few small art schools thrived along the paths of the itinerant painters, well advertised in advance by their instructors:

On March 8, 1817 "Mr. Williams, Portrait Painter, Respectfully informs the Citizens of Newbern, and its vicinity, that he intends (with sufficient encouragement) to open an Academy of Drawing and Painting for the instruction of young Ladies and Gentlemen, in the elegant and useful art of Painting—elegant because it is an art which embraces all the objects of nature for its subject—expands and enlarges the mind, by filling it with ideas of whatever is great and beautiful. . . . To the fair sex, it is highly ornamental and useful; and to them, its utility needs no comment. . . ." In 1819, however, Williams, still painting portraits, announced that he "has removed to the House next to Mrs. Oliver's. . . . He will also take Pupils in Drawing and Painting."

Among the ladies who had painting schools were Mrs. Gerard, of New Bern, who on May 31, 1823 had the "honour to inform the Public in General, and the ladies of Newbern in particular that she will teach Painting on velvet, according to the new method, by which Scholars may obtain a perfect knowledge of the art in twenty lessons." And on July 27, 1827, the following announcement ran in the *Fayetteville North-Carolina Journal*: "Mrs. Beze Perry informs her friends and the public generally, that having returned from Columbia, South Carolina, and settled herself here, she will, on the 16th of this month, open a school for young Ladies—to teach them Music, French, Drawing & Painting on Paper, also, Painting on Velvet."

The early nineteenth century produced several academies seeking students and emphasizing the abilities of their teachers, as well as listing in their advertisements the subjects taught.

In 1806, the Greensboro Academy, already established, announced the addition of a Female Academy "under Miss Polly Paisley who is well qualified to teach all the useful and ornamental branches usually taught in this State, Music excepted." The famous Mordecai Female Seminary, opened in Raleigh in 1808, two years later announced that Alex C. Miller would be "Superintendent of Music, Drawing & Painting." In appreciation to "those Ladies and Gentlemen who have encouraged his endeavors," Miller advised that "few attainments afford more rational amusement, and tend more to excite Genius and amuse the Fancy, than the Pleasing Science of Drawing and Painting." Amusingly, an editorial in the *Raleigh Star*, March 15, 1810, at the end of the school term, praised the art work of Miller's students, but added: "His painters are copyists, but they copy only from the Volume of Nature." But the eighteen subscribers to the school, who attended the examinations that year, noted that "the Specimens of Painting really surpassed any expectations that could reasonably be indulged."

Among other academies of the day where art could be studied were the Salisbury Female Academy (1818), run by Miss Slater and Miss Mitchell, "two young ladies from New York"; and the Tarborough Academy (1826), at which Miss Ragsdale taught painting on "paper and velvet."

Almost half a century passed before a proliferation of colleges and junior colleges emerged to supplement or supplant the earlier academies and private schools; and art and music were usually combined into one department in these schools. Delicate watercolor paintings, painted chinaware, oil portraits, and imaginary or "copied" landscapes, emerged from this era, some of which today is being sought by collectors of "Americana."

Art in the colleges for young men rarely taught more than a smattering of art history, and those desirous of studying art as a profession found little opportunity in North Carolina until well into the twentieth century, when a real awakening to art developed in the state. But there were some cultural highlights, one of which was the action of the Legislature of 1815 to purchase a statue of George Washington.

5. THE CANOVA STATUE

In 1815 the General Assembly authorized Governor William Miller to purchase a full-length statue of George Washington, to embellish a rotunda in the State House, and appropriated $10,000 to pay for it. This event was amazing in the light of North Carolina's reputation as "poor, backward, divided—an unattractive place in which to live because of limited opportunity for advancement." So, it is more likely that patriotic excitement rather than culture motivated the action. The War of 1812 was over and Tarheels were fired with national patriotism. One of them was A. G. Glynn, whose exuberant speech during a Fourth of July celebration at Raleigh in 1815 projected the idea of a memorial statue of George Washington. Glynn's idea caught the imagination of North Carolina's citizens and political leaders and culminated in the 1815 Legislature's venture into art—setting a precedent for a gigantic repetition one hundred and thirty-two years later.

Governor Miller and a committee appointed by the Legislature were quick to seek a sculptor capable of executing this important work, and, much to their credit, sought advice from competent political leaders on the national level. They had no precedent to follow and no museums to consult. (The Boston Museum of Art, the Corcoran Art Gallery, and the Metropolitan Museum of Art did not then exist. Virginia, however, had erected the Houdon statue of Washington in Richmond.)

Senator Nathaniel Macon took hold of the project on the national level—also an amazing fact, since he was considered by John Quincy Adams as "a man of small parts and mean education . . . who votes against all claims and all new appropriations." Others held that Macon thought "his state of North Carolina ideal . . . as a meek state and just people with no grand notions or magnificent opinions." But this grand notion of his home state to honor Washington obviously caught his fancy, for he turned to Thomas Jefferson, the most knowledgeable man of his time, for counsel. Jefferson responded on January 22, 1816, with the suggestion that Antonio Canova of Rome be commissioned to do the statue from Carrara marble. He emphasized the fact that there was no sculptor in this country worthy of the job, nor was there a single marble statuary in the United States. He recommended Thomas Appleton, the American consul in Leghorn, as a suitable agent. His stipulations were that the style should be Roman, the size somewhat larger than life, and the price of from $7,000 to $10,000. Governor Miller followed Jefferson's suggestions to a letter. Appleton hastened to approach the sculptor, whose reply he conveyed to Governor Miller by letter September 20, 1816:

> In Truth, the numerous labors to which I have obligated myself, for many years to come, would seem to require that I should renounce the honor proposed to me; but my admiration for the genius who has performed such sublime deeds, for the safety and liberty of his country, compels me to make every effort to accomplish the statue you have proposed to me to execute; I therefore accept the commission.

Canova completed the more than life-size "seated" figure in 1820—a year before his death. He chose the seated position in the interest of proportions, as the rotunda was only sixteen feet high, and "I can give a greater force to my feeble genius," he wrote, "animated with the ardent zeal with which I am to render myself worthy of so great a subject."

The two-and-one-half-ton statue survived a rigorous journey from Rome to Leghorn whence the USS *Columbus* (sent to Italy for this purpose) brought it to Boston. Transferred to a coastal vessel, it floated down to Wilmington and then up the inland waterway to Fayetteville; there it was loaded on a wagon and drawn overland by twelve pairs of oxen to Raleigh, a sight that drew cheering spectators along the way. Unveiled in the State House on December 24, 1821, it was considered everywhere in America to be the finest work of art in the country, attracting such visitors as General Lafayette.

Perhaps the best description of the statue is the detailed one by Countess Albrizzi in *The Works of Antonio Canova*, illustrated by the English engraver Henry Moses, whose engraving doubtless played a vital role in the later discovery of Canova's original working model. In part the Countess said:

> In this fine composition Canova has not only maintained the dignity of his subject, but (warmed by admiration of the amiable qualities of this illustrious man) has also infused into the statue an expression of the gentleness and benevolence which tempered his severer virtues.

Meanwhile, in the surge of patriotic pride which made possible the commissioning of the statue of Washington for the Capitol rotunda, Governor Miller decided there should also be a portrait of the late General in both the House and the Senate rooms of the building. Accordingly, on January 11, 1817, he wrote to Daniel L. Peck of Philadelphia, asking that he recommend an artist in his city who could paint two portraits of Washington. Peck recommended Thomas Sully.

Mindful of the state's budget, but with an eye toward possibly obtaining one of the most famous portraitists of his day, Governor Miller wrote to Rembrandt Peale, on the same day he wrote to Peck, asking for his estimate for painting the two portraits. Peale's prices, quoted to Governor Miller by letter January 19, 1817, were obviously prohibitive: $1,500.00 for each portrait, if they were to be different; if they were to be repetitions, $1,500.00 for the first and $1,000.00 for the second. Sully's prices for both portraits, quoted directly to Governor Miller on June 3, 1817, were less than Peale's commission for one:

Historical Portrait 10 x 8	$600.00
Frame for ditto	200.00
Copy of Stuart's Washington 3 x 6	400.00
Frame for ditto	100.00
Total	$1,300.00

Sully had expressed a wish to make one full-length portrait of the General and another depicting him in some "well-known incident in the Revolutionary War—for instance, the passage of the Delaware preparatory to the Battle of Princeton." So he was commissioned by the state to copy the Lansdowne portrait of Washington painted by Gilbert Stuart and to paint the original of "Washington at the Passage of the Delaware."

Due to a misunderstanding about the size of the paintings, Sully painted "Washington at the Passage of the Delaware" on a canvas 12' 5" by 17' 3" instead of 10' by 8' as first approved. Too large for the space allocated for it, the painting was rejected by North Carolina and eventually passed into the possession of the Boston Museum of Fine Arts. The portrait he copied from Stuart was delivered on November 26, 1818.

When the Capitol burned on June 21, 1831, the statue of Washington was crushed in the holocaust, but, fortunately, Thomas Sully's portrait of George Washington was rescued.

Although a new cornerstone was laid on June 4, 1833, to begin construction of a new capitol, the building was delayed by politicians agitating for the state capitol to be moved to Fayetteville, and by continuous changes by the architects, Ithiel Towne and David Paton. Completed in 1840, a rotunda had been included with the hope of having the broken statue of Washington repaired and returned to its former prominence. And for a while it appeared that this hope would be fulfilled, for on June 27, 1831, Robert Ball Hughes, an English sculptor of note, wrote to Thomas Devereux of Raleigh expressing regret at the loss of the statue and offering to restore it for a sum that "would be trifling compared to the actual value of the work. . . . Whatever may be its mutilated state," he promised, "it can be repaired and I shall consider my visit to this country most fortunate should I be the means of preserving to the world the statue of your immortal Washington and the work of that great artist Canova."

A committee appointed by the Legislature of 1831 and headed by Judge William Gaston recommended acceptance of the offer and the Legislature appropriated $5,000 for the work. Hughes received several installments of the commission but a multitude of mishaps prevented his finishing it. During the period from February to September, when he was supposed to be working on the statue, he suffered a number of vicissitudes and at intervals requested $500 or $600 to tide him over. Once bad weather prevented his coming to North Carolina; his wife had a baby that occasioned another delay; and, finally, when he planned to bring the whole family South, an epidemic of cholera broke out in New York which prevented their planned visit to Raleigh.

Various newspaper accounts insinuated that Hughes was a thief who absconded with part of the statue and all of the money and was never heard from again, but records indicate that Hughes was a man of character who lived beyond his means and frequently overspent, and, due to a lively social life, often got behind with his work. In November an indignant Hughes wrote that the editor of the *Greensborough Patriot* "has accused me of running away . . . Tis true I have received $2,800.00 . . . but no more than entitled to by contract . . ."

Hughes contracted only to restore the old statue—not to execute a new one. To do this, the head of Washington had to be transported to Hughes's New York studio, and this posed difficulty. His correspondence indicates that he was dependent on others to get marble to him and that he worked accordingly. He finally moved from New York City to Dorchester, Mass., and, according to the *Dictionary of American Biography*, died in Boston in 1868 without finishing the statue.

Left with only the ruins of the statue as a reminder of the treasure that once brought pride and pleasure to North Carolina, and with most of the appropriation gone, the State consoled itself for a time with a bronze replica of Virginia's Houdon statue of Washington, of which Virginia allowed W. J. Hubard of Richmond to make six bronze copies. Raleigh acquired number two of the castings.

In 1907, R. D. W. Connor, secretary of the North Carolina Historical Commission, learned that Canova's original plaster model was "in a good state of preservation" in Canova's studio at Possagno, Italy. He immediately wrote to the Honorable Lloyd C. Griscom, American Ambassador to Italy, requesting that he investigate the possibility of getting a replica of the statue. On August 22, 1908, Robert C. Winthrop, Second Secretary of the Embassy, informed Connor "that the Ambassador is in receipt of a letter from Signore Tittoni, the Italian Minister for Foreign Affairs, stating that 'the Italian Government will take pleasure in having a reproduction of the cast made and is desirous of offering it as a present to the North Carolina Historical Commission.' "

The plaster cast of the statue reached Raleigh in January of 1910 and was placed in the Hall of History. Elated over this windfall, the problem was settled until 1921, when the State of Virginia presented to the British Empire a copy of its famous Houdon statue of Washington, to be set up in Trafalgar Square in London. This gesture prompted Samuel A. Ashe, a North Carolina historian, to write a public letter lauding the North Carolina Canova statue of Washington as infinitely superior to Virginia's Houdon statue. Stirred by this reminder, the General Assembly at a special session in 1923 appointed a Commission on the Reproduction of the Canova Statue of Washington, to investigate again the advisability of having the statue reproduced. But again, efforts were fruitless, due to impending economic stress. The Great Depression was under way.

Mr. R. O. Everett never relinquished his dream of another Canova statue and was constantly on the alert for other champions of the cause. At a Christmas dinner, 1962, he found one in Miss Annie S. Ramsey of Raleigh, a member of the LaFayette Chapter of the Daughters of the American Revolution. The Chapter was named for LaFayette in honor of his visit to the statue in 1825.

Ben F. Williams, curator of the North Carolina Museum of Art, had for years been intrigued by the history of the Canova statue, and in his research had unearthed a letter (long buried in the files of the Department of Archives and History), of November 4, 1838, from William Strickland to David Paton, Capitol architect, establishing that the rotunda was designed for replacement of the statue and that the stairways had been removed to the halls to make room for it. In 1957 Williams and his wife, Margaret, visited the Canova Museum of Possagno and were permitted to explore its attic. There they found a series of small studies Canova had used for the original statue in 1816 and which R. O. Everett had discovered in 1926. While in Possagno Williams arranged with the Instituto di Storia dell'Arte Fondazione Giorgio Cini di Venezia for photographs of these studies. He wrote a glowing account of this visit, illustrated with the photographs, for the 1957 Winter–Spring issue of the North Carolina Museum of Art *Bulletin*.

Concomitantly, Senator Hector MacLean, son of former Governor Angus McLean (father and son spell their names differently), became an advocate of the project. He had long wanted to augment his father's 1928 efforts to get "Washington" back into the Capitol, and at the persuasion of Miss Ramsey, Williams, and others, he introduced Senate Bill 381 to the 1963 General Assembly, "To Be Entitled An Act to Establish the George Washington Statue Commission." The bill was passed, thus revivifying the struggle of more than a century to regain the state's first significant work of art.

Following passage of the bill, Governor Terry Sanford appointed the following members to the Statue Commission: Hector MacLean, Chairman; R. O. Everett, C. Paul Roberts, Dr. Louise Hall, Ben F. Williams, John R. Jordan, Jr., the Honorable Edwin Gill, Miss Annie S. Ramsey, Mrs. Ernest L. Ives, John A. Kellenberger, Dr. Joseph C. Sloane, and Mrs. Albert G. Edwards. North Carolina had two more governors before this group succeeded in its efforts—Governors Dan K. Moore and Robert F. Scott—but the major legislation and negotiations matured during Governor Moore's regime.

More delays followed, occasioned by disagreements with the Memorials Commission and the Capitol Planning Commission. One point at issue was Washington's attire—Senator John Robertson objected to the "Roman garb" of the statue, "reposing in the rotunda." Senator MacLean countered that changing the statue would be "like putting Whistler's Mother in a miniskirt." Another group objected to the supposed disproportion between the statue and the rotunda.

With all hurdles cleared, Ben F. Williams was enabled to conclude arrangements with Professor Romano Vio of the University of Venice to oversee the recarving of the statue by Mario Cacciatori.

On May 13, 1970, the "new George Washington" arrived in Raleigh— by trailer instead of an ox-drawn wagon. Ceremonies followed as closely as possible those of Christmas Eve, 1821, with the statue being escorted by various local military units. After speeches and a salute from the Hillsborough Light Rifles, it was installed in the rotunda of the State House, a symbol not only of the young state's patriotic fervor but of the older state's dogged determination to restore a part of its artistic heritage.

CHAPTER TWO

Organizing

1. THE AWAKENING

North Carolina was a veritable wasteland during the first quarter of the twentieth century so far as art for the public existed. There were few public places devoted to the display of art objects and all state-owned works of art were housed in various state buildings or in the museums of natural or state history. A few colleges and normal schools, as mentioned earlier, were teaching young ladies to paint landscapes, still life, china-ware, and portraits, and no doubt had small exhibition spaces; but nothing existed on the state level.

Louis Round Wilson, in writing of this period, reminds us that "In 1900 North Carolina was far from having regained the economic status it had reached in the 1850's and it had not broken the benumbing spell which defeat in war and the results of Reconstruction had cast over its former leaders. But the State was looking up financially." In this prevailing financial situation the state valiantly expressed its cultural conscience in the occasional acquisition of portraits, sculptures, and monuments honoring its great: In 1903 a monument of Zebulon Baird Vance by Henry J. Ellicott was erected on the Capitol grounds; a monument to Charles D. McIver by Wellington Ruckstuhl followed in 1911; a monument to the Women of the Confederacy by Henry Augustus Lukeman was erected in 1915; and the Charles Brantley Aycock monument (1924) has a bronze plaque of quotations from his speeches. Four busts sculptured by F. Wellington Ruckstuhl between 1900 and 1912 are displayed in niches on the first floor rotunda of the Capitol in Raleigh. Represented are John Motley

Morehead, governor from 1841 to 1845; William A. Graham, governor from 1845–1849 and Secretary of the Navy 1850–1853; Samuel Johnson, governor from 1787–1789 and first United States senator from North Carolina; and Matt W. Ransom, Confederate General, United States Senator, and Minister to Mexico. Of course, many monuments preceded and followed those listed above, but these are representative of this particular period. But more significant cultural fires were being kindled here and there.

Soon after the North Carolina Historical Commission was created by the General Assembly in 1903, some of its members and a few other people scattered around the state began to discuss the possibilities of a Museum of Art for North Carolina and to try through various means to stimulate public interest in the idea. Clarence Poe, brilliant young editor of *The Progressive Farmer*, as early as 1915 urged the appointment of a State Art Commission, and through his farm-oriented magazine did much to awaken children to an appreciation of art. He also influenced the State Board of Agriculture to appropriate funds to buy reproductions of famous pictures relating to country life, to be placed in the schools.

Women of social distinction such as Mrs. Katherine Pendleton Arrington of Warrenton, Mrs. Harold Dwelle of Charlotte, Mrs. Henry London of Raleigh, and Mrs. Henry J. MacMillan of Wilmington, to name a few, were visiting museums in larger cities and in Europe and sharing their experiences on the local level; sowing cultural seed that would blossom later. But it was John J. Blair, head of Schoolhouse Planning for North Carolina, and Robert Burton House, then Secretary of the North Carolina Historical Commission (both members of the State Literary and Historical Association), who in 1924 took the first compelling steps toward developing such a Museum by initiating the idea of a state art organization to sponsor it.

2. THE NORTH CAROLINA
STATE ART SOCIETY

The North Carolina State Art Society, formally organized in 1925, made an immediate cultural impact that has endured for a half century. From its inception its leaders have been forceful advocates of better art for the state and proponents of a museum in which to house its own collections and attract other important collections. Its history is inextricably interwoven with the history of the North Carolina Museum of Art, recorded later in the chapter on Museums.

The Art Society is an outgrowth of the North Carolina Literary and Historical Association formed in 1912. Robert Burton House, secretary of the "Lit and Hist" association, as the group was affectionately called, was among those particularly sensitive to a lack of leadership in the arts in North Carolina. He also felt that the Historical group was becoming "set and stodgy" and needed to develop more new branches, besides the recently formed North Carolina Folk-Lore Society. As he said later, "It seemed to me that Poetry and Art interests were ready to organize." Accordingly, House suggested a poetry society and an art society to the Literary and Historical Association. The proposed poetry society met with little response, so he concentrated on the art society.

Before the annual meeting of the Literary and Historical Association in late 1924, House enlisted the aid of John J. Blair, head of Schoolhouse Planning (now the State Department of Public Instruction), and proposed an informal meeting of art-interested people. He already had consulted Mrs. Elizabeth H. Winnfree, restorer of historical documents for the Historical Commission, who suggested that "we get socially active and public spirited women into it." He also found his "two chief advisers," Mrs. R. L. McMillan and Clarence Poe, the young editor of *The Progressive Farmer*, interested in the idea. All agreed that "John Blair had the interest in art and the diplomacy to nurse things along until interest consolidated."

Interest in a Fine Arts group was immediate, for House selected his supporters with great forethought. Several of those who gathered for that organizational meeting devoted the remainder of their lives to the betterment of art in North Carolina. Present were Mrs. Henry London, Mrs. Katherine Pendleton Arrington, Mrs. R. L. McMillan, Clarence Poe, Robert B. House, Miss Mary Hilliard Hinton, Miss Carrie Jackson, W. L. Polk, Judge R. W. Winston, and John J. Blair, who was elected president. Mrs. H. M. London was elected secretary and treasurer.

The State Literary and Historical Association approved the Fine Arts Society as a new branch at its 1924 annual meeting and authorized the preparation of a constitution and by-laws under that name. At a meeting on December 6, however, the name of the Fine Arts Society was changed to the North Carolina State Art Society, and its first action was endorsement of a museum of art. Mrs. Arrington reported a fund of $1,000 already contributed for procuring art works, doubtless her own contribution. Poe, ever interested in raising the cultural interests of rural children, reported another $1,000 donated by the Agricultural Society, to be duplicated by funds raised in the rural schools for the purchase of paintings depicting rural life, to be hung in those schools.

House soon left Raleigh to join the faculty at the University of North Carolina at Chapel Hill, and his identity as founder of the Art Society became overshadowed by his other fine contributions to the state. Now Chancellor Emeritus of the University of North Carolina at Chapel Hill, he is typically modest about his early role in the Art Society: "If you study my career, you will find the word 'Helper' just about sums it up. Mary Lee McMillan is the living person who deserves more honor for the beginning than I do," he said in a recent letter. Although House soon retired from the Art Society as an active member, his brain child flourished and realized many times over the basic goals adopted in its Constitution:

1. To promote an interest in providing a State Art Museum in Raleigh, the Capital City of the State;
2. To secure by gift, loan, or purchase objects of art which shall form a permanent collection;
3. To aid in the establishment of Art Museums and Art libraries throughout the State;
4. To aid in securing loan exhibitions and collections of paintings and objects of art for different towns and communities in North Carolina;
5. To secure speakers and lecturers of recognized ability upon subjects pertaining to art appreciation.

The State Art Society held its first annual meeting conjointly with the annual meeting of its parent organization in 1925. It already had gained national attention as a cultural venture and was thus able to bring to North Carolina for this meeting an exhibition of important works of art from the Grand Central Galleries in New York City and to lure Homer Saint-Gaudens as its main speaker for the occasion. The paintings were hung in the parlors of Meredith College, then located on Blount Street in Raleigh, and Saint-Gaudens spoke to the group in the college auditorium that evening. The exhibition and Saint-Gaudens's speech were the first of similar annual contributions by the Art Society to the cultural life of the state.

Blair served as president of the Art Society only during its two-year gestation period, but in 1927 he was to become, vicariously, one of its greatest benefactors by securing the Phifer bequest.

The 1926 annual meeting of the Art Society marks its separation from the Literary and Historical Association and its start toward a prominence that has brought international fame to North Carolina more than once. Mrs. Katherine Pendleton Arrington was elected president, and her energetic leadership from the first made her name synonymous with that of the Art Society. "The group contained dynamic leaders, of whom Kate Arrington was from the first the most ambitious and the most energetic," House recalls.

A stately, sophisticated beauty, endowed with considerable wealth, charm, and ingenuity, Mrs. Arrington established liaison with the Knoedler Gallery and the Grand Central Galleries of New York City and the Robert Vose Gallery of Boston, all three of which lent to North Carolina distinguished exhibitions composed of such well-known masters as El Greco, Rembrandt, Ryder, and Eakins. Miss Leila Mechlin of the American Federation of Arts, an art critic of stature, became interested in Mrs. Arrington's endeavors and arranged for some of these exhibitions, which Mrs. Arrington as a patroness of the Art Society often financed personally.

The Art Society received its charter of incorporation on October 7, 1927, enabling it to receive gifts toward one of its major objectives—the founding of a State Museum of Art. The certificate of incorporation was signed by John J. Blair, Clarence Poe, A. W. McLean, W. N. Everett, Mrs. R. L. McMillan, Mrs. Ruth H. Moore, Josephus Daniels, E. C. Brooks, and Mrs. H. M. London, all of Raleigh; R. W. Winston and H. W. Chase of Chapel Hill; Gilbert C. White of Durham; Mrs. W. N.

Reynolds of Winston-Salem; J. I. Foust of Greensboro; F. L. Seely of Asheville; and K. P. Arrington of Warrenton.

With this illustrious group listed on its charter of incorporation, the Art Society immediately attracted gifts toward its future museum. Mrs. Arrington contributed the first gift, a painting by Gari Melchers, later adding four paintings by American artists, Coptic textiles, and numerous smaller items. Through her influence five paintings were given by John Gelatly, as was one by Miss Mary Tannahill of Warrenton. George Pratt, following a report made by Mrs. Arrington at an art meeting in New York City, selected sixty-seven items from his collection of ancient glass and gave them to her for the Art Society.

Art in the schools was emphasized by the Art Society from the beginning, particularly by Poe, Blair, and Mrs. Arrington, and in 1927 North Carolina was honored as the first state to win a national prize (a thousand-dollar painting) for having placed in its public schools five original paintings by notable American artists. Through a cooperative plan with the Grand Central Galleries, Mrs. Arrington offered $500.00 to each of the first five schools in the state that would match her gift and purchase a painting for its building. North Carolina not only won the prize; it was spotlighted by the Grand Central Galleries in a brochure entitled "How North Carolina is Obtaining Pictures for its Public Schools." The brochure contained essays by three North Carolina high-school students. Records of which schools bought paintings, the fate of the thousand-dollar prize painting, and the brochure have disappeared, but the paintings, wherever they are, must have increased in value many times over since 1927.

The crowning event of 1927 came to the Art Society in the form of a bequest which would greatly accelerate its progress toward a future museum. Robert Fullenwider Phifer, a native of Concord, North Carolina, who had resided in New York City for many years, bequeathed his large collection of art and considerable funds to the Art Society, partly through friendship with John J. Blair and partly because he "wanted to do something for art in North Carolina." Blair and Phifer had become acquainted around 1895, and, because of their mutual interests in golf and art, a friendship developed which lasted until Phifer's death in 1928. Phifer was a bachelor and, according to Blair, "the first golfer I ever knew."

"I saw him a number of times in Concord when I was on the Board of

Trustees of the Jackson Training School," Blair recalled when interviewed by a Raleigh *News and Observer* reporter for a story on the Phifer Collection, December 8, 1929. But it would appear from the following letter, dated June 28, 1927, that Blair had not yet discussed the Art Society with Phifer:

> Dear Sir: I have been buying pictures now for quite a number of years. I have about 75 oil paintings, some water colors, some etchings and some Japanese prints. I have been thinking of willing the collection to Concord or Charlotte—my native section. I have had some doubts, however, as to how they would be taken care of and shown—as neither of the towns has an Art Museum. I see from the *Magazine of Art* that you have an Art Society. Will you kindly let me know what your organization is? Is it a State institution? Have you a building? I will be very much obliged if you will give all the particulars. Would you have room to take care of and show such a collection. I am anxious to leave this collection to my native state somewhere. I am writing Charlotte about organizing an Art Museum. They do not seem to be too enthusiastic about it.

(The Mint Museum of Art was founded nine years later. One can only speculate as to the outcome of the Raleigh Museum had this collection gone to Charlotte.)

Blair replied to Phifer assuring him that through the Art Society there would be a place for his collection. Then, on October 13, 1927, Phifer wrote to Blair regarding a December exhibition of some of his paintings, adding: "I am very glad to get in touch with you again. As we go through life, I hope we will meet in the near future—to discuss the golf proposition." Blair immediately arranged an exhibition of a portion of the Phifer Collection at the 1927 State Fair, and later informed Phifer that "a whole booth was set aside for it . . . the show was a great success with over 25,000 visitors . . . the governing board of the Society was most grateful and the Governor himself enthusiastic." Phifer later sent down ten paintings for the December annual meeting of the Art Society, "to remain on permanent loan" should they arrive too late for this particular meeting.

Phifer was not well at this time and went to Battle Creek, Michigan,

for treatment and a possible operation. By now the two men were address-
ing one another as "My Dear Blair" and "My Dear Phifer," and some of
Phifer's letters expressed deep concern about the future of his collection.
Several of his paintings were on loan to the Calumet Club and the Salma-
gundi Club in New York City, where he held memberships, and fifty or
more of them were either hanging or stacked in his New York apartment.
Revealing a pathetic awareness that his time might be running out, he
wrote Blair from Battle Creek on December 28, 1927, that before leaving
New York he had put clauses in his will bequeathing his entire collection
to the North Carolina State Art Society, with additional funds, held in
trust, to become available to the Society under certain conditions. These
conditions involved four principal beneficiaries who were close relatives
and whose portions would come to the Art Society should they leave
no heirs.

When the collection arrived, following the death of Phifer on October
16, 1928, its full monetary value had not yet been determined, but it was
known that he had refused $5,000 for one of his favorites, "The Secretary
of the East India Society" by Hoppner. A portion of the money ($27,500)
came to the Art Society in 1941, and another portion ($300,000) came
later at the death of one of his heirs. Even then it could hardly have been
imagined that eventually the total legacy to the Art Society from Phifer
would be $1,416,599.22.

The Phifer paintings now belong to the North Carolina Museum of
Art—a gift from the State Art Society—but funds from the bequest are
administered by the Art Society and may be used only for the purchase of
art, never for salaries or other expenses. And only the interest may be used
for the purchase of art, unless otherwise voted by the Board of Governors
of the State Art Society.

The collection itself attests to Phifer's perceptivity as a collector and
remains a fitting memorial to this dedicated native son who, in the words
of Robert Lee Humber, "anticipated with confident assurance the birth in
North Carolina of a genuine interest in art and public support of an outstanding gallery." It also affirms the deep trust Phifer placed in Blair, who
personally supervised the care of the collection until his health failed in
the early thirties.

With five years of extraordinary achievement to its credit, several growing collections of art to be protected, and some monies to be invested, the Art Society requested the 1929 General Assembly to place it under state patronage and control. The Assembly passed favorably on the request, and although no appropriation of funds was made at the time, Section Four of the bill declared:

> The Board of Public Buildings and Grounds is authorized and empowered to set apart, for the exhibition of works of art owned, donated, or loaned to the State Art Society, Inc., any space in any of the public buildings in the City of Raleigh which may be so used without interference with the conduct of business of the State; and it shall be the duty of the custodians of such buildings to care for, safeguard, and protect such exhibits and works of art.

Also set forth in the bill were instructions as to government of the Art Society:

> The governing body of the North Carolina State Art Society, Inc., shall be a board of directors consisting of sixteen members, of whom the Governor of the State, the Superintendent of Public Instruction, the Attorney General, and the Chairman of the Art Committee of the N. C. Federation of Women's Clubs shall be ex-officio members, and four others shall be named by the Governor of the State. The remaining eight directors shall be chosen by the members of the Society in such manner and terms as that body shall determine.

The chairman of the North Carolina Federation of Women's Clubs has always been included as an ex-officio member of the Art Society board because of that organization's support of art in the state. Not only does the Federation sponsor open exhibitions with prizes among its members, but contributes purchase awards to the North Carolina Artists' Annual Competition.

When the State assumed "patronage and control" of the Art Society, it provided a temporary art museum (actually just a gallery) in the State Agricultural Building. The gallery opened on February 26, 1929, with an exhibition of paintings from the Phifer bequest and other gift items in the

Art Society's collection. The following December, when the board of directors met for the first time under its new official status, the Society's future seemed assured. A glowing report of the Society's first five years, written in 1931 but unsigned, referred to a proposed "Ten Year Plan," and stated that the early dreams of a State Art Museum had become "a substantial certainty, with only the exact time of its inauguration indefinite."

Then, as later recorded by Miss Lucy Cherry Crisp, "over the bright prospects promised by the encouraging events of 1929, there fell a great dimness, the dimness of the Depression, and the idea of a State Art Museum seemed likely again to become a far distant dream." With work toward a museum temporarily set aside, the Art Society concentrated on promoting Tarheel artists and improving art in the schools. It invited the newly organized North Carolina Association of Professional Artists, more fully covered in another part of this book, to exhibit at several of its annual meetings in Raleigh. At the 1932 board meeting, it also appointed a committee "to write up the work of the North Carolina artists," instructing it to submit this information to the State Library and the State Library Commission.

At this same meeting the board appointed a committee consisting of Mrs. Arrington, Miss Annie L. Petty, and Mrs. J. J. Andoe, "to formulate a plan for circulating pictures in the public schools." Again, Mrs. Arrington's generosity must have made possible the realization of such a plan, for on March 24, 1970, Mrs. James Beckwith of the Warren County Schools wrote to Mrs. Christopher Webster, Secretary of the State Art Society, that "Sylbert Pendleton gave me a bunch of the prints which Kate Arrington used to give to the school children for art appreciation instruction back in the early 1920's. . . . Incidentally, various teachers want to use them for American History, French, an exhibit of Madonnas, etc. Kate would be delighted."

The setbacks to hopes for the museum were balanced, at least in part, by an unexpected benefit of the Depression. The Federal Art Project, whose story is taken up in detail elsewhere, established an art center in Raleigh that was so successful the need for a permanent museum became even more apparent. In 1939, following persistent appeals from the Art Society, the State provided space on the second floor of the former Supreme Court Building to be used for galleries and headquarters for the

Art Society. William C. Fields, a promising young artist from Fayetteville, succeeded James McLean, a Raleigh artist, as director of the FAP art center. Considerable renovation was carried out under his supervision.

The official opening of the new State Art Society Gallery on March 28, 1939, was a memorable one, marked by an exhibition of American paintings assembled from New York galleries by Edmund C. Babcock to celebrate the importance of the occasion. Just as exciting was the December annual meeting of the Art Society, held in its new quarters. Principal speaker at the meetings on Wednesday and Thursday was Alfred M. Frankfurter, editor of *Art News* and a member of the World's Fair committee in charge of the collection of Masterpieces. He was secured by Mrs. Arrington who had served on the State committee for the Fair and the Women's National Advisory Committee. An exhibition of watercolor paintings from the Museum of Modern Art of New York City adorned the walls of the gallery.

The combined Art Society Gallery and FAP Center was in continuous operation from December, 1939, until Federal support ended in March, 1943, leaving supporters of the new gallery apprehensive as to its survival. Interest from the Phifer bequest was yielding approximately a thousand dollars annually, including dividends, and membership dues and patrons' contributions were totalling $800 to $1,000. But these combined funds fell far short of the minimum requirements necessary to maintain the gallery.

Again the Art Society appealed to the State for help, and the 1943 General Assembly appropriated an annual grant-in-aid of $2,000 for the salary of one person to serve as gallery director and executive secretary, "and for occasional extra help." The State continued to furnish gallery and office space and to provide lighting and heating, but the Art Society was responsible for all other expenses—from postage stamps to exhibition fees. In 1947, however, the annual grant-in-aid was raised to $5,000 to provide for an assistant to the director. In 1949 the amount was increased to $6,000 to permit a small raise in salaries; two years later it was increased to $10,000. This last amount sufficed for the following eight years and was expected to include all salaries and operation costs.

Miss Katherine Morris, of Raleigh, served as executive secretary and gallery director from March, 1943, until August, 1945, when she was succeeded by Mrs. Henry London, a charter member of the Art Society who exerted a cohesive force as an active director throughout her lifetime. Legend has it that any man who came into the gallery during Mrs. London's reign, even the Governor, was liable to be called upon to help uncrate paintings, lift boxes, or do any chore requiring male strength.

When the appropriation was granted in 1947 for an assistant, Miss Lucy Cherry Crisp of Falkland, North Carolina, joined the gallery as Mrs. London's assistant, becoming gallery director and executive secretary to the Art Society when Mrs. London resigned in August, 1947. Miss Doris Meekins joined the staff as assistant to Miss Crisp, but resigned in 1949. Mrs. Harold Dwelle of Charlotte, an Art Society vice-president-at-large, had interested Ben F. Williams, just returned from Europe, in the Art Society, which led to his accepting Miss Crisp's invitation to succeed Miss Meekins. Williams remained to eventually become general curator of the North Carolina Museum of Art, and now has the honor of seniority of tenure.

In writing of those lean years, Miss Crisp recalls the increasingly wide and varied programs and services provided by the gallery and the Art Society, now housed in the State Educational Building:

> During the eleven years from March, 1943, to January, 1953, one hundred and twenty-two special exhibitions were shown in the State Art Gallery in its two locations. They included many one-man and group shows of work by North Carolina artists, but they also ranged far and wide to provide items from many areas and to appeal to the many and various interests of the public served by the Gallery. Their scope in time was broad; from medieval manuscripts to Matisse lithographs; from DaVinci models to Winslow Homer drawings; from Coptic textile fragments to fabrics from modern North Carolina mills; from Rubens to Picasso and John Marin. They were broad also in their inclusion of paintings, sculpture, prints, drawings, photography, architecture, furniture, textiles, pottery, pewter, glass, children's art, and objects of good design. Many were drawn from North Carolina and other American sources, but some came from Holland, France, England, Germany, Japan, and the Orient.

Following a successful membership campaign in the summer of 1946, the Art Society celebrated its twentieth annual meeting that December by sponsoring its first juried competition for North Carolina artists, offering $1,000 in prizes. The jury for selection of works to be shown and for awards was composed of Julianna Force, Thomas Colt, and Lamar Dodd. Thought by some to be the first "juried" art show held in the state, it actually had a forerunner in 1931, sponsored by the Professional Artists of North Carolina. It was the first, however, offering sizeable money awards. "Artists appeared from every direction and interest ran high," Miss Crisp recalls. Newspapers across the state carried columns of news and comment on the jury's choices and exclusions.

Of the "growing decade" at the gallery, looking toward a museum, Miss Crisp and her staff aimed at "the establishment, even though in miniature, of as many as possible of the major functions and services of a public Art Museum, in order that beginnings, at least, of all these things might have been made when the goal of a great Museum of Art should finally be achieved." An important parallel development supporting the Society's work toward an art museum was initiated in 1943 when Governor J. Melville Broughton called together a Citizen's Committee for a State Art Gallery. Former Governor J. C. B. Ehringhaus, the Honorable Josephus Daniels, Clarence Poe, Mrs. Arrington, R. D. W. Connor, Robert B. House, and Robert Lee Humber were present; all expressed themselves as in favor of definite action toward early realization of a museum building "as soon as war-time conditions might permit."

Robert Lee Humber, a world-renowned lawyer and a native of Greenville, North Carolina, who had returned from Paris where he had practiced law and was just emerging on the North Carolina art scene through the State Art Society, expressed his willingness to explore the possibilities of attaining a museum for North Carolina. His exploration and subsequent negotiations extended into 1947 when, through his masterful persuasion, the General Assembly appropriated one million dollars for the purchase of art works for a State Art Museum in Raleigh, contingent upon the receipt of a "matching gift" and upon available funds at the end of the year—conditions that few believed would be possible. Humber had assured the Assembly that if they voted this appropriation "there was a bona fide promise of a matching gift by a responsible party . . . outside the State," although he was pledged to withhold the donor's name. This enforced secrecy on the part of Humber while trying to persuade the General Assembly to make such an unprecedented appropriation obviously caused him much embarrassment, and at one period it almost led the Legislature to recall the appropriation and distribute it elsewhere. But with the State Art Society's record of achievement to back him, the support of Governor R. Gregg Cherry, and a telling speech by Representative John Kerr, Jr., all was saved, as is recounted more fully in the section on the State Art Museum.

Upon release of the million dollars to the State Art Society, the 1951 General Assembly authorized Governor W. Kerr Scott to appoint an Art Commission to supervise its expenditure and established procedures by which the museum was to be governed. The five-member commission included Art Society members Robert Lee Humber, chairman; Mrs. Katherine Pendleton Arrington, Clarence Poe, Clemens Sommer, and Edwin Gill. Miss Lucy Cherry Crisp was requested to serve as secretary to the Commission.

The bill releasing the million dollars also stipulated that each purchase from the fund be approved by a recognized art expert and by the board of directors of the Art Society. William R. Valentiner, then director of the Los Angeles County Museum, was engaged as the "art expert" to pass on the value, suitability and other qualifications of each purchase, and Carl Hamilton, a former art dealer and friend of Robert Lee Humber, served as consultant to the Commission.

With the million-dollar appropriation in hand, and with $300,000 contributed by the State Art Society from the Phifer funds, the Commission purchased nearly two hundred paintings "as a nucleus collection, around which many and varied collections might be made in the years to come."

Astute buying of this "nucleus collection," and the attendant publicity attracted by North Carolina's extraordinary venture into the art world, led to magnificent bargains and other generous gifts. The Art Society found itself custodian of over two million dollars' worth of art but still with no museum in which to show it. Furthermore, the "matching gift of a million-dollar collection" (now known to be from the S. H. Kress Foundation) was contingent upon suitable space in which to display it. Even so, it was not until 1953 that the General Assembly authorized the conversion of the former State Highway Building in downtown Raleigh into an art museum and appropriated funds for its renovation, operation, and maintenance, and for salaries of an enlarged staff—all with strong support from Governor William B. Umstead, Governor Luther B. Hodges who succeeded him, and D. S. Coltrane, Assistant Budget Director.

While the old Highway Building was being converted into an art museum, Miss Crisp and Williams were busy over at the State Art Gallery assembling a museum staff, purchasing equipment, training volunteers, and generally preparing for the greater responsibilities near at hand. They also were in constant demand as speakers by impatient art groups and others around the state interested in the progress of what seemed to be a mythical museum.

One of the most devoted workers for the museum, Mrs. Katherine Arrington, died at her home in Warrenton on April 12, 1955. After more than a quarter-century's work she would not witness the fruition of her efforts. Mrs. Arrington was succeeded as president of the Art Society by Robert Lee Humber. In December of 1953, the Art Society had created the position of vice-president especially for Humber, in addition to its usual three vice-presidents-at-large. This new office enabled Humber to preside during Mrs. Arrington's illness and later to accede to the presidency.

The Society's most pressing obligation at this time was to hire a museum director. With W. R. Valentiner already familiar with the Society's collections, Humber prevailed upon him to remain as the museum's first director. He accepted on November 1, 1955, and immediately began cataloguing the various collections. Under the new regime, Miss Crisp was appointed director of art education but resigned in 1956 to work in another southern state. Edgar Thorne, assistant director of the new museum, resigned at the same time.

When the museum was officially opened in April of 1956, the State Art Society, headed by Humber, had twelve hundred members; the future appeared bright indeed. But Humber's reign as president, despite the many rewarding events to come, was to be a turbulent one. Almost immediately he was confronted by Valentiner's discontent over the authority vested in Carl Hamilton as consultant to the Art Commission. Valentiner wrote to Humber on January 2, 1957, that "under these circumstances I do not think it wise for me to hold on to my position any longer—the position of a 'figurehead,'—as it does not correspond to the position of other museum directors in our country. I have made up my mind to resign if this situation is not changed very soon."

Valentiner died in New York on September 6, 1958, following a curtailed trip to Europe, and although he had resigned earlier, apparently it was without malice, for he willed his entire collection to the museum. When he resigned it was his wish that his assistant, James Byrnes, become director of the museum. Edwin Gill, a long-time member of the State Art Society Board of Directors, and several other board members also favored Byrnes as director. Humber and other board members wanted a man of "more scholarly attainments." The state newspapers, shut out of several closed-door sessions, had a field day over the division of the board regarding Byrnes and confused the public with such terms as "fired," "ousted," "given his walking papers," and "left dangling in uncertainty." As the dispute gained momentum Clarence Poe, who had voted against Byrnes, was moved to write a long letter to the *News and Observer* in which he criticized the publicity as "unjustifiably hurtful to Mr. Byrnes." And Byrnes, in defense of his own "shortcomings" (often referred to but not explained by the Art Society board), was led to unfold the story of his early struggle to surmount poverty and achieve a place in the art world.

Machinations of the two factions resulted in Edwin Gill's obtaining proxy votes from Mrs. Charles Cannon, ill in Concord, and Mrs. George Paschal of Raleigh, then on a trip to Europe, both of whom favored Byrnes; but proxy votes were ruled invalid. Intrigue also led to two surprise flights from Europe to the United States and back by Clemens Sommer, another board member. Sommer, then teaching abroad, favored a new museum director and was also fearful, along with many others, that Gregory D. Ivy would not be re-elected to the sixteen-member board which also served as a guide to the North Carolina Museum of Art. (A considerable number of "Ivy-leaguers" joined the Art Society that day in time to vote, if necessary, to get him re-elected.) The newly organized Associated

Artists of North Carolina was credited with payment of Sommer's traveling expenses. It did lend its name to the cause, but the flights were paid for privately.

The Board of Directors voted seven to six to seek a new full-time director and to release Byrnes as of September 1 of that year, a move that drew the ire of Governor Luther Hodges, who described the handling of the Byrnes case as "ridiculous," and threatened to withhold the expansion funds for the museum which Humber had pushed through the 1959 Assembly while he was Senator. Governor Hodges met with the Art Society board on April 1, 1960, and insisted that Byrnes be retained until January 1, 1961, and that "unanimity" prevail in whatever the board decided. "There should be no minorities or majorities," he said. "We are seriously interested in one thing—uniting in the development of this great institution. The state is expecting us to stop this haranguing."

A motion was then made by Poe that Byrnes be retained as full director for the balance of the year, noting that this would "not only mean increased prestige but increased salary." The *Greensboro Daily News* reported that "after Poe's motion had been discussed and approved, there was a torrent of praise for all concerned," and that "Mrs. O. Max Gardner of Raleigh summed up the feeling of her fellow directors with the exclamation: 'I love everybody.'" Clemens Sommer again returned to Europe, after allaying rumors that he would serve as an interim museum director.

Then arose the question of "Who owns the paintings in the State Art Museum—the State or the Old Masters of Politics in the State Art Society?" For an answer Governor Hodges, who had proposed that the museum be taken out of the hands of the privately run Art Society, turned to the Commission on Reorganization of State Government. The Governor also wrote a letter to Humber stating that he believed the state would be "far better served" if state cultural agencies were brought together in a "cultural center," and that he would follow the suggestions of the Commission on the use of the expansion appropriation referred to previously.

Following a lengthy study of "the present statutory arrangement for the government of the North Carolina Museum of Art and the possible need for changes in that arrangement," the Commission on Reorganization of State Government reported to the Governor on September 23,

1960. The report recommended that the museum be turned over to complete state control, with minimal representation from the State Art Society, and that the position of director of the museum be established and filled by an appointee of the new board of trustees of the museum.

Throughout the stormy controversies of 1960 regarding the Art Society's activities, the newspapers often slanted their reporting toward dispraise of Robert Lee Humber, leading Egbert L. Davis, a board member, to write to the Raleigh *News and Observer* on November 14, 1960, that "these statements are in absolute contradiction of the facts and gross misrepresentations of the truth. . . . During my several years as a member of the Board of Directors of the North Carolina State Art Society, I have always found Dr. Humber to be completely honest, fair, and democratic in every respect. He is always willing to abide by the decisions of the Board made by majority rule." A month later, Watts Hill, Jr., another board member, voiced disapproval of Humber at the annual meeting of the Art Society on November 30, stating that during his year as a director he had never received a written reply to any letter he wrote to Humber, that he was not informed adequately of approaching board meetings, and that important problems facing the museum were not discussed at board meetings. He also said that "Humber was chairman of all the committees of the present board of directors." Humber acknowledged that he was head of the board's executive committee and building committee but would be "perfectly happy to give it up at any time." At the December quarterly meeting of the board of directors Humber stated that he "considered it advisable that the Chairman of the Executive Committee be someone other than the President of the Art Society and that he would like to retire from that position . . . that he would, at any time, be happy to relinquish the reins of the State Art Society, and that he wished members of the Board to feel no obligation at all to him in this matter." According to the minutes, Hill then nominated Humber for president.

Two great rewards came to the Art Society in 1960 that more than offset the dissident notes that year. First, the Samuel H. Kress Collection arrived, but instead of the promised one million-dollar collection, it now amounted to two-and-one-half million dollars worth of paintings. Secondly, on November 25, 1960, Humber was able to announce in a letter to the Art Society members the coming of Justus Bier who, as the new director of the North Carolina Museum of Art, "was elected by an overwhelming vote of the Board of Directors."

The 1961 General Assembly officially divorced the State Art Society and the North Carolina Museum of Art, as the Governor's Commission had suggested. Pursuant to the decision, the Art Society on July 1, 1961, relinquished to the museum the art collection purchased with the $1,000,000 appropriated by the General Assembly in 1947; the Phifer Collection which by this time had increased in value to $500,000; its collection of works by North Carolina artists and other gifts appraised at approximately $750,000; and the Kress gift of $2,500,000. It had truly achieved its goal—a Museum of Art for the State of North Carolina.

Humber resigned as president of the Art Society at the annual meeting on November 29, 1961, ending seven years of leadership, and became chairman of the museum's board of trustees. The Art Society expressed its gratitude in a glowing tribute, ending with:

> We wish by this minute to record forever the deep sense of gratitude felt by the North Carolina State Art Society for his notable accomplishments, to assure him of our continuing respect for his leadership, and to promise him that the Society will continue, by every means in its power, to promote the best interests of the arts in the State of North Carolina.

Set adrift from the museum by legislation, and stripped of its major purpose, the Art Society might well have foundered. Instead, it began 1962 with a new president and new visions. Joseph C. Sloane, director of the Ackland Art Center and Art Department at the University of North Carolina at Chapel Hill, was elected president of the Art Society the day Humber resigned. He became the third president of the 37-year-old organization and the first president to be chosen from the professional art field. Sloane began his tenure with a seven-point program at the February, 1962, board meeting. His spirited vision was contagious, and the following December, at the Art Society's annual meeting, he reported all of his seven-point program as having been accomplished.

The first point of the program, involving regional representatives, yielded fabulous returns socially and financially early in Sloane's regime, through a project masterminded by Mrs. Ira Julian and Smith W. Bagley of the Winston-Salem Division of the Art Society. The project was called "Collectors' Opportunity," and paintings valued at more than $1,500,000 —all of museum caliber—were borrowed from New York galleries for the occasion. Bagley, a grandson of R. J. Reynolds of tobacco fame, described the primary purpose of the exhibition as being an effort to create collectors in North Carolina: He reasoned that "if you can create an interest in collecting, the collectors will ultimately support a great Museum." A steering committee composed of Mrs. Julian, Bagley, Mrs. Agnew Bahnson, Jr., Mrs. Gordon Hanes, Philip Hanes, Jr., William Herring, and George Mountcastle had as advisers Justus Bier and Joseph Sloane. Dr. and Mrs. Bier spent many weeks of research in authenticating the works. Sloane introduced the exhibition in the catalogue as "a frank invitation from an interested group of citizens addressed to their fellow North Carolinians, to join them in the pleasures of art collecting." Hope prevailed, of course, that many of the works would find their way to the museum at Raleigh. Some of them did, immediately. Three paintings and a fifteenth century sculpture were presented to the North Carolina Museum of Art; one painting was given to the Ackland Art Center at Chapel Hill; and another was presented to the Mint Museum in Charlotte, with the stipulation that it be exhibited at the museum in Raleigh during certain periods each year.

Until 1963 all Purchase Award works of art from the North Carolina Artists' Annual Competition had been given to the museum in Raleigh by the Art Society, and these gifts throughout the years built the nucleus of the museum's collection of contemporary Tarheel art. Under the new regime, however, the Society, no longer obligated to continue this custom, initiated a program of donating award works to young galleries and smaller museums around the state. Policy governing such gifts, set forth in *Summaries of Reports of Officers and Committees* as of December, 1963, reads:

"The N. C. Museum of Art will have first selection of one of the four purchase awards. The other three (or four, if the Museum does not select one) will be offered to other communities of the Art Society's choice which have permanent collections and adequate museum facilities. Insofar as is possible, the Art Society intends to make these awards from year to year on a rotating basis among the eligible communities.

"Members of this committee are as follows: Mrs. Howard Manning, Gregory Ivy, Mrs. Ira Julian, George Bireline, Ben Williams, Mrs. George Paschal, Jr., representing the President." Later, this committee became known as "The Museum Committee," and was composed of Mrs. John M. Foushee, chairman, and Mrs. Ira Julian, and Dr. George S. Welsh. Among North Carolina museums and galleries which have profited from this policy are the Rocky Mount Art Center, the Statesville Museum of Arts and Sciences, Wake Forest College Gallery, the Mint Museum, the Asheville Museum, and East Carolina College School of Art.

Over the years the State Art Society has honored members who have rendered unusual service to the arts in the state. The following have been honored with Certificates of Merit, some posthumously: 1951, John J. Blair and William Meade Prince; 1954, John H. Kerr, Jr.; 1958, Miss Katherine Morris and Mrs. Julianna Busbee (Mrs. James Cordon of Raleigh received a silver bowl for her twenty-five years as Society treasurer); 1962, Mrs. Helen P. Bell, Mrs. John Foushee, Mrs. John A. Kellenberger, Miss Jeta Pace, Miss Ruth Faison Shaw, Mrs. Louis V. Sutton, Mrs. W. L. Thorp, Jr., Mrs. Lois B. Tracy, and Peter B. Young; 1963, Mrs. Arthur Levy, Jr., Mrs. R. R. Sermon, Mrs. Mary Beth Buchholtz, Mrs. Norman Wishart, Mrs. J. H. B. Moore, Mrs. Ira Julian, Smith Bagley, Miss Mary Virginia Horne, and Harold Allred; 1967, Robert Lee Humber, Edwin Gill, Clarence Poe, Katherine Pendleton Arrington, and Clemens Sommer; 1968, Mrs. Mary Myers Dwelle, Lloyd Griffin, Robert Burton House, and Robert Phifer; 1970, Miss Lucy Cherry Crisp.

Memberships increased significantly in 1962 through a new system of Regional Representatives working under the guidance of Mrs. Agnew H. Bahnson, Jr., of Winston-Salem, membership chairman. And the largest sum ever offered as prize money for the North Carolina Artists' Annual was raised by Joseph Cox, of the School of Design in Raleigh, $2,000 of which was provided by the Mary Reynolds Babcock Foundation.

In 1964 Sloane expressed concern for the financial future of the Art Society, partly based on a new legal opinion limiting the income from the

Robert F. Phifer estate to the acquisition of art works only, as mentioned earlier. Self-imposed obligations of the Art Society to provide for all social entertaining for the museum's benefit, its participation in at least one retirement fund, increase in the North Carolina Artists' Annual Competition, and art education projects, necessitated a request for subsidization from the Advisory Budget Commission. Encouraged by George Geohagan, the Commission granted the Society $14,000 for the biennium, which enabled it to maintain the high standards set for its service programs.

Mrs. George W. Paschal, Jr., followed Joseph Sloane as president of the Art Society in 1965, "via the museum's volunteer program." As a former professional journalist, Mrs. Paschal was articulate and able to communicate to others her concern and interest in the welfare of the museum, to implement the various programs started by Sloane, and to initiate other innovations. Her reign might well be considered the "social" era of the revised Art Society, so many events were accompanied by "sparkling" social entertainment. One such event was the elegant dinner on May 3, 1965, for Feodor Zakharov, the Russian-born artist whose eighty-third birthday was honored by a retrospective exhibition of his paintings at the museum. Mrs. Charles Babcock of Winston-Salem, a friend of the artist and collector of his works, was hostess. Other glamorous affairs included a reception for members of the Legislature, and "Community Days" at the museum, celebrating the twentieth anniversary of the million-dollar appropriation by the State Legislature back in 1947. The reception for the 1967 Legislature not only acquainted that body with the Society's work with the museum but served as an expression of appreciation to the Legislature for its part in making the museum possible. Following the reception, the five-member State Art Commission appointed by Governor Kerr Scott in 1947, was honored—Mrs. Katherine Arrington and Clemens Sommer, posthumously.

"Community Days" brought thousands of visitors to the museum. Whole communities and their mayors came and met their various legislators and literally received "red carpet" treatment. In return several communities held their own celebrations and raised money for paintings for the museum. The Chapel Hill Chapter of the Art Society, for instance, presented a $1,200 watercolor, "Schnee Wetter" by George Grosz, to the museum, a distinct addition to its modern collection which is lacking in works by artists from foreign lands. And, "as a demonstration of its affection and concern for the museum," the State Art Society purchased and presented to it "Le Repose" by Edgar Degas, filling another conspicuous gap in the museum's collection.

Also, in an effort to aid the inadequate staff of the growing museum, Mrs. Paschal developed a widely-based corps of volunteers called Museum Aides, who provide clerical assistance for the curators, the library, the book shop, and the information and reception desks, as well as the usual hospitality pleasantries. Acoustiguides, making possible an hour-long tour of the museum and a "formula-speech" with slides and projector to be used by Regional Representatives, or others interested in getting the museum story to the public, were invaluable additions to the Art Society's program during this period. Mrs. Paschal credits the success of her regime to good public relations administered by Art Society personnel, particularly Mrs. Lunsford Long, the late Margaret Ehringhaus, Mrs. Stella Suberman, and Mrs. Christopher Webster.

In 1968, Mrs. Agnew H. Bahnson, Jr., of Winston-Salem became the fifth president of the Art Society. Through her influence the Society purchased two outstanding gifts for the museum: the Greek sculpture of "Aphrodite" and the Kenneth Clark film series, *Civilisation*. Mrs. Bahnson designated the year 1967–68 as "The Year of Choices, Responsibilities and Decisions." The Society had received the remainder of the Phifer bequest. "Involved in this has been recognition of the trusts laid on us as the recipient and guardian of the funds—responsibility for discharging these obligations with thoughtfulness and care to enable us to make choices concerning the use of this trust in a way which would, to the best of our ability fulfill the aspirations behind them and benefit most significantly and appropriately the people of our State," Mrs. Bahnson charged the Society, in her annual report.

She further reported that sixty-seven Art Kits had been placed in various schools and communities; the third annual Teacher's Study Tour (a program initiated during Mrs. Paschal's presidency) was conducted again by Perry Kelly; the North Carolina Collectors, with much help and the careful planning of Ben Williams, visited important collections and galleries in Washington, D. C.; and eight traveling exhibitions of works from the North Carolina Museum were financed by the Society. (The framing, crating and shipping charges for these traveling exhibitions are underwritten by the Art Society.)

The Society has been described as a bridge connecting the museum, the state government, and the people of North Carolina in ways both large and small. It has several memorial funds to which people may contribute for the purchase of works of art for the museum, such as the Margaret Peoples Ehringhaus Memorial, through which a lithograph by Mary Cassatt, "Sara Wearing Her Bonnet and Coat," has been given.

From time to time the Art Society has moved some of its annual meetings to cities other than Raleigh, to participate in celebrating various anniversaries of those cities. It met in Winston-Salem in 1966, in Charlotte in 1968, and in Greensboro in 1970. One of its earlier moves was to Charlotte in 1938, just two years after the opening of the Mint.

When Finley T. White of Durham was elected president of the North Carolina State Art Society at its annual meeting in Greensboro December 2, 1970, the Society unknowingly made a direct link with the past. When White began studying the early history of the Society he was surprised to find that his father, Gilbert C. White, had signed the certificate of incorporation, thus bringing the Society full-circle.

3. THE FEDERAL ART PROJECT

The federal government is responsible for the liveliest period in the history of art in this country, and particularly in North Carolina, when during the latter days of the Big Depression and the early days of World War II it shouldered a major responsibility for the plight of living American artists and their inability to earn a livelihood. This concern culminated in the organization of the Federal Art Project (FAP), a branch of the Work Projects Administration providing work for needy artists, architects, photographers, and craftsmen. Through a turn of fate, North Carolina became headquarters for FAP, a circumstance which doubtless saved the

State Art Society from temporary obscurity and breathed new life into its plans for a State Art Museum.

Holger Cahill, who had just spent some eighteen months in the southern states collecting colonial art objects from attics and junk shops to be used in the restored museum at Williamsburg, Virginia, was appointed National Director of FAP. Simultaneously, a group of art-conscious citizens of Raleigh applied for help in expanding the development of art in that area. And Cahill, his southern travels fresh in his mind, decided a "southern city asking for aid" would be ideal for the first experiment as well as for headquarters for the Federal Art Project. Thus Raleigh became the first city in the United States to have a federal-supported art center and to become a model for other centers throughout North Carolina and the United States.

Daniel S. Defenbacher, then of Chapel Hill, had gained attention through an exhibition of his watercolor paintings in a show sponsored by the Southern Art Projects, a Carnegie Foundation project, which led to his appointment as State Supervisor of FAP by Mrs. May E. Campbell, State Director of Professional and Service Projects of the WPA. Defenbacher was followed by Gene Erwin of Durham in 1938, and subsequently by Miss Katherine Morris of Raleigh in 1940.

Dr. Elizabeth Gilmore, instructor in Fine Arts at Duke University, was appointed District Art Supervisor of FAP in this state, "to assist the WPA office in approving the technical quality of all art projects and to act as chairman of the State Advisory Committee." Members of the advisory committee were Mrs. Katherine Pendleton Arrington, Warrenton; Mrs. John Sprunt Hill, Durham; C. C. Crittenden, secretary of the State Historical Commission, Raleigh; Mrs. L. V. Sutton, Raleigh; Mrs. John MacRae, Asheville; Miss Juanita MacDougald, Raleigh; William Kenneth Boyd, Duke University, Durham; Louis Vorhees, artist, High Point; and Mrs. Corrine McNair, curator of Person Hall Art Gallery, University of North Carolina, Chapel Hill.

At the time of Defenbacher's appointment there were only two artists registered for WPA jobs, but about forty qualified persons were thought to be registered in other classifications. Artists, to be employed, must have been on the relief rolls prior to November 1, 1935. Projects planned for

North Carolina included lectures by artists to leisure-time groups, exhibitions by local and national artists and craftsmen, and preparation of a catalogue of works of art in North Carolina.

Apparently North Carolina artists were in less need of subsidy than were many artists in other states, for William C. Fields, a former director, recalls that WPA never sponsored an individual artist in this state as it did in other areas of the country. Through FAP, however, nine Tarheel artists were represented by twelve works of art in a preview exhibition in the Virginia Museum of Fine Arts in Richmond, in December of 1938, as a screening process for the World's Fair exhibition in New York City. Artists included were Callie O. Braswell, Robert M. Skelton, Hermione Hamlet, and Frederick Whiteman, Greensboro; Claude Howell and Henry J. MacMillan, Wilmington; Richard Lofton, Winston-Salem; and Elizabeth Cordell Masters and Nathan Ornoff, Durham. From the hundreds of paintings previewed in Richmond to represent the southern states at the World's Fair, four of the above artists had work accepted for the exhibition: Claude F. Howell, Henry J. MacMillan, Richard Lofton, and Nathan Ornoff. All were subjected to the scrutiny of a series of juries and a stringent process of elimination or acceptance after reaching New York.

North Carolina's real awakening to art came through the many art centers FAP established throughout the state. To stimulate interest in the development of these art centers, Cahill traveled about the state speaking to civic, art, and social groups. "The WPA project does more than provide a livelihood for artists," Cahill declared, pointing out that more than 95,000 works of art had been created and allocated to schools, libraries, and other tax-supported institutions over the country. "The program tends to make art 'the property of all rather than the hobby of a few.' It checks 'cultural erosion,' the flocking of artists to big cities, leaving communities bare. It has helped to rediscover America's cultural past, and has brought together art interests and resources in communities."

Cahill's enthusiasm inspired the establishment of art centers in nine North Carolina towns and cities: Raleigh, Winston-Salem, Asheville, Concord, Greensboro, Sanford, Greenville, Kinston, and Wilmington. Each center had its own director and an active personnel, and the general plan consisted of three main units—gallery, school, and extension work.

Inherent in each program were art exhibitions, including crafts and industries; gallery talks; school classes in drawing and painting with much emphasis on the creative work of children, both white and Negro; and modeling and commercial art. Downtown areas were usually selected for the centers, with the definite idea of making them a permanent addition to the cultural life of the city.

Response was phenomenal. By December, 1938—a period of only three years—more than 4,000,000 people had attended art centers in North Carolina, and the *Charlotte Observer*, in praise of the rapid strides in North Carolina's projects, recalled that "Irvin Cobb once said that North Carolina and Kansas were the butt of the 48 states of the union, but Cobb has lived to see North Carolina grow away from this opprobrium." The same article reported that Sanford, the smallest town in the state to have a center and with a population of only 5,000, had more than 200 people register for instruction the first day the center was open. The center was established purely as an experiment, with one instructor, as the result of a speech by Greensboro's director, Frederick J. Whiteman, but the unexpected enrollment necessitated the engagement of others. William C. Fields, just graduated from the University of North Carolina as one of the first recipients of the B.A. degree in Fine Arts given by the University, was director of the Sanford Center from 1938 to 1939, when he moved up to the state level.

Criticized from its beginning to its demise for "its wasteful and trivial projects" (junior colleges, theatre groups, orchestras, murals, etc.), in its eight years of operation WPA proved a vital stop gap "that performed among its many other useful services the considerable one of restoring self-respect to many of the 8.5 million individuals it employed at one time or another," at a cost of nearly $11 billion.

Usually sponsored by state and local agencies, but paid for chiefly by the Federal government, FAP by 1938 had produced 2,500 murals and placed over 42,000 paintings on loan in public buildings all over the country. Several post offices in North Carolina were decorated with these murals, and at least one North Carolina artist painted one of them. A preliminary jury of selection, headed by Miss Elizabeth A. Chant and including Miss Ethel Williams, Miss Monimia MacRae, Tom Orrell, and Herbert Cavanaugh, was elected to choose a painter for a mural to be placed in the Wilmington Post Office. Artists in Maryland, the District of Columbia, Virginia, and North Carolina were eligible to enter the competition. William F. Pfohl of Winston-Salem won the commission. Claude Howell recalls that Pfohl painted the mural in Winston-Salem on canvases which he carried to Wilmington in large rolls, and then mounted them like wallpaper.

North Carolina's cultural outlook profited enormously by its Art Centers, as the following sketches of some of them will reveal; and while most of the centers closed with the termination of WPA, others survived to give impetus to larger and more permanent achievements.

The Raleigh Center, under the directorship of James McLean for its first four years and of William C. Fields as his successor, maintained two sub-galleries—one at Needham Broughton High School and one at the Crosby-Garfield School for Negroes. Art classes were conducted at both places, as well as at the Hugh Morson High School, until 1939. At that time the State Art Society and the Raleigh WPA Art Center established an uptown art gallery on the second floor of the Supreme Court Building, under the joint sponsorship of the Society and the WPA Art Program. The sub-galleries were closed, but Miss Katherine Morris, the State Supervisor, maintained offices in the old Academy Building. On January 6, 1940, the *News and Observer* reported that "about 400 Raleigh school children take WPA art courses."

In August of 1942, Fields resigned as assistant state director of the WPA art project and director of the Raleigh Art Center, to accept a year's scholarship at the Boston Museum School of Fine Arts. Clayton Charles succeeded Fields as secretary of the State Art Society, and Mrs. Ann Harris succeeded him as director of the Raleigh Art Center. The end of WPA was already in sight, so no appointment was made to replace Fields as assistant director of the state art project.

The Greensboro Art Center, with $1,500 subscribed by citizens, began its activities in July of 1936. By 1938 its staff included a director (Frederick J. Whiteman), a supervisor of teaching, several instructors, a gallery attaché, gallery technicians, research workers, a secretary, a carpenter, and a janitor. The Richardson family gave the center its quarters. From the opening of the Greensboro Art Center through February 1, 1938, attendance reached 66,000. Twelve thousand attended the school, and 7,000 attended special events—a total of 85,000 persons reached by this one center.

The Wilmington Art Center got its start in a downtown building formerly occupied by an undertaking establishment, which at the time was reported as "undergoing a cheerful change" while WPA carpenters and painters remodeled it for an art gallery and museum. It was formally opened on the night of October 31, 1938. Irving Guyer, of the Exhibition and Graphic Arts Division of FAP, spent three months in Wilmington assisting with exhibitions and the establishment of the museum. It had a phenomenal attendance record, due in part to the nearby camps of World War II. Its first exhibition was made up of American watercolor paintings lent by the Museum of Fine Arts, Boston; the Museum of Modern Art and the Metropolitan Museum of Art, New York; and by watercolorist Eliot O'Hara and others.

Henry MacMillan, the director, and his two assistants, Miss Rosalie Oliver and Miss Margaret Williams, conducted 150 classes for children. Claude Howell recalls the project's sponsorship of two other galleries—one at Wrightsville Beach during the summer and one at the Woodrow Wilson hut. Gallery attendance for the year 1940–1941 reached a peak of 36,965 persons.

Although the museum had the endorsement of the City Council, the Chamber of Commerce, the County Commissioners, the Exchange Club, the Kiwanis Club, the Rotary Club, the Lions Club, the North Carolina Sorosis Club, the Thalians, the Daughters of the American Revolution, and the United Daughters of the Confederacy, as well as of private citizens, it closed in 1943 for lack of money after Federal aid was withdrawn. But it left in its wake many interested people who continued to work toward the development of art in Wilmington.

Another legacy from FAP was the Wilmington Art Association, which grew from a charter group of fifteen art-minded people to a much larger group that inaugurated and for several years directed the Cottage Lane art show—a major attraction of the annual Azalea Festival. By 1961, these outdoor exhibitions had grown from a mere handful of paintings to nearly five hundred pieces of art work and were attracting an estimated attendance of around sixty thousand people. Held near the little white cottage in which Miss Elizabeth Augusta Chant had lived, they have been a tribute to this artist and teacher who established herself in Wilmington as a professional painter in the late twenties.

Under the directorship of Mrs. Chester Marsh, the Winston-Salem project was called the Arts and Crafts Workshop and had its headquarters at 404 North Main Street. Mrs. Marsh enlivened state interest in art by sponsoring art exhibitions and by honoring the exhibiting artists. Many North Carolina artists had their first one-man show at this center, and through it the Piedmont Art Festival (1943–1950) evolved.

The Piedmont Art Festival attracted topnotch painters and art teachers in the state. Among them, to name a few, were Manuel Bromberg, Robert Broderson, James T. Diggs, Ben F. Williams, Callie Braswell, Anne Wall, Elizabeth Mack, and Susan Moore. The Workshop and the Festival were later absorbed by the Winston-Salem Art Center, after which Mrs. Marsh, in March of 1952, retired to her Blue Ridge mountain lodge, "Saloge," to weave and write.

In November of 1941, the Federal Art Project crowned its achievements by joining the National Council and the American Artists Professional League in observing National Art Week. Labeled "the biggest sales exhibition of art works ever held in this or any other nation," its slogan was "American Art for American Homes." President Roosevelt endorsed the project as a means of livelihood for the artists and craftsmen of America, "that would safeguard the cultural resources of America."

North Carolina joined in the celebration wholeheartedly, as evidenced by the professional status of its leaders. North Carolina's Chairman of National Art Week was B. W. Wells, professor of botany at North Carolina State College, who appointed the following persons to the state committee: T. A. Wilson, chairman of the Industrial Commission; Governor J. Melville Broughton; John Lang, NYA administrator; Miss Ila Holman, supervisor of Public Activities program, WPA; Howard C. Ford, WPA craft project; Miss Katherine Morris and William Fields, supervisor and assistant, respectively, WPA art; John Park, Jr., of the Raleigh *Times*; Jonathan Daniels, editor of the *News and Observer*; Mrs. Cornelia Morris, marketing economist, Agricultural Extension Service; Mrs. C. A. Richardson, chairman of the Raleigh Women's Club Art Department, all of Raleigh; Frank Porter Graham, president of the University of North Carolina; Mrs. E. N. Meekins, state chairman of the Women's Club Art Department; Donald McDonald, of the Art Department of Duke University; Mrs. J. H. B. Moore of Greenville; Mrs. Katherine P. Arrington, president of the State Art Society, Warrenton; and Mrs. Lewis Burwell, curator of the Mint Museum, Charlotte.

At local levels, the chairmen were: Mrs. C. A. Richardson, Raleigh; Gregory Ivy, head of the Art Department of Woman's College, University of North Carolina, Greensboro; Mrs. John Hood, Kinston; Mrs. J. H. B. Moore, Greenville; Mrs. Martin Lafferty, Concord; William Pfohl, Winston-Salem; Mrs. Lewis Burwell, Charlotte; John Allcott, head of the Art Department of the University of North Carolina, Chapel Hill; and Miss Ethel Messick, Wilmington.

The Work Projects Administration and its Federal Art Project expired on Friday, April 30, 1943, when all of its projects were closed. Probably the most controversial of all federal agencies, the WPA did much to "lift the shadow of poverty from our land" and to encourage cultural pursuits that otherwise would have withered and died. Among its more permanent monuments are the museums and art galleries it subsidized, the college and university programs it enriched, and the thousands of pictures and murals it commissioned for public buildings. Of even greater significance was its child-centered programs in the public schools that awakened an art interest in millions of children whose lives otherwise might never have been touched by creative opportunity. And since North Carolina was headquarters for FAP, this state probably profited more than any other from this federal project.

4. NORTH CAROLINA ASSOCIATION
OF PROFESSIONAL ARTISTS

Although the State Art Society was thriving by 1931, its concern was centered on a future Museum of Art rather than on native artists, despite the fact that quite a few Tarheels had attained professional status in their particular fields of art. These artists felt the need to organize and to promote their own work through exhibitions; and even though North Carolina has produced a number of professional artists and art organizations since, this is the first and only statewide group which has categorized itself as "Professional," with the express goal of selling its art works.

They met early in 1931 at the Chapel Hill studio of Mary deB. Graves, soon to be Mrs. Pembroke Rees, and organized as the North Carolina Association of Professional Artists intent upon "giving the people of North Carolina an opportunity to see what their own artists are doing and of giving the artists an opportunity of showing their work to the public."

Prerequisites for membership were that all members work for their living by means of brush or pencil and be native Tarheels, or to have worked in the state for as long as five years.

Charter members and officers were: Miss Graves, president; Charles Baskerville, Jr., of New York, vice-president; Miss Isabelle Bowen (later Mrs. Henderson), of Raleigh, secretary; and William Steene, of Chapel Hill, treasurer; James McLean, Miss Mabel Pugh, and Mary Tillery, Raleigh; Francis Speight, Philadelphia; Gene Erwin, Durham; Elliot Daingerfield, Blowing Rock; Louis Vorhees, High Point; William Pfohl, Winston-Salem; Miss Marie B. Hunt, and Clement Strudwick, Hillsborough; Henry Jay MacMillan, Wilmington; and Mary Tannahill, New York City.

Most of these members were represented in the group's first exhibition, held in Hill Hall on the University of North Carolina campus during April of 1931, at the invitation of President Frank Graham. This first exhibition by the Professional Artists of North Carolina drew the attention of the State Art Society and its subsequent invitation to exhibit their work at its annual meeting in Raleigh in December of 1931.

Little information appears to have been recorded on the first and second annual exhibitions by this group, but the third one was held in conjunction with the Chapel Hill Dogwood Festival in April of 1933, with the prospect of traveling to Winston-Salem, High Point, and Danville, Virginia, and of becoming the first traveling show of work by Tarheel artists. Since there was still no art gallery in Chapel Hill, this exhibition of more than seventy pieces was arranged around the walls of the spacious lobby of Hill Hall. The Art Department of the North Carolina Federation of Women's Clubs sponsored the 1934 annual exhibition of works by these prolific artists, scheduling it for travel to Oxford, Winston-Salem, Reidsville, and Morganton. In 1935 the State Art Society again invited them to show, along with a New England exhibition sent south by the Guild of Boston Artists. Listed among non-members invited by the North Carolina Professional Artists to exhibit in the 1935 show were Henry J. MacMillan of Wilmington, "whose strong, modern work drew most enthusiastic comments from members of the club"; Primrose McPherson of Raleigh, "whose drawings and portrait drawings received special mention"; Mrs. Alex Johnson, "whose canvases were described as brilliant"; Jaques Dement, Katherine Davis, Irene Price, William Blackburn, William Cannon, and William Temple.

A feature story on the group by R. W. Madry of the University News Bureau, said "there was no exhibition during 1936, but through the efforts of the president, Miss Elizabeth Dortch, it was arranged that the 1937 exhibition be held at the new Person Hall Art Gallery at the University." This was a juried show, open to all North Carolina artists—the first statewide juried show to be held in North Carolina. Jury members for the event were Russell T. Smith, chairman of the University Art Department; Gregory D. Ivy, head of the Art Department of Woman's College, Greensboro; and Alexander D. McDonald, head of the Art Department of Duke University. A hundred and thirty-two pieces of art work were submitted by 39 artists, of which 42 works were accepted. They ranged in scope from "Modernistic ideas, bordering on cubism," to a magnolia scene "highly modeled and faithfully colored."

Non-members represented in this exhibit were Claude Howell and Helen MacMillan of Wilmington; Evelyn Kernodle, Conrad Lindeman, Mary Leath Stewart, Ben Earl Looney, Miriam Sloan, and Ann L. Myrick of Greensboro; Margaret Munch and Wautel Selden of Chapel Hill; Irene Price of Raleigh and Wilmington; Elizabeth Reeves of Pittsboro; and Edmund Strudwick of Hillsboro. Association members whose work was accepted by the jury included Charles Baskerville, Jr., William Blackburn, Gene Erwin, Isabelle Bowen Henderson, Richard Lofton, Henry Jay MacMillan, Mabel Pugh, Clement Strudwick, Mary Tannahill, Mary Tillery, and Louis Vorhees.

The North Carolina Association of Professional Artists had four presidents during its short life of seven years. The first was Mary deB. Graves, sister of the late Louis Graves of *Chapel Hill Weekly* fame. She was a native of Chapel Hill, and it was in her quaint woodland studio that the Association was inaugurated and many of its meetings were held. Her training in art included a period in Baltimore, work at the Pennsylvania Academy of Fine Arts in Philadelphia, and study in New York City under William Chase and Henri. Although better known for her pastel portraits of children, Miss Graves also painted portraits of a number of prominent men and women. Several of her portraits may be seen on the University of North Carolina campus at Chapel Hill; among them, Edward Kidder Graham, and the two Mason sisters—Martha and Varina—whose mother willed the Mason Farm to the University, with the stipulation that portraits of the sisters and of their father hang in halls of the University. A cousin, Miss Lena Mae Williams of Chapel Hill, posed for the Mason sisters' portraits to insure that they be as life-like as possible.

The second president, Louis F. Vorhees, was born in Michigan and educated at the University of Michigan Department of Architecture. He studied painting under Hugh Breckenridge and taught architecture at the University of Virginia. His work was described then as "distinctly modern and known for its individuality of handling and unusualness of subject matter."

Elizabeth Dortch, a native of Goldsboro, became the third president. She studied in Raleigh at both St. Mary's and Peace Institute, and in New York at the Grand Central Art School under Weyman Adams, Howard S. Hildebrandt, George Pearce, and Erid Pape. For a number of years she conducted a studio art school for children in Raleigh and was active in the State Art Society. Flowers and portraits were her main subjects.

Gene Erwin, a Durham native, was the fourth and final president of N. C. P. A. After graduating from the University of North Carolina, where he received his Teacher's Training Certificate, he studied at the New York School of Fine and Applied Arts, and later at the Harvard summer school on a Carnegie Cooperation Scholarship. In 1935 he received a second Carnegie Fellowship to study with Grant Wood at the State University of Iowa. From Iowa he returned to North Carolina as state supervisor of the Federal Art Project. During this period his work consisted mainly of decorative flower paintings, done in gouache, and watercolor landscapes.

No record exists of a formal dissolution of this group, nor of any activity after 1937. The organization seems to have faded out of existence, perhaps because some of its members disliked juried exhibitions, which they felt belonged to amateurs. In addition, several members lived out of the state and their ties with the group gradually weakened. Despite its muted ending, however, the group remains memorable for its achievements and the individual successes of a number of its members, some of whose biographical sketches will appear later in the book.

CHAPTER THREE

Teaching

Although art courses were introduced into the curricula of North Carolina schools as they proliferated during the late nineteenth and early twentieth centuries, no art degrees were given until well after 1900. With few exceptions the colleges were church-supported and were female institutes or normal schools and consequently teacher-oriented. Eventually many of the art courses developed into art departments, but not until 1950, when the M.F.A. was added by the universities, was real progress made in spreading art instruction in the state.

Several important occurrences during the third decade of 1900 changed the trend in the teaching of art in North Carolina: (1) In 1931 the State College of Agriculture and Engineering at Raleigh, the University of North Carolina at Chapel Hill, and the North Carolina College for Women at Greensboro, merged into the Consolidated University of North Carolina. And, although this move by the General Assembly was to save money in this depression period by prevention of overlapping and duplicating some areas of instruction, the savings provided money for new educational programs such as art instruction. (2) In 1933 Black Mountain College was established with an art department under the distinguished Josef Albers, whose influence generated an international flavor to the awareness of art in North Carolina. (3) In 1934 Walter Clinton Jackson, new Chancellor of the Woman's College at Greensboro, established the first Art Department in the Consolidated University.

Quickened by these events, progress in the teaching of art was accelerated, enabling this state by the mid-1940's to enter the mainstream of an already art-conscious nation.

There are now approximately seventy colleges and universities in North Carolina, the majority of which include some art in their curricula. Space forbids a detailed account of each, and as found by Wellington B. Gray of East Carolina University, who made an in-depth survey of the art activity in all of them for 1970 publication, "the first hurdle was in securing the information." It takes several proddings and often months to secure a minute, but important, bit of information. The following selected few indicate the trend in all of them to provide some art knowledge for students who are interested.

THE UNIVERSITY OF NORTH CAROLINA AT GREENSBORO

Prior to consolidation, the Greensboro division of the University had been from 1892 to 1919 the State Normal and Industrial College, and then the Woman's College at Greensboro, with art training teacher-oriented. But when Chancellor W. C. Jackson inaugurated a new Department of Art in 1934, he brought in as director Gregory D. Ivy, a distinguished, creative artist and art educator from Missouri who already had made his mark nationally. Ivy plunged into his new job with the determination to build the best art department in the South, and to provide for women students opportunities to develop artistically in ways hitherto not possible in this part of the country. His often stated philosophy was that "a state-owned institution should be aware of the new dimensions and the new vitality developing in and around it, and of its obligations to meet the needs not only of students but of community and state as well—in groups or as individuals."

Art Education continued to be of prime importance, but from the start Ivy's curricula-planning embraced new courses to meet prevailing needs. In 1936–37 he introduced the first industrial design class in the United States for college women. And during World War II, in order to prepare young women to fill positions in industries requiring technical skills, courses in mechanical drawing and production illustration were added. Then there were summer art colonies for advanced painting, with locations alternating between Beaufort-by-the-Sea and Burnsville-in-the-Mountains.

Soon the entire state was feeling the impact of Ivy's efforts and witnessing a tremendous surge of interest in art. As early as 1942 the Southeastern Arts Association met at Woman's College, attracting 500 artists and teachers to Greensboro. Other events spurring the growth of the Art Department were its participation in the Arts Festivals (combining the dance, dramatics, literature and art), and the International Textile Design exhibition inaugurated in 1944.

The Annual Arts Forum, initiated in February of that same year, drew over 200 persons from thirty-two colleges in ten states and subsequently became national in scope. And although the Forum included all the arts, the Art Department was more visually represented by its exhibitions of art works by artists of national and international importance. Ivy's master *coup* was the year he brought Phillip Guston, Franz Kline, Jack Tworkov, and Mark Rothko and an exhibition of their paintings to the Art Forum at the same time. Walter Gropius, William Stanley Hayter, Lewis Mumford, and James Johnson Sweeney were some of the other prestigious figures who spoke at various Forums.

Until 1950, when the Art Department at the University at Chapel Hill added the M.F.A., Ivy's department was the only Art Department in North Carolina offering the B.F.A. and M.F.A. degrees, thus being able to supply other colleges with highly trained teachers and department heads, and the state with outstanding art supervisors who raised the tenor of art in the public schools throughout North Carolina. Among this latter group have been the late Callie Braswell, Greensboro; Mrs. Elizabeth Mack, Charlotte; Mrs. Elinor Reuer, Raleigh; Mrs. Tom Sneed, Chapel Hill; Miss Elsie Smith, Durham; and Miss Mary Burgess, Durham County.

In 1958 the Art Department, in cooperation with the Home Economics Department, developed a course in residential design, which won national favor and a four-page color-spread feature in *McCall's* magazine for November, 1958. Outlined for art and home economics majors, the project was designed to provide students with special knowledge of problems they might face in making homes for themselves and their families. Supervised by an architect-instructor, the late Edward Loewenstein of Greensboro, students designed and supervised the building of a house for client-builder Eugene Gulledge, also of Greensboro. Another "first" for women college students, and named "Commencement House" by the college, *McCall's* referred to it as "a honey of a home."

Some of the Woman's College graduates who went on to head other College Art Departments in North Carolina are Mrs. Margaret Click Williams, Peace College; Mrs. Ruth Clarke, at one time head of the Art Department at Meredith College and now teaching part time at Greensboro College; Mrs. Mackey Jeffries, who also was a director of Meredith's Art Department and now teaches art at the Governor's School in Winston-Salem. Out-of-state placements have included Warren Brandt, now a prominent New York artist who became head of the Art Department of the University of Mississippi after getting his M.F.A. at Greensboro; Miss Lee Hall, State University of New York; Miss Martyanne Dehoney, State Teachers College of Jersey City; and Miss Margaret Crawford, head of the Art Department at Russell Sage College, Troy, New York.

On the permanent staff of instructors Ivy brought to the Art Department were Miss Helen Thrush, who became one of the leading teachers of print-making in the South; Dr. Elizabeth Jastrow in art history; Miss Noma Hardin, crafts and textile design; John Courtney, painting; Susan Barkesdale, fashion design and illustration; and later John Kehoe, art education; and John Partin, painting.

When Ivy became impatient over the many delays in providing adequate space for the fast-growing Art Department, which he found "utterly frustrating," he resigned in 1961. Miss Thrush was acting head of the Art Department until Gilbert F. Carpenter assumed the position in 1963. Carpenter came to Greensboro from the University of Hawaii, where he was associate professor of art from 1959 to 1961. He had previously taught at Columbia University, Hunter College, and St. Joseph's College for Women, all in New York City. Under his direction the staff has continued to increase, and the degrees now given are the B.A., B.F.A., M.F.A., and M.Ed.

The Weatherspoon Gallery, adjunct of the Art Department, is more fully covered in the section on Galleries.

THE UNIVERSITY OF NORTH CAROLINA
AT CHAPEL HILL

There was no Art Department at the University of North Carolina when President Frank Porter Graham took office in June of 1930—one hundred and thirty-five years after the University opened its doors. The young president was confronted with so many urgent needs created by the fast-expanding student body at the University and the onset of the Depression that the addition of an Art Department might have been postponed indefinitely had it not been for President Franklin Delano Roosevelt's vast program of public works. But, as Archibald Henderson says in *The Campus of the First State University,* "The ill wind of financial depression at least blew some good toward the Old North State."

The introduction of an Art Department to the campus was a dramatic occasion accompanied by the opening of old Person Hall as an Art Gallery as well as a teaching facility. President Graham was a member of the North Carolina State Art Society and a good friend of its president, Mrs. Katherine Pendleton Arrington, and of administrative Dean Robert Burton House, who had been a founding member of the Society. All three felt the urgency of such a cultural addition to this growing intellectual center, and doubtless the three brought pressure to bear upon the University trustees; for the executive committee of that body, on October 14, 1933, adopted a building program totaling $700,000 "providing for, among other items, a Fine Arts Building." The Fine Arts Building had not yet materialized when the Legislature of North Carolina passed an act in 1935 enabling state institutions to participate in the program of the Federal Emergency Administration of Public Works. Neither did much, if any, of the $700,000 find its way toward an art building. For it was the federal government and private contributors that made possible the renovation of Person Hall, the second oldest building on the campus, to be known as Person Hall Art Gallery, and to be opened to the public in 1937 as the home of the Art Department.

Although there was no Art Department at the University prior to 1937, some activity in this field went on. For instance, J. Penrose Harland, professor of archaeology, maintained a valiant effort to creditably fill the University's deficiency in art instruction. Through his courses on general archaeology and Greek archaeology he covered not only the architecture of the times, but also the paintings. And to meet the state's requirements that all elementary public school teachers have courses in art, the Department of Education brought visiting artists to the University to teach in the summer school. The University also provided space, when possible, for groups of townspeople and students who periodically organized sketching classes and imported private teachers to conduct them. These groups worked in the basement of Hill Hall, the attic of Peabody, and finally the (then) dirt floor of Person Hall.

Miss Alice Tuttle (who later became Mrs. Harold Steadman and the first art teacher at the Mint Museum of Art in Charlotte) was the last private teacher preceding the inauguration of the University's Art Department. She had been a student in the 1934 summer school art class of the Education Department taught by Francis Speight, a Bertie County native who had migrated North to study art at the Pennsylvania Academy of Fine Arts at Philadelphia. Miss Tuttle's work had been so outstanding that, upon Speight's departure, she was asked to teach the second term of summer school art.

Speight's return to North Carolina to teach at the University, even for such a brief period of time, created quite a stir among art lovers and newspaper reporters, who quoted him as saying that "it was with a sort of patriotic feeling that he accepted the invitation to teach here." (Even though he was quite young, Speight already was represented in the permanent collections of the Metropolitan Museum of Art, the Toronto Museum, and the Pennsylvania Academy, as well as in private collections in Chicago, Detroit, New York, Philadelphia, Pittsburgh, Chattanooga, and elsewhere.) It was the popularity of Speight's classes during the summer of 1934 that convinced the University officials that a permanent art curriculum was imperative at the University. Enrolled in his class were twenty-one pupils instead of the six to fifteen expected, which led Speight to emphasize the University's need for art instruction by pointing out that many of his Honor Roll students at the Pennsylvania Academy were from the South.

The state's newspapers echoed the University's news release that "the six-weeks' course here marked the first time in the history of Southern universities that such a course, equal to those offered in the best art schools in the cities of the North, had been embodied in summer school curricula, and Speight expressed his pleasure with the interest manifested." Administrative Dean Robert B. House admitted that "we fully realize the need of such a department and the success of the class this summer confirms our belief of the interest in art, but we lack money and had rather not announce any plans which we may not be able to carry out."

Events moved swiftly, however, for on December 3, of the same year, President Graham happily announced at the annual meeting of the State Art Society in Raleigh that "through the generosity of an anonymous donor and aid from the federal government, the state is going to have an art museum on the University of North Carolina campus at Chapel Hill." He told of the many and varied phases Person Hall had gone through before its present condition of being gutted by workmen laying the groundwork for the art museum. He also reviewed briefly the Southern Arts Projects in which the University was sharing, sponsored by the Carnegie Foundation and directed by Miss Leila Mechlin.

Following President Graham on the program Miss Mechlin explained that the Southern Arts Projects had been initiated by the American Federation of Arts as an experiment at Telfair Academy in Savannah, had been successful there and extended to Charlottesville and Chapel Hill. Then funds for the work had been exhausted, but the Carnegie Foundation stepped in and saved the endeavor, for the time, at least.

Optimism prevailed, and President Graham announced that "the Chapel Hill unit of the project also will, possibly in the spring, send out a travelling exhibit through the state, as is being done at Charlottesville in a successful program of taking art to the people." Miss Mechlin concurred in the dream of Mrs. Arrington who, in her presidential report to the State Art Society, said that she hoped "for the future that every town or city in North Carolina would have an art museum and an art building . . . that the idea was no more fantastic than the idea of a library for every town had been fifty years ago."

Remodeling of Person Hall was completed toward the end of 1936, and while it did not attain the dimensions of an art museum *per se*, it was a fine gallery for its day and served as the home of the new Art Department. Dedication exercises were held in Hill Music Hall on January 15, 1937, at which time the "new" Person Hall was turned over to Professor Russell T. Smith, who had come to Chapel Hill in 1936 to develop an Art Department. An illustrious crowd attended the dedication ceremonies. Speakers Dean Everett V. Meeks, of the Yale University School of Fine Arts, Miss Mechlin, and President Graham delivered glowing speeches on the role of art in our society. All rejoiced in the culmination of earlier hopes, expressed by Miss Mechlin at a State Art Society meeting in Raleigh in 1934, "that a school or department of creative arts may be founded [at Chapel Hill] to eventually match the fine work being done in the drama and in music."

Mrs. Arrington, a moving spirit behind the arts in North Carolina, had been revealed as the anonymous donor referred to earlier by President Graham. She had given $10,000 toward the renovation of Person Hall as a memorial to her brother, Milo M. Pendleton of the class of 1902. Other contributors, according to Archibald Henderson's *The Campus of the First State University*, were Mrs. Rufus L. Patterson, William D. Carmichael, Frank L. Fuller, and Mrs. B. H. Griffin. Henderson also credits the Civil Works Administration, in conjunction with FERA and WPA, as granting the sum of $10,000. These gifts made possible the renovation of Person Hall.

During the dedication exercises President Graham in his inimitable style paid the following tribute to Mrs. Arrington and the federal government:

> This little hall has a story which it could tell of a University's decision in slender times to make an investment in art, with no assurances of a roof for many months to keep out the rain which beat upon its inner walls. . . . Today it stands, roof and all, with most of the original bricks and all the original simple lines, the work of many hands, the blending of three centuries, and the final result of the cooperation of Uncle Sam's CWA and North Carolina's KPA (Kate Pendleton Arrington), the beautiful home of the De-

partment of Art, the youngest of all our departments in the next oldest of all our buildings.

Following the dedication program, the élite gathering moved from Hill Hall to Person Hall (led by its regal benefactor, Mrs. Kate Pendleton Arrington, who, if memory serves me right, was clad in a flowing chiffon evening gown in subtle shades of mauve and lavender) for a reception and the viewing of its premiere exhibition of *modern* American paintings and a small group of earlier English and American paintings. Among the artists represented were John LaFarge, Mary Cassatt, James McNeill Whistler, Childe Hassam, Eliott O'Hara, John Singleton Copley, Sir Thomas Lawrence, and many others shown in this area for the first time.

As early as 1930 a feature writer had predicted that Chapel Hill might become an art center, based on the fact that three portrait painters were residing in the village: Mrs. Arthur C. Nash, wife of a prominent architect, Mrs. Mary deB. Graves Rees, and William Steen. The opening of the Person Hall Art Gallery strengthened this prediction by stimulating anew the interest and imagination of art-minded people around the state.

Smith remained as art chairman only until 1940, at which time he left to become the director of the Boston Museum School of Fine Arts. Before leaving, however, he lured his old friend, John Allcott, away from Hunter College in New York to Chapel Hill to become his successor, with a friendly agreement to exchange jobs from time to time—a plan that never quite materialized, Smith said, as he reminisced about Chapel Hill when the writer visited him at the Boston Museum in 1965.

When Allcott arrived in the fall of 1940 the state was on its way to recovery from the Depression, except for the public schools and institutions of higher learning, about which some of our political leaders showed little concern. Also, World War II was casting its shadow over future plans for expansion.

Conscious of the struggle of the Art Department, a group of Chapel Hill women met and offered their aid to John Allcott. In January, 1941, the following notice appeared in the *Bulletin of Person Hall*: "Many plans for the better presentation of exhibitions and lectures to the public and for the encouragement of the students were not quite possible this year.

And the staff [Art Department] would not want to undertake again, unsupported, this work of 1940. The gallery needs help. To prevent the blackout of Person Hall, and to make possible many fine activities, an association is proposed: *The Friends of Person Hall.*"

The organization was formally organized on the evening of February 2, 1941, marked by the preview of an exhibition of Van Gogh's work and a lecture by Clemens Sommer on "Van Gogh and His Time." The organizing committee of the group included Mrs. W. D. Carmichael, chairman; Mrs. Collier Cobb, Jr., vice chairman; and Mrs. George S. Lane, treasurer. Other members were Mesdames H. M. Burlage, W. E. Caldwell, W. C. Coker, Lyman Cotten, F. H. Edmister, D. Franklin Milam, Larry Flinn, Joseph Pratt, M. J. Rosenau, Clemens Sommer, and M. T. Van Hecke—all faculty wives except Mrs. Flinn and Mrs. Cobb.

This group immediately initiated through the Art Gallery a gigantic art program for the Orange County schools, providing rental pictures, lecturers, and transportation for parents, teachers, and students to Person Hall for exhibits and lectures. When gasoline rationing interfered with the delivery of pictures, Mrs. Russell Grumman, director of the rental project, used Parcel Post. *The Story of Person Hall*, written in 1942 by Mrs. Gladys Hall Coates, chairman of the organization, recounts among other achievements the cataloguing of University portraits, the rental of educational films, sponsorship of lectures, the beginning of a loan fund inspired by "the generous donation made by the Cobb family as a nucleus." The Friends often financed the printing of the *Bulletin,* and exerted extensive efforts to "make new groups in our midst, on account of the war, feel at home in the Art Gallery."

After cataloguing the rich heritage of portraits on the University campus, the Friends gathered historical data about the subjects and employed Arthur E. Bye, official restorer for Princeton University, to restore and bring new life "to the faded features of prominent North Carolina men portrayed on canvases long neglected, sometimes mutilated, and often relegated to dark closets." In a stirring speech during the celebration of the 150th anniversary of the cornerstone laying of Old East—oldest State University building in the country and now a historical shrine—Bye refers to the experience as surprising and exhilarating: "As I grew to know these casualties from the past, brought to me literally on stretchers, torn and wounded, but yet alive, made immortal by the brush of Peale, Sully, Harding, or Garl Browne, I grew to revere them as men of ennobling influence whose lives still touch upon our own."

The Friends financed speakers such as William Stanley Hayter, head of Atelier 17 in Paris (and New York City during World War II); Josef Albers, Sibyl Moholy-Nagy, whose husband played a leading role in the Bauhaus in Germany; and underwrote numerous exhibitions. They provided salary supplements for gallery workers and arranged guided tours to New York City and Washington art galleries for groups of University students. Herman Weil, a Goldsboro member, placed in the Art Department over a hundred volumes containing eight thousand cross-indexed photographs, to aid in studies in Italian art under the distinguished Renaissance scholar, Clemens Sommer.

By 1949 membership was statewide and an Art Foundation was planned to further augment the Art Department, but efforts toward this were discouraged by the University, already developing its own fundraising Foundation and preparing to embrace its newly-inherited Ackland bequest.

May 18, 1950, marked the final gesture of The Friends of Person Hall, when it entertained Sibyl Moholy-Nagy, friend and guest of George Kachergis of the Art Department, and financed her talk on her late husband's work with the Bauhaus and her book about his work.

Class enrollment in the Art Department had grown to 336 by 1941, and art was incorporated into the freshman program of the University for the first time. The teaching staff had expanded, too. Clemens Sommer had come in 1939 to inaugurate a program of graduate study in art history; and Kenneth Ness followed in 1941, as resident-artist on a Carnegie Foundation grant (one of the few such appointments in the country). His job was not to conduct regular classes but to teach through example by painting and commenting while students looked on, and to give criticism to students seeking advice. In this same manner he also enlivened an occasional Sunday afternoon in the then sleepy little university village by demonstrating portrait painting in the studio of Person Hall.

Choosing a model from the audience, he would paint vigorously while the surrounding spectators listened to his comments and watched his dexterous brush in hypnotic fascination. On November 20, 1941, the *Raleigh Times* ran a feature story and a picture of Ness doing a portrait demonstration in celebration of National Art Week, using as his model William C. Fields, a recent graduate of the Art Department who was then assistant director of the State WPA Art Project.

Born in Michigan in 1903, Ness studied at the Art Institute of Chicago, the University of Detroit, the Detroit School of Applied Art, and the Wicker School of Fine Art. In 1948 he was described by Allcott as having special value, "because of his double experience: as a painter and as an advertising designer."

When World War II cast its shadow over the University, the Art Department was chosen as a new War Art Center. Ness was asked to take charge of it, and under his instruction posters, charts, and displays for such agencies as ODC, OWI, the Red Cross, and the University War Information Center were designed and executed through different media, the most fascinating of which was the silk-screen process of quantity printing—a method made popular among creative artists by federal arts and crafts workshops and later developed as a fine arts technique for printmaking.

Through this wartime expediency, students were kept busy "learning by doing." Among their projects were a series of War Bond and Stamp posters, executed in compliance with a request from the United States Treasury Department's section on education; a Tin Can Salvage Poster; and morale posters for the National Munitions Corporations. A bulletin sent out on May 8, 1943, by the University News Bureau, told of the War Art Center and of its comprehensive background of studio methods and practices open to art students engaged in the poster-making projects. As a local project the graphic design class prepared a series of slides and film plates for projection in Health Department clinics in Orange, Chatham, Durham, and Person counties, to aid in the study of epidemiology. Person Hall, of course, was far too small for these major projects, and much of the work and teaching was done in other campus buildings.

Another wartime effort of the Art Department was the arts and crafts workshop, designed to meet the increasing demand for occupational therapists in rehabilitation centers, army camps, and army hospitals. Those of us who took the course were given certificates leading to credit in the fields of education, sociology, or art. Instruction was given in the evenings at the Person Hall studios by Stephen Hopkins Walker, artist-craftsman of Washington, D. C., who had taught sculpture and allied arts at the University of Virginia and had been director of art in Fairfax County, Virginia. He had studied with the famous Russian sculptor, Alexander Archipenko, and with the Danish craftsmen Lauritz Eichner and Adda Husted-Anderson, two of the world's leading silversmiths.

Brightening the wartime gloom were the many fine gifts that continued to come to the Art Department, enriching the library and the teaching program. A small reference library of books and photographs was made possible by The Friends of Person Hall and the Henry Clay Frick Foundation. Gifts of money came from Lawrence Flinn, a wealthy member who was later killed in combat, and from the family of Collier Cobb, Jr., and special grants of books came from the University Library Board and the Carnegie Foundation of New York. Mr. and Mrs. George Lurcy of Paris, New York, and High Point, made significant contributions, and Mrs. George Westervelt underwrote many expenses of the gallery. She and her husband, a retired Navy Captain, paid the expenses of faculty and students on New York study trips and among other things financed the cost of life models for a summer session. Mrs. Arrington continued to make contributions and to use her influence to bring fine exhibitions to the gallery. She provided several scholarships and made possible an important course of lectures (illustrated by lantern slides, beginning with David and Ingres around 1800 and continuing up to Picasso and Dali in 1942), paving the way for exhibitions of more modern paintings. "North Carolina students enjoy and are seeking to enlarge their understanding of modern art," Allcott said.

The handsome desk of General Person, for whom the gallery was named, was given by Miss Ellen Hale Wilson in memory of Peter Mitchell Wilson, the great-great-great nephew of the General. An equestrian statue entitled "Youth," was given to the gallery by sculptress Anna Hyatt Huntington for the front courtyard of Person Hall.

Somewhat indicative of propaganda was an assemblage of art works displayed in Person Hall during February of 1942. At that time the University was conducting a "winter" summer school for Latin American students gathered in Chapel Hill from all parts of the world, a program inaugurated by Sturgis Leavitt of the Romance Languages Department. The exhibit, together with accompanying charts and statistics, was provided by the Government to "set forth the character and the purpose of the WPA art program" which was enabling twentieth-century American artists to keep working at their professions, and was especially prepared to acquaint the visiting Latin American students with the philosophy behind the WPA project.

By this time John Allcott had been on loan to the Government for a period of two years, doing Navy educational work in Washington, leaving Kenneth Ness as acting chairman of the Art Department. But on July 28, 1945, Chancellor House announced that both Allcott and Ness had been selected by the War Department to serve on the faculty of the University Study Center of the Army Education Program for troops in the Mediterranean theatre of operations; that "while Ness is on leave to join Allcott in Italy for a four-month period of army instruction, William Meade Prince, artist-illustrator and visiting lecturer in the University's Art Department, will serve as acting head and will direct art studio classes until both Allcott and Ness return to Chapel Hill in December." The two men met in Florence, Italy, where they served as civilian education specialists in the Study Center which opened with an enrollment of 1,300 men.

With only a skeletal staff, and aid from Clemens Sommer, Prince and Miss Harriet Dyer Adams, curator, maintained a lively program, despite the clouds of war. Sommer worked quietly with his students in art history (behind a large screen in the library of Person Hall), meanwhile dreaming of the future when the department might offer the Ph.D. in that field. Statesman-like in bearing and charming of manner, he possessed a fine sense of humor and often found time for a good story. One he particularly liked to tell was about his coming to Chapel Hill: "When Dr. Frank Graham hired me to teach art history, he thought he was also hiring a painter," he would chuckle, "and he could hardly wait to see what kind of painting his European acquisition would turn out. Every time we met at a party or on the campus, he would ask me when I was going to start painting. He never seemed to believe me when I said I was not a painter."

Finally, as the story goes, at a party being held in Chapel Hill for Mrs. Franklin D. Roosevelt, President Graham got a convincing though surprising answer from another source. He cornered the young son of Sommer and inquired: "Why doesn't your father start painting?" "Because he doesn't know how," was Sebastian's laconic reply. From then on, Sommer recalled, he was left in peace to teach his beloved course in art history, a job he cherished until his fatal automobile accident on the night of March 11, 1962.

Following several earlier assistants, Miss Lynette Warren joined the Art Department May 1, 1946, as curator and hostess for the gallery, and with the help of graduate students maintained the library and managed the studio store and a collection of rental pictures. She remained on the staff until January, 1959.

George Kachergis joined the Art Department staff in 1949, coming to Chapel Hill from Bradley University. A native of Waterbury, Connecticut, he received the B.F.A. and M.F.A. from the University of Chicago. His long list of one-man shows, purchase awards, and his inclusion in the Metropolitan Museum of Art exhibitions of American painters in 1950 and 1952 brought not only personal distinction but importance to the young Art Department. Other striking honors were a $1,000 Tiffany Fellowship in 1951 and another $1,000 purchase prize from the Terry Art Institute International Exhibition held in Miami, Florida, to be followed by numerous recognitions over the years. He became the first director of art education in the University Art Department, contributing generously toward the development of better art in the public schools. He served as a panel member at the 1948 National Art Conference of the Museum of Modern Art in New York City.

Among a number of other excellent teachers brought in by Allcott for short periods were Emma Lou Davis, sculptress, who flew her own airplane, and John Rembert, a fine painter who later became paralyzed. Rembert's painting, "By the Winds Grieved," won a purchase award in the 1948 North Carolina Artists' Annual and is now in the North Carolina Museum of Art collection. Robert Howard came in 1951 to teach sculpture, and almost immediately gained international recognition for his unusual sculpture. *La Revue Moderne* not only devoted much of an issue to his work but featured his "Pasage II" on its cover. For a number of years his work averaged more than a prize a year. Allcott, Ness, Kachergis and Howard are still members of the University Art Department at this writing in 1970.

It would be difficult to look back at those days without paying tribute to Archie Daniels, a frail bachelor who for fifteen years went quietly about his many odd jobs, dignified by the title of "assistant curator." His skills in wood-working and carpentry were put to use in repairing picture frames, and his self-taught knowledge of painting enabled him to do a great deal of "touching up" of paintings for the gallery as well as for outsiders who often had him restore family heirlooms.

On the side, Archie painted for hours at a time, his style neither primitive nor contemporary, but often competent. "I never want to paint a pessimistic picture," he once said, "but I would like to paint a masterpiece that would live on and on after I leave life's stage." This he almost did. Many offices on the campus are brightened by his interpretations of the campus or of a country scene, and I bought one of his watercolors that had drifted from a fine estate into a junk shop. Entitled "Silence," it hangs in an upstairs hall and is so reflected in a mirror as to make it visible from every bedroom. Archie had a manuscript of over 300 typewritten pages, entitled "Sunshine and Shadows," which he felt was about ready for publication when he passed away, as quietly as he had lived. He was found dead at his home on May 20, 1955, but not before being honored by the Chancellor of the University when he retired at age seventy-two. A small group of friends and admirers met at the office of Chancellor House for the occasion, at which time the University conferred upon Archie the title of "Honorary Curator-Emeritus of Person Hall Art Gallery."

Upon the return of Allcott and Ness from World War II, the Art Department was recharged by their new curricular ideas designed to meet the needs of the community as well as students. In 1948 Allcott contributed a glowing report to the *Chapel Hill Weekly* on the continuous growth of the Art Department, enumerating many of its achievements. "There are about 50 students majoring in art . . . training for careers in advertising design . . . to become painters, sculptors, architects, art historians, museum workers, teachers. . . . Over 400 general students in the University elect art courses during the year. . . . There are noncredit courses sponsored by the Person Hall Art Gallery for the general public. . . . These courses last year included an evening sketch class, Saturday and summer classes for children; a class in arts and crafts, conducted by Ola Maie Foushee; and the Orange County art teaching project, directed by Emily Pollard for the Friends of Person Hall."

A graduate course in creative art leading to a Master of Arts degree was announced by Allcott on February 3, 1950: "This program will be the only course in this area which naturally follows for our A.B. graduates interested in continuing with a graduate major in creative art," Allcott said, pointing out that formerly students had had to go afield to continue their work in creative art, or else had registered for a minor in creative art with a major in some other subject. The reference library containing 1,500 art books, ten files of current art magazines, 11,000 photographs, and 200 facsimile color reproductions Allcott considered an excellent basis for the serious and distinguished work in art history in the University, and for a type of instruction not available in most professional art schools; "a mark of the creative art instruction possible at a good university."

Kenneth Ness became acting director of Person Hall and the Art Department in 1957. By then the Ackland bequest was a certainty and the Ackland Museum building was in progress. Ness not only created the impressive interior design and decor, but selected the furnishings for the building. On September 20, 1958, friendly and intimate Person Hall relinquished its priority on culture to its successor, and Ness and his staff moved across campus to Columbia Street where they joined the new staff of the new Ackland Art Center. There, despite its mausoleum-like façade, its interior throbs with constantly expanding art activities. Only a few members of the present art staff know more than hearsay of the once thriving Friends of Person Hall, which for nearly two decades supported the Art Department and Person Hall Art Gallery.

THE SCHOOL OF DESIGN, NORTH CAROLINA STATE UNIVERSITY, RALEIGH

In 1948 the world-renowned School of Design was organized through the combination of the existing Departments of Architecture and Landscape Architecture. Devoted and dedicated to the development of a native architecture and its accompanying forms for the southern region, it would not be within the scope of this book but for the immense amount of art instruction inherent in the curricula. Since art is part of four parallel programs (architecture, art, humanities and social sciences, and science and engineering), many of its students become prize-winning painters. Also, among its teachers there are several artists whose work is widely collected and who, through example, inspire a uniquely disciplined quality in painting.

Duncan Stuart, Associate Professor of Design, for example, won first prize in graphics at the Oklahoma Artists Annual in 1947; was represented in the Chicago Art Institute Invitational Annual, 1948; the Metropolitan Museum of Art's first Contemporary Annual, 1950; the Whitney Museum of Art, 1951; and has won numerous purchase awards. His work is well represented in the North Carolina Museum of Art at Raleigh. Manuel Bromberg stacked up a similar record, as did Roy Gussow with his sculpture, when they taught there. Joseph H. Cox, who teaches visual communications, painting, and graphics, was recipient of a Tiffany Scholarship in 1941, and is represented through purchase awards in the North Carolina Museum of Art; the Mint Museum of Art, Charlotte; and the Norfolk Museum of Art. He has murals in Indiana, Michigan, Tennessee, and North Carolina. The most recent of these is an exterior panel in stained glass and anodized aluminum on the Branch Banking and Trust Company, Raleigh, North Carolina, and a thirty-six foot by eight foot sculptural aluminum mural, using colored light, in the Southern National Bank in Lumberton, North Carolina.

The honors received by George Bireline, Jr., are too numerous to list. In this state alone he has won first prize in competitions at the Winston-Salem Gallery of Fine Arts and in the North Carolina Artists Annual, and has won the Harrelson Purchase Award. His work was shown in the Fourth International Young Artists Exhibition, U. S. A., in Tokyo, Japan, and used as a catalogue illustration; and was included in the American Federation of Arts circulating exhibition in 1967–68. A John Simon Guggenheim Memorial Foundation Fellowship has assisted his research and artistic creation.

In 1950 the students of the School of Design established the *Student Publication of the School of Design*, a slick, well-illustrated organ which is circulated internationally. An independent student project, it has been supported by student fees, patrons, and subscriptions, but primarily from the proceeds of an annual art auction which draws hundreds of art-interested people from a wide area who are anxious to add to their private collections of art. In the foreword of an early issue of the publication, Dean Henry L. Kamphoefner described the goals of the school:

> The school in its teaching recognizes the dangers inherent in a materialist-mechanistic civilization where there may be an over-reliance on the machine and the mechanical devices available for use to man in his constructions for shelter. We give attention, therefore, to that larger responsibility of architecture, the art of humanizing the environment. . . . To combat the dangers of over-specialization we seek to develop the personality and character as a whole. The goal in the growth of the student is not only the mastery of the architectural techniques of the profession, but through the stimulation and development of the intellect and emotional capacities together, a readiness is developed to meet the challenge of any environment.

EAST CAROLINA UNIVERSITY

Art has been a part of the curriculum of this university since its early days as East Carolina Teachers College. Miss Kate Lewis kept a lively art program going for future public school teachers from 1909 until her retirement in 1946. Service courses and skill courses continued to be taught basically to education majors until after World War II. During its transitional period, after Miss Lewis retired, Mrs. Jean Lane Fonville was acting director from 1946 to 1948. The first art education candidate was graduated in 1946, when all aspects of the college began a phenomenal growth. The art faculty was increased to four and the A.B. degree in studio and the B.S. degree in art education were added.

Acceleration of the art program began in 1956 when Wellington B. Gray came to the then East Carolina College as head of the Art Department. At the end of six fast-paced years the Department became the first School of Art in the South, necessitating a reorganization of the faculty to include a dean, an assistant dean, and nine departments. That same year the School gained approval to offer the B.F.A. and M.F.A. degrees and now offers the A.B. (art history), B.S. (art education), B.F.A. (studio), M.A. (art-studio), M.A. in Education (art education), and M.F.A. (studio-professional). In 1965 the National Association of Schools of Art gave the School accreditation—thus endowing it at that time as the only accredited art school or department in the tri-state area of Virginia, North Carolina, and South Carolina.

Gray says that "in order to have attained this status, the Department has worked toward rigid professional standards, diversifying its program within the school by the addition of professional degrees. . . . NASA membership puts official sanction on the professional standards developed in recent years which have launched East Carolina's entrance into the national mainstream of professional schools of art." He maintains that his faculty is one of the most professional and prolific in terms of professional involvement. Of the twenty-nine full-time faculty members under contract in the fall of 1970, three hold doctorates, thirteen the M.F.A., nine the M.A., two the M.S., one the M.Ed., and one a professional diploma.

Well-known for their own works, which are exhibited nationally and are in leading collections in the state and elsewhere, are faculty members Tran and Marilyn Gordley for their paintings, Paul R. Minnis for his ceramics, and Donald R. Sexauer for his prints. Under Sexauer's direction, the graphics department of the School of Art is the largest in the South. It is well equipped with etching presses and lithograph stones, and the first (possibly the only) serigraph machine in the area.

By 1962 the eight large classrooms were equipped with eighteen potter's wheels, three tremendous kilns, six jeweler's tables, and many drafting tables. It was the only school in the state with its own pug wheel, enabling the students to mix their own clays mechanically. Numerous looms provide opportunity for students of industrial arts and home economics to do experimental yardage as well as finished products, but "always with emphasis on design."

Gray holds the degrees of B.S. in art education, the M.A., and the Doctor of Education. He has contributed numerous articles on various art subjects to many art periodicals. His book, *Student Teaching in Art*, was published by the International Textbook Company, Scranton, Pennsylvania.

NORTH CAROLINA CENTRAL UNIVERSITY

North Carolina Central University was chartered in 1909 as a private institution named the National Religious Training School and Chautauqua. Founded by its late president, Dr. James E. Shepard, it was maintained by gifts, student fees, and some help from the State. By legislative act in 1925, it became a liberal arts college—the only state-supported liberal arts college for Blacks in the United States.

The Art Department has slowly developed from courses in art, according to Mrs. Lynn M. Igoe, chairman since 1966. It made great strides in the late 1950's when Edward Wilson, internationally known sculptor, was chairman. It has continued to grow under the leadership of Mrs. Igoe and an expanding faculty that as of 1970 includes Robert F. Kennedy, with a B.A. from Mexico City College and an M.F.A. from the University of Michigan; and instructors Lana T. Henderson, Samuel B. Molina, and Norman E. Pendergraft. A museum has been added and the Art Department awards the B.A. for art majors in Art Education, Fine Arts, and Visual Communication.

L'Atelier, a student organization, is open to art majors and others interested in the visual arts. Activities include talks on art, visits to museums, galleries, and exhibitions, and sponsorship of student art exhibitions.

NORTH CAROLINA AGRICULTURAL AND TECHNICAL STATE UNIVERSITY

A. and T. University at Greensboro has offered a major in art since 1932. The major sequence offers art education, design, and painting. Professor H. Clinton Taylor served as chairman of the Art Department from 1932 until his death in 1958 when he was succeeded by Professor LeRoy F. Holmes.

A. and T. students have been well represented in art exhibitions of note. Marvin Outterbridge, for instance, won a $50 purchase prize for his woodblock print in the first Associated Artists' Annual Print and Drawing exhibition held at East Carolina College in March, 1965. Four A. and T. students were represented in that show. Alumni who have reached some degree of recognition include Harold James, an illustrator; H. D. Bullock, F. B. Baird, Theolander Taylor, and Clarence Bullock, artists; Theodore Wells, an artist-teacher; and Preston Haygood, who owns an art shop.

From the beginning the Art Department has emphasized instruction for prospective teachers of art as well as prospective painters, acording to Professor Holmes. The four-year program leads to the B.S. degree in art, whereas the initial program, general in nature, was modified in 1965 to permit concentration in three years. A graduate program is in the preparatory stages.

ELIZABETH CITY STATE COLLEGE

Inaugurated first as a Normal School in 1891, this area college's art was teacher-oriented and was part of the curriculum from the turn of the century. According to Professor Vincent J. de Gregorio, chairman of the Art Department in 1958, the art program then required 58 semester hours, and an art major received the B.S. degree upon completion of 127 semester hours. He was expecting to move to new quarters in the 1966–67 college year and to expand the art program.

WESTERN CAROLINA UNIVERSITY

Art at Western Carolina College (now Western Carolina University) has been offered "as far back as I can check the catalogues," wrote Rodney L. Leftwich, head of the Department of Fine and Industrial Arts, in 1965, "although a major in this field was not started until 1947." At his writing the department was offering three degrees in art (the B.S., A.B., and a B.S. in Education), and had a staff of seven art teachers. Leftwich also noted that a new building was projected and hoped for in the near future.

"We have approximately 100 art majors and, in addition to this, teach a survey course in Art History required of all students, and special art courses for elementary majors." Leftwich headed the department from 1947 until about 1969 when Perry Kelly, former State Art Supervisor, assumed the directorship. The staff soon doubled and the B.F.A. and a double major in art are offered under the combined Departments of Industrial Education and Technology and Art.

WINSTON-SALEM STATE UNIVERSITY

Formerly the Winston-Salem Teachers College, this university has been teacher-oriented from the beginning. It developed a strong Department of Art Education under the directorship of Professor J. T. Diggs, who for more than twenty-five years developed unique methods of helping teachers of art in the public schools. Haywood Oubre followed Professor Diggs as director of the Art Department, which along with the new trend of the university as a whole is moving toward the liberal arts approach, with a major in art becoming effective in 1971. Since Professor Oubre came in 1965, the art staff has grown to four: Diggs teaches an introduction to art and art appreciation; Roland S. Watts, art education; Mrs. Mitzi Shewmake, sculpture and art history. Oubre himself gives instruction in drawing (the only prerequisite), color and design, and teaches a course in Afro-American art, which is also an art history or art appreciation course.

Along with other state-supported colleges, which the Legislature of 1969 raised to university status, Winston-Salem State University became integrated, and although in a minority, a number of white students are already taking advantage of this expanding Department of Art, according to Professor Oubre.

THE UNIVERSITY OF NORTH CAROLINA AT WILMINGTON

This branch of the Consolidated University of North Carolina was established in September of 1947. Art was introduced through night classes for adults, taught by Wilmington artist Claude Howell. Soon the popularity of these classes indicated the need for a Department of Art, and Howell became its director. Howell designed the spacious art quarters of the Fine Arts Building, the hallways of which serve as exhibition space. The Art Department is a one-man operation and does not offer a degree in art at this writing, but through its outstanding exhibition program it is wielding a significant influence on culture in the state and particularly Eastern North Carolina.

SHAW UNIVERSITY

An independent, non-profit institution, this Negro university in Raleigh gives the B.S. degree, with instruction in painting, sculpture, printmaking, and ceramics. In 1969 Mrs. Herbert Collins stated that Shaw is in the process of revising its entire curriculum, the new program to require a three-year humanities sequence of all students. She further reported that "Art History will be part of this sequence. . . . In the past Shaw has offered a limited amount of art geared mainly to the needs of elementary education majors." To implement this program, Mrs. Collins initiated a monthly series of art exhibits. Students also are encouraged to take field trips to view exhibits of artistic significance.

THE UNIVERSITY OF NORTH
CAROLINA AT ASHEVILLE

Originally a community college, the University of North Carolina at Asheville has a Department of Art and Music, inaugurated in 1965, with Professor Eugene F. Bunker, head of the visual arts faculty, and S. Tucker Cooke, instructor.

The role of the art instruction, as interpreted by Bunker, is to offer its major students, the student body, and the community quality education in three primary areas of the visual arts, which he describes as (a) two-dimensional theory and studio (drawing, painting, print-making; (b) three dimensional theory (design, sculpture, metal, and glass); and (c) art history. Referring to the department as "experimental," Bunker would like to have the students "question the relation of the visual arts to their environment." An art major must produce a creative project or an art history thesis before graduation.

SALEM COLLEGE

Founded in 1772 by the Moravians as the first college established in North Carolina, Salem has had some art instruction from the beginning, but the Art Department averages only six to eighteen graduates annually with an art major as late as 1970. From 1950 until the last few years the Art Department has been a one-man operation under the direction of Edwin F. Shewmake, chairman. With the added space provided by Salem's Fine Arts Center (a multi-purpose building completed in 1965), the Art Department expanded to include William G. Mangum, associate professor; James M. Moon, instructor in studio art; and Antony Swider, part-time lecturer in art education. Shewmake reports that equal emphasis is placed on art history and studio art. The major in art requires a minimum of six courses above certain other courses, and an exhibit of work or a thesis in art history is mandatory for each major at the end of the senior year. For a teaching certificate in art, eight courses are required.

GREENSBORO COLLEGE

The Methodists chartered Greensboro Female College, as it was first called, in 1838, and Professor Irene Cullis, long-time chairman of the Art Department says that "earliest accounts record the inclusion of 'art instruction.'"

"For many years a girls' school," she continues in her report, "the college has always stressed the importance of music and art in the training of young ladies. Changes have been made from time to time—notably, the admission of men students in 1955—and the art program has developed from charcoal drawing and china painting to become an integral part of a liberal arts curriculum. For some years now, at least one course in art or music has been required of all bachelor of arts candidates."

Now housed in a new building providing a tremendous amount of space for art instruction, the Art Department offers courses in sculpture, printmaking, art history, crafts, painting, arts and crafts for the exceptional child, and art methods in the public schools, among others. The expanded faculty includes Assistant Professor John C. Bott, and lecturer Ruth Clarke. Some of the expansion in course offerings is provided through the Art Departments of Guilford College and Bennett College, giving the art majors a choice of three different emphases: "the North Carolina teaching certificate; preparation for graduate work in art history; and extra studio courses for the future professional painter."

ST. MARY'S COLLEGE

Founded at Raleigh under Episcopal influences by the Reverend Albert Smedes in 1842, St. Mary's, until recently a preparatory school, has offered some type of art instruction from its beginning. St. Mary's publication, the *Muse*, a Music Department magazine, contains numerous articles on artists and lectures to art students in the 1880's and 1890's. All of these courses required additional tuitional charges.

In 1937, when other colleges were expanding their art instruction, St. Mary's dropped the additional tuition charges. Basically a one-person department, usually having a student enrollment of about one-fifth of the student body, the emphasis has been on developing basic skills and knowledge of the arts. Miss Katherine Currie Morris, who graduated from St. Mary's Junior College in 1925, taught art there in 1925–26. After a distinguished career and many art honors in other art areas, she returned to teach art again at her Alma Mater from 1945 to 1958. Mrs. Margaret Click Williams followed Miss Morris and has succeeded in building a collection of prints and slides for the teaching of art history.

PEACE COLLEGE

The Presbyterians chartered Peace Female Institute as a junior college in Raleigh in 1857 but, due to the Civil War, opening was delayed until 1872. Its Art Department was shared with Music, and the gymnasium doubled as an art gallery. The first art teacher at Peace was Miss Frances Fowler. Miss June J. Spencer, a former pupil of Miss Fowler's, was the art teacher from 1880 to 1885. James Lee Love of Burlington, in 1946 established the June J. Spencer Scholarship in Art.

At its 1954 Commencement, Peace exhibited art works by thirty-eight of its former art students. Among its distinguished alumnae practicing art in North Carolina are Mrs. J. Francis Paschal (Primrose McPherson), represented in the North Carolina Museum of Art's permanent collection, and an illustrator of note; and Miss Mabel Pugh, whose story is more fully told elsewhere in this book. For a time Mrs. Ruth Huntington Moore was head of the Art Department at Peace. Following Mrs. Moore's death in 1936 Miss Pugh returned to become head of the Art Department, a position she held until her retirement in 1960.

Under the present direction of Mrs. J. Olmsted, basic courses are offered in painting, commercial art, ceramics, art history, and art appreciation. *High Time to Tell It*, an autobiography written by Miss Mary Alves Long, an alumna, in 1950 when she was past eighty, gives us this glimpse of art in the early days of Peace College: "The gymnasium was at the top of the building—it was also the art gallery by day, gym hours being from nine to ten at night. Here with the easels, pictures and statues all being pushed to one side, we repaired the first three nights in the week to exercise. . . ."

MEREDITH COLLEGE

The Art Department at Meredith in Raleigh grew from courses in art taught by Miss Ida Poteat in the early 1900's and later by Miss Mary

Tillery. As a Department of Art it gained momentum under the leadership
of Mrs. Ruth Clarke who became head of the department in 1957. She
was followed in 1961 by Mrs. Mackey Jeffries. The present director is
Leonard White of Chapel Hill. When "Mackey," as she now signs her
work, was in her second year at Meredith, she said in an interview that
she was "impressed with the potential growth of the art department and
encouraged by the seriousness and capabilities of students choosing art as
a major. It was these qualities, in fact, developed by Mrs. Ruth Clarke
(also a product of Woman's College at Greensboro) that lured me to
Raleigh."

Meredith gives the A.B. in art, and while it does not emphasize art
education, it does give courses whereby a student may get certification to
teach art in the public schools, according to White. Dean Peacock, in an
interview in 1962 said, "Through our teacher program we hope to get
better art into the schools, and if our own students missed this ingredient
in their own education, we have them pick it up while at Meredith." Each
student is required to take at least three hours in either art or music, as
"art is a part of basic education in the esthetics."

WAKE FOREST UNIVERSITY

Chartered in 1833 as the Baptist Literary Institute, this forerunner of
Wake Forest College opened in Wake Forest in 1834. It is doubtful that
much art existed in this controversial school, which contributed to a rift
among the Baptists just prior to its opening. Beginning in 1929, however,
Professor A. Lewis Aycock began offering courses in art history, adding
an additional course in the early 'thirties and another in 1963. These art
appreciation courses covered ancient and medieval art, Renaissance and
modern art, and American art. In 1965 Aycock wrote that "all courses in
art history are elective, but they are used as related courses by many departments in the College, and classes have had from twenty-five to sixty-five
students each semester they are offered: 265 in the fall semester; and 266
and 268 in the spring." At that time a library of 12,000 slides had been
collected in preparation for establishing a full art department.

Wake Forest College was moved to Winston-Salem about 1951. An

Art Committee of the Student Union began building a permanent collection of art in the early 'sixties and in 1964 was given an award-winning sculpture by the State Art Society from the North Carolina Artists' Annual of that year to encourage its efforts.

DAVIDSON COLLEGE

Although Davidson was founded in 1837 by the Presbyterians, like most early church schools it confined its art instruction to the history of art or art appreciation, with a minimum of studio instruction. Art instruction gained considerable momentum when Professor Douglas Houchens came as art director in 1953, at which time additional courses were added, with considerable emphasis on graphics.

Under the leadership of Houchens, the Art Department played an important role in the Fine Arts Festivals sponsored annually by the Music Department at Davidson until about 1968. To implement the instruction in art, a growing collection of films, slides, and reproductions of masterworks to "introduce the student to key modes of expression throughout the range of art history, as well as serving as prime examples of order, unity, and content," has been built up. And a provocative program of art exhibitions of international scope has numbered as many as fifteen annually.

Student work, as well as the creative work of the teachers of art at Davidson, has been well accepted in competitive art exhibitions around the country and is comparable to that of large university art departments.

In 1958 Houchens reported that, "Ours is a one-man art department and I am it. Subjects taught are art history, painting and drawing, sculpture, and graphics." Now on his staff of assistants are Larry Ligo, teaching art history, and Herbert Jackson, studio. Professor Houchens teaches studio and films. As of 1970 an art major was being anticipated for 1971.

GUILFORD COLLEGE

This Quaker college was inaugurated in 1837 and has offered some art, mostly art history, for a number of years. At this writing James C. Mc-

Millan is head of the Art Department and teaches advanced studio. His assistants are Mrs. Emily E. Huntley, Jack Berkman, and Mrs. Catherine Montgomery, all of whom teach drawing, painting, and the history of art embracing the Renaissance, ancient, and medieval periods. Through a cooperative teaching program with Bennett College and Greensboro College, the Art Department at Guilford offers a cooperative A.B. with a major in art.

QUEENS COLLEGE

In the rash of colleges established by the Presbyterians in the late nineteenth century, Charlotte Female Institute was chartered about 1857. After other changes in its name, it was moved to its present site as Queens College in 1912. Some art was taught from the beginning, although available information is somewhat meager on the early phase of its instruction. Art history, studio, art education, and ceramics are now taught at Queens and George A. Shealy has been head of the department since 1960. The B.A. with a major in applied arts is offered by the college. Distinguished Tarheel painter Philip Moose served on the art staff for a number of years.

ATLANTIC CHRISTIAN COLLEGE

When Russell Arnold returned to his Alma Mater in 1951, as a teacher in the Department of Philosophy, Art, and Music, this college, supported by the Disciples of Christ, was merely considering a separate department for art. Under Arnold's influence, however, this nebulous plan became a reality in 1953 and he was made chairman of the new Art Department. Starting with just two courses, the department was soon offering the A.B. and the B.S. degrees, with or without a teaching certificate.

Due to the emphasis on teacher-training at Atlantic Christian, the art program has accented art education. Within the chosen degree program, the student may emphasize one of three programs: fine arts, commercial

20

arts, and art education, the latter meeting the state requirements for both elementary teachers and art supervisors.

This fast-growing Art Department has gained considerable attention for the well-trained artists it produces who enter universities for graduate work. Jim Farlowe of Raleigh, and William Minchew of Wilson, are two well-established examples.

Arnold is himself a versatile artist. A number of his works are in museum collections, including the North Carolina Museum of Art. He earned his M.A.C.A. degree at the University of North Carolina in 1951. Prior to that he studied four years at the Art Students League in New York, six months with Hans Hoffman, and had courses in industrial and architectural design at Pratt Institute. His architectural knowledge and influence are reflected in the new buildings on the college campus and particularly in his own art building which he designed and believes, "is without doubt one of the finer art facilities anywhere in this whole area of the country."

In the fall of 1964 *The Crucible*, a "little magazine," made its appearance as a cooperative venture of the English and the Art Departments at Atlantic Christian. Made up of writing, poetry, and art by students, one of its most expensive and alluring features is a centerfold of an original print.

In our last communication with Arnold, the Art Department had grown to four and he anticipated that the Art Department will grow gradually along with the remainder of the college.

HIGH POINT COLLEGE

This United Methodist college was opened in 1924. Music and Art are incorporated in the Fine Arts Department, with Raiford Porter as chairman of the art division. Under the direction of Porter, art instruction has been expanded in art history through a slide collection, exhibitions, and night classes "for teachers with the need for certificate renewal and laymen of the community with an interest in art."

The A.B. in art provides enough courses in education to meet state requirements for those wishing to teach in the public schools.

Porter, a native of Winston-Salem, has exhibited his own work (painting and sculpture) extensively. He has also ventured into book illustrating, his first being of Omar Ben Sufi, a cat in Edward Henry Peple's book, *A Night Out*, published by John F. Blair.

DUKE UNIVERSITY

Soon after the death of James Buchanan Duke in 1925, his already established endowment to Trinity College was doubled and the name of the college was changed to Duke University. Six years later, the Fine Arts Department was created through the efforts of Dr. Louise Hall. The *Duke Alumni Register* for February, 1932, carried a two-page story entitled "Art Activities Along Various Lines are Being Developed." Some of the activities listed were the fast-growing art library, several loan exhibitions centered in the East Campus Library under the direction of Mrs. Lillian B. Griggs, and an extensive collection placed in the library by Mrs. Margaret Barber of Missouri "for a period of twenty-five years." (Exhibits were held at Trinity College as early as 1923 under the auspices of the Elk-L scholarship fraternity and included Miss Mabel Pugh's work, exhibited in the main hall of Southgate Building. A news clipping on the exhibition says: "The members of the Elk-L as well as the other young women of the college will appreciate all the support given Miss Pugh's exhibition.")

The *Alumni Register* also noted that in October, 1930, W. K. Boyd called together a group of art interested people who organized the Art Association of Duke University "for the purpose of promoting interest in the Fine Arts . . . and to sponsor exhibitions"; that Mrs. Hope E. Chamberlain, head of Pegram House, since her arrival had set up her own studio, complete with etching press, and had two students; Miss Elizabeth H. Brodel had come from Johns Hopkins as Hospital Artist; and thirty-two students elected the survey course in the History of Art. Courses were offered in architecture, sculpture, and painting (all art history); and the Department of Education was offering Drawing and Industrial Art for professional credit for those who needed to teach these subjects in public schools. Katharine Gilbert was reported as teaching the Philosophy of Art, and Mrs. Gifford Davis and Mrs. Richard Shyrock were giving art guidance in the Nursery School—"letting the children scribble, etc."

From other records it appears that the fine arts, aesthetics, and music were combined as the Department of Aesthetics, Art, and Music from 1942 to 1960. Meanwhile, studio courses were added along with a distinguished art staff, and in 1960 a full-fledged Department of Art evolved, with Earl Mueller, already professor of art history, becoming chairman pro tem of the new Art Department. During the 1942–1960 period, practicing artists Charles Sibley, Robert Broderson, and Edith London joined the staff.

In 1962 the Mary Duke Biddle Foundation and the Department of Art established a small gallery in the Woman's College Library and together with the Duke University Student Union inaugurated an exhibition program of international scope. Also during that year Duke inaugurated an "Artist in Residence" program, bringing Ibram Lassaw, world-known sculptor, to Duke as the first participant.

In 1963 the Benjamin N. Duke Professorship in Art was established and William S. Heckscher became the first full-tenured Benjamin N. Duke Professor. In 1966 he also assumed the chairmanship of the Department of Art which he held until 1970, when he became director of the newly opened Duke Museum of Art. At that time Dario Alessandro Covi, art historian who had headed the Department of Art at the University of Louisville for a decade, came to Duke as chairman of the Art Department.

As of 1970 the distinguished staff included Louise Hall, Mueller, and associate professors Marianna Jenkins, Sidney Markman, Elizabeth Sunderland, Karlo Langedijk, Vernon Pratt, Edith London, and W. K. Stars. Stars, in addition to teaching art education, serves as curator of the Duke Museum of Art. Justus Bier, director of the North Carolina Museum of Art, was adjunct professor in 1970.

BENNETT COLLEGE

James C. McMillan, an artist of note, taught most of the art courses at Bennett College, a Methodist school in Greensboro, from 1947, which appears to be the beginning of the Art Department, until 1960 when he received a Danforth Scholarship for study. During that period he managed to acquire an M.F.A. from Catholic University, Washington, D. C., a fellowship to the Skowhegan School of Painting and Sculpture in Maine, a Certificate from the Academie Julien in Paris, and to have exhibited at most of these places. His work was shown in the Corcoran 82nd Annual in this country, the 1956 area show at the Smithsonian Institution, and at the Raymond Duncan Galerie in Paris, when he was studying abroad. In our last contact with McMillan, in 1960, he hoped to use the Danforth Scholarship to do further study toward his doctorate in fine arts at Syracuse University.

By 1970 Bennett College had increased its art staff to include two teachers, and through a cooperative plan with Greensboro College and Guilford College was able to offer a major in Art.

ST. ANDREWS PRESBYTERIAN COLLEGE

Even though St. Andrews is among the younger colleges in the state, having opened its doors in Laurinburg in 1961, it immediately offered six courses in the visual arts. By the beginning of the 1964–65 term the fine arts major was introduced in which a student could earn his B.A. in either studio or dramatic arts, and the arts program included eight courses in creative art, four in art history, and eight in drama. An active exhibition schedule keeps on display art from various areas in the gallery area of the Vardell Music Building.

Although the Art Department is small, John I. Dahl, its director, is working toward continuous expansion.

PRIVATE ART SCHOOLS

North Carolina's mountains and beautiful coastal areas, with their changing moods, have attracted several private art schools. One of the earliest and most prominent of the mountain schools was Elliott Daingerfield's, situated just above Blowing Rock. A close second was the Ringling Art School at Little Switzerland, followed by Seecelo at Burnsville, now revived as "Painting in the Mountain" summer school of art. Less well known, perhaps, were the Flat Rock School of Art at Hendersonville, N. C., and the Huckleberry Mountain School.

Seecelo, founded in 1945 by Frank Stanley Herring, was situated on a magnificent site overlooking Mt. Celo which inspired its name, and maintained two lodges, ten cottages to house its students, a dining room, a library, and a small swimming pool and lake. Herring, an indefatigable painter and teacher, ran this school until just before his death in 1965, at which time Mrs. Herring sold most of the property.

In 1953 the Outer Banks Gallery and Studio was opened at Kill Devil Hills. Founded by Miss Dorothy Bowie and Miss Pat Donnan, it drew students from Maryland, Washington, D. C., Ohio, Wisconsin, Pennsylvania, New York, Virginia, and North Carolina. For a time, beginning in 1954, the John Brady School of Art thrived at Blowing Rock.

Penland School of Arts and Crafts is, of course, internationally known, but is outside the scope of this book, which has dealt more with the fine arts. At the opposite end of the state is EEII's Little Korners of the World at Belhaven, which, in addition to instruction in art puts great emphasis on the crafts.

The Ferree School of Art was established in Raleigh, North Carolina, in June of 1947 by T. S. Ferree. A four-year accredited school, the curriculum included instruction in art history, drawing, anatomy, portraiture, fashion designing, and sculpture, with intensive training in commercial art. In 1952 the student body represented fifteen states. The distinguished faculty included two Tarheels: Jeff Hill and Ben F. Williams, both of Raleigh.

Since the majority of students were male, the Korean War drew heavily on the enrollment, a loss from which the school never recovered, Mr. Ferree recalls. The Ferree School closed in 1953.

While none of these schools offered degrees, they have added immeasurably to the enrichment of art in North Carolina.

BLACK MOUNTAIN COLLEGE

The life of Black Mountain College was short but meteoric. It is remembered mostly for its Art Department headed by Josef Albers, and the distinguished teachers he brought there; all giants in the field of art. Walter Gropius, Robert Motherwell, Ossip Zadkine, Lyonel Feininger, F. W. Goro, and Mary Callery, some of them former colleagues of Albers at the Bauhaus in Germany, made this small western North Carolina school one of the world centers for art thought and creativity.

Born in Germany in 1888, Albers had a distinguished career in that country. In 1920 he joined the Bauhaus school in Weimar to do advanced study. In just two years he was conducting the Bauhaus glass workshop and in 1925 was invited to join the Bauhausmeisters—a distinguished group including Lyonel Feininger, Walter Gropius, Kandinsky, Klee, Moholy-Nagy, and Schlemmer. When the German government closed the Bauhaus school in 1933, Albers came to North Carolina and became Professor of Art at the newly organized Black Mountain College. He left North Carolina in 1949 to head the Yale Art Department and served there until his retirement in 1958.

Long fascinated by the "infinite possibilities and endless relationships of color and light," he has employed cut construction paper as well as paint (generally on masonite) to illustrate "simultaneous contrast," sometimes creating the illusion of flickering lights by the simple use of two contrasting colors. When he had his first one-man show in North Carolina at the old Person Hall Art Gallery in Chapel Hill in the early thirties, the writer peeped behind one "free" wall, sure that he had hidden lights behind the paintings. Of course, there were no lights. It was all *trompe l'oeil*.

During his sixteen years at Black Mountain College Albers gained the reputation of being one of the greatest teachers of this century. Since then he has been honored by the Museum of Modern Art and the Metropolitan Museum of Art among other high ranking museums. He was paid tribute by the North Carolina Museum of Art in Raleigh in January of 1962, when seventy paintings and prints by this "master of the geometrically 'precise' school of painting" were exhibited. The University of North Carolina at Chapel Hill honored him with the degree of Doctor of Fine Arts at its 173rd annual commencement on June 5, 1967. In 1970, under the direction of Ben F. Williams, the North Carolina Museum of Art began a survey of material on Black Mountain College, looking toward an in-depth study of its widespread influence on art in this country.

CHAPTER FOUR

Museums and Galleries

From 1936 to 1956 North Carolina gained six museums: the Mint Museum of Art of Charlotte in 1936; the Wilmington Museum of Art, 1938; the Hickory Museum, 1944; the Asheville Museum, 1948; the North Carolina Museum of Art, Raleigh, and the Statesville Arts and Science Museum, 1956. With the exception of the Hickory and the Statesville museums, all of them profited, directly or indirectly, from the Federal Arts Project from which they received financial assistance. The story of the Wilmington Museum, phenomenally successful but short-lived, appears in the section on the Federal Arts Project.

1. THE MINT MUSEUM OF ART

On October 22, 1936, the old Mint building in Charlotte was dedicated as North Carolina's first art museum. This historic structure, originally built to house a branch of the United States Mint, parallels in interest the museum's growing collection of art, now valued at nearly a million dollars. From its very outset the Mint had a slight connection with art. Colonel John Hill Wheeler, its first superintendent—also known as the author of *A History of North Carolina*—was the son-in-law of the noted painter Thomas Sully.

Established by an Act of Congress on March 3, 1835, the branch Mint was erected at a cost of $29,000.00. It was destroyed by fire on July 27, 1844, but reconstructed on the same architectural plan two years later. At this time the Southern Appalachian region was the principal gold mining territory in the United States and over five million dollars in gold was coined in the Charlotte mint between 1837 and 1861. The Mint suspended operations during the Civil War, and the building was used as district headquarters for the Confederate Army. When it was reopened after the war, increasing availability of gold in California lessened the importance of Charlotte as a gold center and coinage was gradually abandoned. Thomas A. Edison conducted experiments in the building from 1901 to 1903, but became discouraged upon finding that gold did not exist in sufficient quantities in that area to warrant the kind of operations in which he was interested.

Some thirty years later, when the building was scheduled for demolition to make room for a new Post Office wing, Mrs. Harold C. Dwelle and several other historically-minded citizens who were dreaming of an art museum for Charlotte, seized this opportunity to retain a bit of Charlotte's past and at the same time obtain the nucleus of a longed-for art museum. This small group of Charlotteans met on February 14, 1933, to discuss the rescue of the Mint building for this purpose. Present were James E. Steere, in whose office they met, Martin E. Boyer, Charles W. Tillett, Jr., Dr. J. Rush Shull, Burton H. Smith, Clarence O. Kuester, Mrs. William H. Belk, Mrs. John D. Shaw, Mrs. William I. Henderson, Mrs. Dwelle, and Mrs. Ralph Van Landingham.

In order to attract others who might support this cultural venture, Mrs. Dwelle, the leading enthusiast of the project, sponsored a lecture and luncheon at the Woman's Club and invited the art critic of the *Washington Star* to speak. But, instead of giving an enlightening lecture on art, as expected, the critic urged the men and women present to preserve the old Mint which Mrs. Dwelle had shown her on that chilly February morning. Mrs. Katherine Pendleton Arrington, who as president of the State Art Society was also a guest for the occasion, responded with an encouraging offer of $200.00 toward the undertaking. Other small donations followed, totaling around $400.00—a generous sum for those days of the Great Depression.

The rubble of the old building was purchased for $1,200.00 and literally "dumped" on a four-acre site in Eastover Park contributed by E. C.

Griffith. With the help of PWA funds and the joint efforts of many prominent Charlotteans the structure was reassembled, and in just three years, despite an inordinate number of obstacles, was converted into a museum—the core of its present impressive structure.

The opening of the museum on that October evening of 1936 was indeed a festive event for North Carolina and particularly for Charlotte. Collectors, galleries, and museums around the country lent paintings for its premiere exhibition, and, as further encouragement, Samuel H. Kress presented the museum with a Florentine Tondo painting by Granacci, entitled "Madonna and Child." But the crowning joy of the occasion was the arrival from England that morning of a portrait of Queen Charlotte, then attributed to Allan Ramsey—a surprise gift from Mrs. Westray Battle.

From its beginning the Mint Museum of Art has supplied teachers to meet the various needs of the community for art instruction. Mrs. Harold Steadman, its first art teacher, has remained through the years to conduct classes for adults and children. In her reminiscences of the "old days," she recalls many of the early struggles:

"Mrs. Harold Dwelle was the first president and the only one for many years. That first summer they went looking for a teacher who was enthusiastic, understood many media, and loved and understood children. Miss McDougal, head of the Adult Education Department in Raleigh, recommended me. . . . They offered me all cooperation in getting up classes, with the stipulation that I pay to the Museum only a small percent of what I took in over a hundred dollars per month. . . . In those depression years I averaged about $500.00 per year, as students paid only fifty cents per lesson. Mrs. Lewis Burwell, the godmother and curator of the Mint for many years, gleaned a salary of $50.00 per month, much of which went back into its expenses, I am sure.

"Edith Harwell made pottery on the wheel, fired, glazed and sold it there. At times there was a weaver, and as visitors streamed through the museum, we demonstrated for them. I made thousands of finger-paintings and water color paintings and demonstrated plaster casting, modeling of statues, oil painting (portraits, landscapes and still lifes) for teachers and school children."

Mrs. Katheryn Kortheuer, present curator who joined the Mint as a teacher in 1938, recalls the hard times the museum suffered during the Depression and World War II, and that Joseph Hutchinson, who followed Mrs. Burwell as director, pulled the loose ends together and initiated the first lectures on art appreciation. Bruce St. John followed Hutchinson as director and expanded the program until it became necessary to hire a curator. Meanwhile, little had been done about maintenance, and without humidity control the museum was handicapped in getting good exhibitions. Mrs. Kortheuer served as director for three years, during which time a general renovation of the museum took place. A series of concerts, lectures by outside specialists, and art demonstrations inaugurated during this period began to draw the interest of Charlotteans and to necessitate a larger staff.

The Museum's greatest strides in keeping pace with the growing art needs of the area were made during the years from June, 1958, until November, 1966, when Robert W. Schlageter was director. A native of Illinois, with a distinguished background in art history, foreign travel, and training in museum administration, he came to Charlotte from Tennessee, where he had taught at the University of Tennessee and lectured at the Oak Ridge Art Center and Knoxville College. His first efforts were toward creating a "new look" for the building; rearranging the museum's collections by periods for better study; and projecting a definite program for these purposes, embodying three categories—*creative patronage*, to increase the museum's support of contemporary artists through exhibitions and competitions; *museum standards*, to raise the quality of the museum's displays; and *education*, to strengthen the museum's educational programs for the community.

Facilities were enlarged with the opening of a new wing, incorporating a theatre-in-the-round with a seating capacity of two hundred people. The theatre is used for lectures, concerts, film presentations, and performances of the Mint Drama Guild. A gallery area around the theatre almost doubles exhibition space, and at either side are walled sculpture gardens. The top floor of this wing contains offices, a library, and an exhibit area of the M. Mellanay Delhom Institute of Ceramic Studies. Miss Delhom serves as curator of her collection which spans more than 1,000 years of ceramic arts, and draws such study groups as the International Wedgewood Seminar.

The growing permanent collection of the Mint Museum provides an introduction to Western art from Italo-Byzantine painting to Contemporary. Among important works in its various collections are the "Madonna and Child," from the Samuel H. Kress Collection, originally attributed to Granacci but now listed as anonymous; "Madonna and Child with Four Saints" by Ridolfo Ghirlandaio; "Christ and the Samaritan Woman" by Sisto Badalocchio (gift of the Charlotte Debutante Club); "Country Lane" by John La Farge (acquired by the Woman's Auxiliary Purchase Fund); "Rest on Flight into Egypt" by Francesco Zuccarelli (a second major gift by Mrs. Arthur G. McGee, at that time of Cleveland, Ohio); "My Friend Brien O'Malley" by Robert Henri (gift from the John Crist, Sr., Memorial); and a "Pair of Kneeling Angels with Candlesticks" in terra cotta, by Benedetto da Majano of Florence, Italy—1442–1497 (gift of Mrs. Harry Winkler in memory of her husband and son); in addition to numerous gifts from Mrs. Dwelle, Mrs. Katherine Pendleton Arrington, Mrs. Martin Cannon, Sr., Mr. and Mrs. Morris Speizman, and Mr. and Mrs. Sam Galabow.

Among a generous number of area painters represented by purchase awards are J. Bardin, "Blue Trellis"; Don Harris, "The Relic Hunter"; Claude Howell, "Buoy"; John Kehoe, "Cuban Cockfight"; John Waddill, "Bay Blossom Reflecting on an Evening Star"; and George Bireline, "W–59" (gift of the Ford Foundation program for visual artists).

The Mint Museum has profited greatly by the services and projects developed by the Woman's Auxiliary, which gleans thousands of dollars from its annual tour of Charlotte homes and its antique shows, used for enriching the many programs of the Museum.

The museum library contains a 26-volume Thieme-Becker German Kunstler-Lexikon, an eight-volume Benezit & Bryan dictionary, 1200 art reference books, and 5,000 color slides. Furthermore, a consultive service on restoration and on fine art collections sometimes brings unattributed paintings to the museum. As Director Cleve K. Scarbrough reported to the membership in a letter dated January 1, 1970, "the Museum is not only a depository for one of the largest public art collections in the region, but is an active educational institution as well."

To sum up the achievements of the Mint Museum at Charlotte, words from its February, 1959, *Bulletin* are just as appropriate today: "Rich in history, rich in the intellectual and aesthetic pleasures of its total program, this is a magnificent return on nine hundred dollars, three acres, and the devotion of countless volunteer services."

2. THE HICKORY MUSEUM OF ART

North Carolina gained its second permanent museum of art when the Hickory Museum of Art was dedicated on February 4, 1944, with the Honorable Clyde Hoey, ex-Governor and Senator, as speaker for the occasion. Culmination of "a dream born in the heart of a former Duke University football player," its story and that of Paul W. Whitener, founder and director for fourteen years, are intertwined.

Upon graduation from Duke in 1936, where he had been a star football player, Paul Whitener took a job with the Good Roads Association, requiring much tramping over the countryside. On one of these jaunts he came across a beautiful young lady who sat sketching. Fascinated, he said: "I believe I could do that." She handed him the brush with the suggestion that he try it! He did, and never stopped. He also became enamoured of the young lady, Mildred M. McKinney, whom he later married. He began studying art at the Ringling Summer School of Art at Little Switzerland and became a private pupil of Wilford S. Conrow, Frank Stanley Herring, and Donald Blake, studying from time to time at the Grand Central Art Galleries' school in New York City.

During this time Whitener began to envision an art museum in Hickory that would serve all the people in the Catawba Valley, and even though he had become a prolific and professional painter, he dedicated most of his time to promoting interest in the museum project. It was indeed a great day for Hickory and the surrounding area when the old Bradshaw Building on First Avenue was dedicated as the Hickory Museum of Art.

Even before its dedication, the museum received national recognition in 1943 by celebrating National Art Week—a project of WPA. Hickory placed second in the nation and won a bronze figure by E. Bruce Douglas entitled "The Skier," valued at the time of its award at $750.00. Through his work with the National Art Week program, Whitener gained many friendships among museum directors and artists throughout the United States, many of whom caught his enthusiasm and helped him gradually acquire a permanent collection for the Hickory Museum which he hoped "would be second to none in the South." And, according to Whitener, the museum's collection of American art was the largest in the South until the opening of the North Carolina Museum of Art in Raleigh. The local citizens of Hickory and his wife "Mickey" also were caught up in Whitener's dream and faithfully and constantly supported him in his struggle to develop a museum.

A strikingly handsome and persuasive man, Whitener elicited gifts of as many as twenty-eight art items at a time from New York galleries. In 1954 Allan Gerdau's New York gallery gave the museum a collection of ceramics and other artifacts from the Inca and Nazca periods valued at several thousand dollars. One gift, an unusual sculpture, is so large it had to be divided and shipped in two pieces. Four men and the artist, Pietro Montana of New York, reassembled it in Hickory. Entitled "Civilization" it consists of some thirty figures in plaster, each representing some phase of civilization. The collection of more than two hundred paintings includes among its European treasures works by John Hoppner, Mather Brown, Thomas Lawrence, and Paul Hubner; a Tintoretto, and a valuable work by Honoré Daumier. A few of the many American painters represented are Andrew Winter, Chauncey Ryder, William H. Singer, J. M. Whistler, Lawrence Sisson, Jon Corbino, and George Innis, Jr., the latter represented by eleven works. An oil portrait of the "Rt. Hon. Sir Thomas Parker," attributed to Gilbert Stuart (1755–1828) and valued at $8,-000.00, was presented to the museum a few years ago by Clark Hartwell of Los Angeles, through the efforts of New York art dealer Jay Coe, formerly of Greensboro.

Among North Carolina artists whose works are included in the collection are Douglas Grant, Asheville; Shirley Pruden, Greensboro; George Donehue, High Point; Peggy Link, Reidsville; Phillip Moose, Newton; Charles Tucker, Charlotte; Anne Moore, Granite Falls; John Brady, Hickory; and Whitener himself.

Gifts continue to expand this collection. In 1960, for instance, the museum received a pastel "Self-Portrait" of Pietro Montana, who gave the large sculpture referred to earlier, a wood-carving by Vernon Smith of Orleans, Massachusetts, an oil and a watercolor by Walter Frandon, New York, and a painting of "General Lafayette" by Henri Pierre Danloux, presented by Mrs. Eli T. Watson.

When I first heard of the museum in 1958, I went to Hickory to write a feature story about it. At that time the museum had just moved into a new home to more adequately accommodate its collection by then valued at more than $200,000.00. But Whitener, its director, was at home convalescing from an operation for a brain tumor that had left him partially paralyzed on his right side. His right eye was covered with a jaunty black patch to offset double vision produced by the operation, and he had to force his hoarse voice to speak of his all-consuming interest: not football, but the museum. He told of the "Picture of the Month" the museum placed in the First National Bank of Hickory, of the museum's influence in the high school, and its working arrangement with the Mint Museum of Charlotte whereby outstanding exhibits to both museums were made possible. Then, apologetically, he asked: "What do you think of these sketches I am doing with a felt pen? I am having to learn to paint with my left hand now that I can't use my right one, and these are soon to be exhibited at the Mint Museum in Charlotte."

Soon after this visit Whitener returned to Duke Hospital, where he succumbed to cancer of the brain on May 19, 1959. But before his death, he was apprised of plans for a larger and finer museum.

Remodeling was begun almost immediately on what once was the Shuford Mills office building, situated downtown at the corner of Third Street, N. W., and First Avenue, N. W., preparatory to converting its spacious quarters into the new Hickory Museum of Art. Alex Shuford, president of Shuford Mills and long-time benefactor of the Museum, underwrote the entire renovation project and contributed to it a relic room containing a fine collection of coins. A total of 650 linear feet of wall space was provided for picture hanging, and concealed lighting was installed for both floors, which cover more than 5,300 square feet.

The old brick façade gave way to modern semi-gloss black squares outlined in metal and topped with a wide band of gently ruffled precast concrete, designed by James N. Sherrill, a Hickory architect, who also designed and remodeled the interior.

The new building was dedicated on Sunday afternoon, October 30, 1960. Robert Lee Humber, of Greenville, and Gregory D. Ivy, head of the Art Department at the University of North Carolina at Greensboro, were the main speakers. Harry D. Althouse, president of the museum board of directors, paid tribute to its founder in these words: "We have all helped a little, but Paul Whitener was solely responsible for this museum. His perseverance and passion for art was a remarkable thing." As a Whitener Memorial Collection, the Burr Galleries of New York, through Mrs. Eleanor Gay Lee (director of one-man shows), sent the museum sixteen paintings and graphics and one sculpture.

Under the direction of Mrs. Whitener (now Mrs. R. F. Coe), the museum continues to thrive by bringing to the area outstanding exhibitions, searching for new acquisitions, and keeping its doors "open, free, to people of all ages," a cultural fountain for the entire Catawba Valley and its environs. The Museum Art Guild, composed of a number of young people, is augmenting the services of the museum to the community.

3. THE ASHEVILLE ART MUSEUM

The Asheville Art Museum Association, Inc., was organized on November 29, 1948, "to promote cooperation in all matters of public interest; to develop and increase civic interest; to create and maintain higher standards in art and the museum; to teach and educate the public in art; to establish and maintain a museum wherein all kinds of art, sculptures and paintings may be exhibited to the public; to sell outright, or on commission, or trade and deal in pieces of art."

Until this time Asheville's only museum had been a room in the City Hall where the Asheville Artists Guild, organized in 1926 by Mrs. Eva D. Barnett, exhibited its works. With the cooperation of the Department of Parks and Recreation and the Grove Park Commission, the newly organized museum group was able to lease the tiny stone gatehouse at the corner of Charlotte Street and Celia Place, which they opened on December 26, 1948, with a gala reception. In 1958 the Artists Guild merged with the Art Museum, raising its membership to seventy-six people.

Although this museum was tiny, with only two small galleries, its program was gigantic. Manned entirely by volunteer help, it was kept open afternoons, and one morning a week for school tours. Exhibits were changed every two weeks. Annual dinners and receptions kept interest alive, and benefit bridge parties and canasta games helped finance the project. Also, in addition to changing exhibitions, it held two annual events— a sidewalk show and "Art in the Park."

James E. Neumann, first paid director of the museum, wrote in 1965 that "in January we will move to the 11th floor of the new Northwestern Bank Building, increasing our space by more than 1,000 percent. Here we will be able to expand our exhibit space and also develop an educational program as a regular part of the museum's activities. . . . Our permanent collection is small and for all practical purposes doesn't exist . . . the collection is not catalogued, so it is rather difficult to know what belongs to the museum. . . . The museum owns a Persian Bowl valued at $1,000 but the source and period are unknown at this time. There are also six or seven Piranesi Prints. Their value and edition cannot be stated at this time."

In 1966 the new Northwestern Bank Building turned over to the museum its entire eleventh floor; and in July of that year F. Edward Barnwell became its director. The Junior League of Asheville inaugurated an art education project through the museum, now able to add studio classes for adults and children and to incorporate a sales and rental gallery where member-artists could display their work.

The following year it was able to play host to the 29th North Carolina Artists Annual exhibition, and the "Muses," a museum auxiliary, organized and opened a museum shop and originated an annual art auction. At the close of 1969 the museum had over seven hundred members and had received over 20,000 visitors. The outlook was indeed bright. But troubles came at the end of the year. The city withdrew its financial support and Northwestern required the use of its eleventh floor. But what appeared to be a disaster was a blessing in disguise. Forced to move from the bank building, the Asheville Art Museum acquired a home of its own. The former Gay Green house on Pearson Drive, a handsome Georgian with lawns and gardens, was available, and with the financial assistance of the museum auxiliary, the Muses, and the cooperation of the trustees of the Green property, the museum established itself in its new quarters. The membership, once seventy-six, had grown to over eleven hundred, and the museum now attracted support from all of western North Carolina.

The museum's strength lies largely in the many interested people who volunteer their services, since all revenues come from membership dues, art sales, and fund-raising projects of the Muses. Its programs include a wide variety of exhibits, films, lectures and demonstrations, a useful art library, and a monthly bulletin. The museum is a member of the Asheville Civic Arts Council.

4. STATESVILLE ARTS AND
SCIENCE MUSEUM

Possibly inspired by the success of the Mint and the Asheville museums of art, a group of civic-minded citizens in Statesville met in 1956 and organized the Statesville Arts and Science Museum. They leased from the city an old abandoned pump station and restored it room by room until it had four galleries—three for monthly exhibitions and one which doubles as a gallery for the permanent collection and as an auditorium for a Little Theatre group. By 1965 membership had grown to about five hundred persons and included several manufacturing firms and business organizations, and three affiliated groups: the Little Henkel Theatre, the Artists' Guild, and the Poetry Society.

A non-profit organization, dependent chiefly on memberships for operating funds, for a number of years the museum was open only on Sunday afternoons and by special arrangements for community groups wishing to use its facilities. Now, due to subsidization by the North Carolina Arts Council, the museum has a full-time curator and is open to the public six days a week. And, according to Miss Louise Gilbert, a former president, "The adults come to see the art exhibitions but the children always head for the gallery that houses our mummy and skeleton, dated around 1500 by the University of North Carolina."

The Statesville Museum began early to sponsor an annual Spring Arts Festival for out-of-state invitational exhibitions. Its permanent collection now numbers about forty-five paintings and several sculptures. In recognition of its contribution to art in North Carolina, the museum was given one of the award-winning paintings by the State Art Society from its 1964 N. C. Artists' Annual exhibition in Raleigh.

Early leaders in the Arts and Science Museum have been Eugene Gregg, L. B. Grier, William T. Leonard, Miss Dorothy Nicholson, Mr. and Mrs. J. P. Huskins, Mrs. Mickey Mizell, Mrs. E. V. Brumley, Ben A. Stimson, and W. E. Webb, Jr., to name a few. Perhaps the most active of this group was Eugene Gregg. A founder of the museum, Gregg had been in charge of foreign operations for the Bell System for many years. In his travels to all parts of the world, he had visited most of the great museums, including the Hermitage in Russia, and had over the years built up a fine private collection of paintings and wood carvings. Despite his cosmopolitan background, Gregg was keenly interested in the new museum and expressed pleasure at "watching this new artistic yeast ferment."

When Gregg began to take life easier and relinquish some of his responsibilities at the museum, Statesville was fortunate in the timely arrival of Frans Van Bergen. Van Bergen brought with him a wealth of experience as a European painter; his works have been exhibited all over Europe, including Holland, Belgium, Germany and Sweden. Mr. and Mrs. Van Bergen became involved in the art life of Statesville immediately and he soon became curator of the little museum, ably assisted by Mrs. Van Bergen whom he met while a student at the Maastricht Academy of Art in Holland. In this country he has had a one-man show at the High Museum in Atlanta, Georgia, had paintings accepted in important exhibitions, including the Southeastern Exhibition, and is now a member of the State Art Society, Charlotte's Mint Museum, and the Winston-Salem Gallery of Contemporary Art.

His works are in museums in Stockholm, Brussels, and The Hague and are owned in this country by residents of Atlanta, Marietta, and Augusta, Georgia, as well as by North Carolinians. His works include portraits, land-

scapes, still lifes, mosaics, murals and stained glass designs. He designed
the stained glass windows for Statesville's St. Pius X Catholic Church and
a window representing the arts and sciences in symbols, presented to the
Statesville Museum by Laws Studios.

The role of the Arts and Science Museum in the cultural atmosphere
of the upper Piedmont area is immeasurable and early qualified the museum as a charter member of the Tri-States Arts Council.

5. THE NORTH CAROLINA
MUSEUM OF ART

Governor Luther Hodges cut the ribbons at 9 p.m. on the evening of April
6, 1956, and the new and long-awaited North Carolina Museum of Art was
opened to the taxpayers of North Carolina. Ringing in the ears of the
waiting throng were words spoken by Robert Lee Humber a few hours
earlier at the largest banquet the Sir Walter Hotel in Raleigh had ever
served:

"Let it never be forgotten that the people of North Carolina ordained
this institution, forged its nativity on the anvil of unprecedented legislation and accepted forthright both the challenge and the responsibility of
permanent survival."

The waiting throng, predominantly members of the North Carolina
State Art Society who had attended the banquet earlier, were astonished
at the grandeur of the interior of the old renovated Highway Building
turned museum, and at the fabulous exhibition of art that embellished
its walls. Eight schools of painting traversing four centuries, with stress
on the seventeenth and eighteenth centuries, were represented. Franz
Hals, Rembrandt van Rijn, Van Dyke, Jan Brueghel the Elder, Peter de
Hooch, and Rubens; paintings contributed by the State Art Society from
the Phifer funds and other collections; and numerous other works of art
given by such donors as Doris Duke, Mrs. Frank LaForge, Walter Chrysler, Jr., Cornelius Vanderbilt Whitney, John Hay Whitney, Mrs. James
Forrestal, Chauncey McCormick, and others, dazzled the onlookers. In
all, here was a collection valued at more than $2,000,000; and the
$1,000,000 promised by the Kress Foundation was still to come.

The day leading up to the dedication of the Museum's opening had been one of glittering social events, planned by Mrs. J. Melville Broughton, chairman, and her entertainment committee. Dr. and Mrs. Humber honored donors and out-of-state guests at a buffet luncheon at the Sir Walter Hotel. Governor and Mrs. Hodges held an afternoon reception at the Governor's mansion for members of the General Assembly, donors, members of the State Art Society, and diplomatic representatives from Great Britain, France, Holland, Belgium, Germany, Spain, and Italy—countries represented by paintings in the Museum. Dedicatory prayers were offered up by Bishop Edwin A. Penick, bishop of the Episcopal Diocese of North Carolina; Rabbi Harry Caplan of Temple Beth Or; and Bishop Vincent Waters of the Catholic Diocese of Raleigh. The Wake Forest Choir, directed by Thane McDonald, sang.

Governor Hodges told the banquet audience that the museum was a logical outgrowth of a mental attitude regarding education which had dominated North Carolinians since 1900, as expressed in Governor Charles Brantley Aycock's educational vision, embracing not only things that are useful and practical, but also those intangibles that nurture the soul of man.

William R. Valentiner, director of the museum, praised his predecessor, Miss Lucy Cherry Crisp, and his staff, and called attention to "the amazing fact that small pieces of canvas covered with bits of color are treasured so much by men that enormous sums are given for them so as to have them preserved for so long as the earth exists as examples of the best that man has created . . . that we value the spirit which induces people to give whatever they have for greater intangible things."

Alfred M. Frankfurter of New York, editor of *Art News* and key speaker for the occasion, praised the Museum as "the South's first museum of consequence," stating that "it houses the most important public collection south of Richmond and east of the Pacific."

Governor Hodges and Humber both commended the work of the late Mrs. Katherine Pendleton Arrington of Warrenton who for twenty-five years served as president of the State Art Society, which from its inception had worked toward achieving such a museum. Tributes also were paid to Representative John Kerr of Warren County whose "Man Cannot Live by Bread Alone" speech turned the tide toward victory when the 1947 legislature faltered at the thought of spending a million dollars of the tax-payers' money for art, and to Carl Hamilton for his distinguished service to the state in helping round up the fine collection paid for with the million dollars. But among the most cogent words delivered that evening were Humber's: "The birth of this institution is a sovereign confirmation that faith is still the most potent force on earth." But this birth might be likened to a woman in travail, only the gestation period consumed years instead of months, and it might be well to recall the arduous years of planning, as well as the faith Humber cites, that led up to this magnificent art collection, appraised and insured in 1970 for $18,000,000.

As we know from the history of the State Art Society, organized in 1925, its directors were ever on the alert for a building to house a Museum of Art. One of their early explorations involved the Cameron house on Hillsboro Street in Raleigh, one of the finest antebellum mansions in this area in 1936, when they hoped to get financial aid from WPA. The owners objected to necessary renovations, however, and were unwilling to rent the house for more than a year. The Art Society had hoped to open the museum on November 1 and celebrate its tenth annual December meeting with "an unusually fine exhibition." Instead, the executive committee of the Art Society adopted the following motions suggesting that further attempts be made to purchase the Cameron house:

"Since the owners of the Cameron house are not willing in leasing to have the house converted into a gallery by partitioning, by remodeling with Celotex walls, or by any change in the house as it now stands, and are not willing to rent it for more than one year; and since the Federal Art Project is not willing to use the house unremodeled or unless it can be rented by the State Art Society for more than one year, the State Art Society withdraws from its agreement with the Federal Art Project to take over the Raleigh Art Center under the supervision of the Federal Art Project with the plan of opening a State Museum. . . . The executive committee of the society passes this motion with the hope that in six months' time sufficient interest can be raised to warrant purchasing the Cameron house with a down payment of $6,000 and other payments to be arranged, since the committee considers the house desirable as a museum not only for present use but also as a site for a permanent museum."

A federally-supported museum of art building evidently had been discussed for some time, for during a two-day convention of the State Council of the Federation of Women's Clubs at New Bern in October, 1935, Mrs. L. V. Sutton of Raleigh, Federation art chairman, proposed the establishment of a State Art Museum in Raleigh with the aid of Federal relief funds. Her recommendation was approved at the closing session of the convention and declared to be "a much more worthy way to spend government money than on the erection of so many National Guard armories in North Carolina."

The State Art Society, of course, found other temporary quarters, but by 1944 the emphasis on financing a state art museum had shifted toward the idea of a memorial not only for those who had served in World War I but particularly in World War II, in which North Carolina "had more than a third of a million men" serving in every war theatre in the world, and gave the lives of between 7,000 and 8,000 of her young men, with other thousands wounded for life. Kenneth C. Royall of Goldsboro, Secretary of War, wrote that "these are the men to whom our State and every part thereof should never fail to pay tribute." The "memorial" idea gained impetus, with the full support of the Women's Clubs around the state. On April 12, 1944, Mrs. R. O. Self, chairman of the Art Committee of the Raleigh Women's Clubs, invited Gregory D. Ivy, head of the Art Department at Woman's College of the University of North Carolina, Greensboro, to speak at their meeting in Raleigh. Mayor Graham H. Andrews introduced Ivy who spoke not only of the future of the memorial gallery but of its implications in a democracy.

Governor Broughton's term included the first wartime legislature in the state since 1865, but, as Hugh Lefler has said in his *History of North Carolina*, "World War II did more to bring the nation out of the Depression than had 'pump priming' and the various nostrums of the New Deal." Patriotism equalled that of 1815 when the legislature voted the appropriation for the Canova statue. Governor Broughton's program brought a nine months' school term, and the first financial aid to art and music, including the North Carolina State Art Society and the North Carolina Symphony Society. This was a propitious time to raise the cultural sights of the state.

So, on June 15, 1943, Governor Broughton appointed a Citizens' Committee for a State Art Gallery, with William T. Polk, associate editor of the *Greensboro Daily News*, chairman; Clarence Poe, editor of the

Progressive Farmer in Raleigh, vice chairman; and C. C. Crittenden of the Department of Archives and History, secretary. Appointed to the Executive Committee to work with the officers were Josephus Daniels, editor; Mayor Graham H. Andrews, former Governor J. C. B. Ehringhaus, Col. William T. Joyner, and Mrs. Louis V. Sutton, all of Raleigh. Other members were Mrs. Katherine Pendleton Arrington, Warrenton; Robert Lee Humber, Greenville; Mrs. Charles A. Cannon, Concord; R. D. W. Connor, Chapel Hill; Mrs. W. N. Reynolds, Winston-Salem; Mrs. J. Lawrence Sprunt, Wilmington; Mrs. S. Westray Battle, Asheville; Mrs. W. H. Belk, Charlotte; Mrs. Henry MacMillan, Wilmington; and Dr. Frederick Hanes and John Sprunt Hill of Durham. This group voted unanimously to launch a movement for the construction of a North Carolina State Art Gallery [Museum] in Raleigh—as a memorial to North Carolinians who had served in the First and Second World Wars. Even so, the committee could not raise the $50,000 in private donations thought to be necessary. Humber startled the group by his estimation that $1,000,000 was needed, and, as recorded earlier, expressed his willingness to explore the possibilities in this field.

Recalling his search for funds for a Museum of Art, Mr. Humber said in a letter to me on June 29, 1967: "Being unable to obtain a million dollars from any private source in North Carolina, with which to buy art, I went to New York to explore the possibility of interesting national patrons of art in this project. Through Mr. Carl Hamilton, I met Mr. Stephen Pechetto, the right hand man of Mr. Samuel H. Kress, with whom I conducted negotiations, which lasted for four years, embracing the period from 1943 to 1947.

"In making this offer [the gift of $1,000,000] Mr. Samuel H. Kress imposed two basic conditions: (1) that neither his name nor that of his Foundation would be disclosed; and (2) that his commitment be verbal and not in writing, in order to avoid the solicitation from other States, where he operated stores, asking for a similar donation. He stated that he was not going to give a million dollars to each of the southern states. A written commitment, he added, could seriously embarrass him in this regard."

Humber accepted these terms and immediately drafted Senate Bill 395, signed by thirteen persons, to be presented to the 1947 Legislature, asking that the state appropriate $1,000,000 to match private potential but unidentified gifts in an equal amount, on which the Kress gift was contingent. The thirteen signers were Joe L. Blythe, Wade Barber, L. M. Chaffin, Julian Alsbrook, Willie Lee Lumpkin, Thomas O'Berry, Hugh G. Horton, Oscar L. Richardson, R. Grady Rankin, Lawrence H. Fountain, Arthur B. Corey, Mrs. R. S. Ferguson, and John C. Rodman. Representative John Kerr, Jr., of Warrenton, displaying the mutual trust he and Humber placed in each other, presented Humber's bill, and made what Humber later described as "one of the most important speeches delivered in recent North Carolina legislative history." A former speaker of the House, who has been described as "an oldtime spellbinder who laced his addresses with classical allusions," Kerr opened his speech with words now indelibly stamped on North Carolina history: "Mistuh Speakuh, I know that I am facing a hostile audience, but man cannot live by bread alone." Then, when opponents of the bill had exhausted every other argument against it and Representative R. L. Harris of Person County introduced a resolution calling for a *sine die* adjournment that might well have defeated the bill, Representative Kerr allegedly jumped to his feet and shouted: "I think I know what's up. If we adopt this adjournment resolution, meaning we must adjourn at the specified time, opponents of this art gallery proposition can object to its coming up on final reading. That would mean it would take a two thirds vote to suspend the rules in order that it be put on second and third readings in the same day."

When Harris interrupted with "I certainly never dreamed there would be opposition to an adjournment resolution," Kerr replied: "Well, maybe you didn't dream it, but there is. Gentlemen, this is nothing but a maneuver to keep the House from passing the art gallery bill."

Representative F. E. Wallace of Lenoir joined Representative Kerr in criticizing the alleged attempts to block the bill, declaring that "the only purpose of this resolution is to put the art bill off for another reading, requiring a two thirds vote."

Speaker Thomas Pearsall cleared himself as well as Representative Harris of any efforts to delay the art bill, by insisting that "the resolution was drawn several days ago and introduced a few minutes ago after I learned that it will be possible for us to complete work by tonight."

Although Governor R. Gregg Cherry favored passage of the bill, several administration followers claimed that enactment of the measure would be unwise; that "we may be dealing with a mirage."

A leading opponent of the art bill was Representative Arch Allen of Wake County, chairman of the House Appropriations Committee, who believed that such requests as $1,000,000 for the State Ports Authority and $10,000,000 for a school building program, and others, should have precedence. Representative Frank Huskins of Yancey, also an opponent, declared that "until we feed our people bread, you can't put them on a diet of caviar."

Debate of the bill was long and at times acrimonious, but the tired legislators closed the page on the 1947 General Assembly by passing it, and thus providing a million dollars to buy works of art, "contingent upon that sum being matched by donations and where there is that amount in the General Fund surplus at the end of the ensuing biennium." Voting was close; 45 to 43; and doubtless with "tongue in cheek," for many still doubted that Humber's "man in the North" would deliver, and raising a million dollars in private donations was a long and tedious, if not impossible, job. And certainly there was little likelihood that the General Fund would have a surplus of $1,000,000 at "the end of the ensuing biennium."

The newspapers had their debates, too. In an editorial entitled "Art vs. Schools" the *High Point Enterprise* characterized the extremely contingent appropriation of $1,000,000 for a state art gallery as "about as foolish a piece of business as any the late Legislature enacted into law," insisting that "the school system needs the money far more than any art gallery," and that "before North Carolina is in position to take the lead in any cultural field it must give its children a better education so that they can appreciate culture." The *Greensboro Daily News*, using the *Enterprise* editorial as a subject for one of its own, admitted difficulty in separating education and culture in its mind as easily as did the *Enterprise*, stating that, "We are strong for more money for schools and so are the teachers, but we haven't heard that the teachers have raised any kick against the proposed art gallery, and that may be because they consider art and education to be closely linked . . . There is no competition among lighthouses.

"The *Enterprise* considers that the secrecy surrounding the donor in itself makes the proposition questionable to our suspicious mind," the

Greensboro editorial continued, cautioning that "This may be natural but the fact is that if the foundation's name were broadcast now, it would be likely to be deluged with requests by other states for the million, a result which neither donor nor North Carolina would welcome. The *Enterprise* might also consider the possibility that Governor Cherry is solidly behind the art gallery proposition and knows the Foundation in question, and is neither so innocent nor so blinded by an esthetic sunstroke as to welcome a Trojan horse in the name of art."

The first of a series of crises followed upon the heels of the successful legislative battle. Samuel Kress became fatally ill and was unable to conduct any business, and since Humber had nothing in writing, the Kress Foundation ignored his pleas for a hearing; and when they eventually arranged for a conference with Humber, they refused to give a money grant, offering a million dollars worth of art instead. Whether paintings instead of money would comply with the spirit of the legislative act of 1947 now had to be determined by another legislature. The *News and Observer* of March 2, 1951, gave this report on the sub-committee's attitude:

"Representative William B. Rodman of Beaufort, who was House chairman of the sub-committee, said he thought the Kress proposal perhaps met in spirit the terms of the 1947 act making the State's $1,000,000 available when a matching sum of $1,000,000 had been paid into the State treasury.

"He conceded that since the Kress million is not in cash it has not complied with the letter of the Act but 'I feel there is a deep sense of moral obligation on the part of the State.' "

But there were others less amenable, and the *News and Observer's* headline, "Bill Would Retrieve Fund," on Saturday morning, April 7, 1951, chilled the hearts of those who thought the art museum battle won. Senator Alton Lennon of New Hanover and thirteen other senators had signed a bill to reallocate the $1,000,000 voted for art in the closing days of the 1947 session. "It has been there for four years without being used," said Senator Thomas B. Sawyer of Durham. "I think it ought to be used either for art or for something else." Another suggestion was that it be parceled out as bonuses to state employees, estimated by someone as

amounting to about $50 per employee. But, although the Appropriations
Committee members strongly opposed the Bill, they presented it, "without prejudice," as a majority of the members felt that the question should
be decided on the Senate floor.

It had been known for some time that the "rich man from up North"
was the S. H. Kress Foundation, but various vicissitudes clouded the legal
concept of the gift. Meanwhile, Governor W. Kerr Scott, House Speaker
W. Frank Taylor, and Lieutenant Governor H. P. Taylor, who was president of the Senate, had agreed to support the Art Society in its fight to
retain the $1,000,000, and Representative W. B. Rodman of Beaufort
and forty-seven other members of the House had signed a bill designed to
untie the legal knots holding back the Kress bequest.

Before the Senate and the House committee acted, a joint message by
Governor Scott and the two Taylors advocating enactment of the Rodman Bill was read to the legislators. "In our measured judgment," they
said, "we cannot afford to reject the Kress offer. In the 175 years of our
history, the State never has been able to establish a great art gallery; but
it is now within our grasp. Any state of this Union would not only welcome
such an opportunity, but would exert itself zealously to obtain it. Surely,
it would be unwise for us now to fumble the ball."

Robert Lee Humber, Mrs. Arrington and other representatives of the
Art Society had appeared before the Joint Appropriations Committee on
the afternoon of February 27, 1951, to argue for the retention of the
$1,000,000. Mrs. Arrington, president of the Society, reminded the com-
mittee that in 1928 the State lost out on a $3,000,000 arts collection, and
urged that "full advantage be taken of the present offer." In the Senate
debate that followed, they were fully supported by Senator L. H. Fountain
of Edgecombe, who "took the floor with a ten-minute talk in favor of
keeping the art fund for art, while whispered conferences went on in
several portions of the Senate Chamber," it was reported, and when the
vote was taken on the Lennon Bill it was defeated 23 to 17. Senator Julian
Allsbrook of Halifax promptly applied "the legislative clincher, putting
any motion to reconsider the vote under the two thirds rule."

Senator Lennon attempted an amendment to put the fund back into
the general fund as a "cushion," claiming that "if the art appropriation

The manner of their fishing.

INDIANS FISHING, drawing by John White. Original in British Museum,
London. *Courtesy of North Carolina Museum of Art, Raleigh.*

STATUE OF GEORGE WASHINGTON by Antonio Canova.

Courtesy of North Carolina Museum of Art, Raleigh.

PORTRAIT OF KATHERINE PENDLETON ARRINGTON by Irving
Wiles. Mrs. Arrington was a long-time benefactor of the arts in North Carolina.

Left: Ben F. Williams, General Curator of the North Carolina Museum of Art and long-time supporter of the arts in North Carolina. *Below*: Mrs. Dan K. Moore, wife of Governor Moore, and Charles Stanford, Director of the North Carolina Museum of Art, talking with a blind student in the Mary Duke Biddle Gallery for the Blind. *Opposite top*: The Honorable Robert Lee Humber, President of the North Carolina Art Society and Chairman of the Board of Directors of the North Carolina Museum of Art, lecturing in the Museum on October 5, 1958. *Opposite bottom*: President Harry S Truman visits the North Carolina Museum of Art, December 5, 1958.

Courtesy of North Carolina Museum of Art, Raleigh.

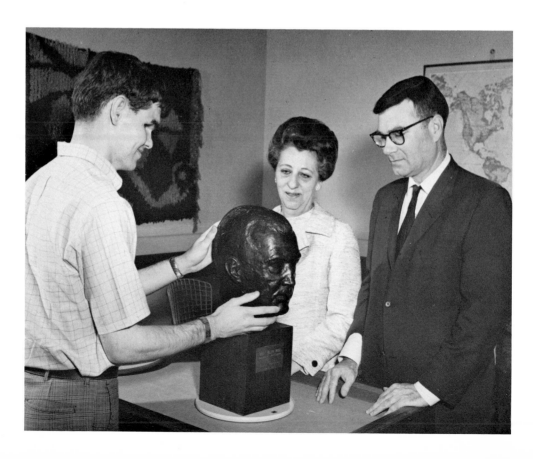

A MILE OF ART AT FORTY OAKS FARM, sponsored by Durham Art Guild and Chapel Hill School Art Guild.

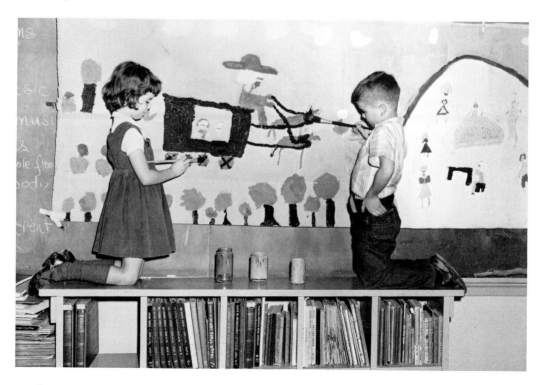

In preparation for a performance by the North Carolina Symphony Orchestra, seven-year-olds put the finishing touches on a frieze inspired by the story of Mozart's early life. Instruction by Mrs. Adeline McCall.

Before and after pictures of the Rocky Mount Arts Center in old water tank and pumping station.

THE UNITED STATES MINT.

C. Hanscn

Before and after pictures of the Mint Museum of Art in Charlotte.

Courtesy of Mint Museum of Art, Charlotte.

were the subject of a referendum, it wouldn't get ten per cent of the votes."
Senator Charles F. Gold of Rutherford threw on more cold water by con-
tending that the state would have to spend more millions to provide a
place in which to keep the paintings to be purchased with the $1,000,000
and those the Kress Foundation would give. "It is a luxury, not an essential
function," he claimed, "and North Carolina is not yet rich enough to
afford a luxury."

The debate in many ways resembled those of 1815 when the Canova
statue of George Washington was being considered and "when the legislature was torn between the fundamental and the cultural needs of the
state."

Mrs. Frank Taylor, wife of the speaker of the House, recalls that
". . . members of the legislature were exerting every effort to take this
million lying idle and return it to the General Fund for Educational purposes. This brought about the grand 'free for all' as you can imagine. Mr.
Kress had not delivered a single picture at the time which gave the opposition a good talking point . . . fights were bitter and long . . . Many people
worked very hard. Practically all night sessions in rooms all over the Sir
Walter were held. No one will ever know, except those of us there, the
extent of Mr. Humber's work for this money."

Legend portrays Humber's persistent appeals as he went from senator to representative, and vice versa, as bridging their naps fallen into
through fatigue. He would still be talking when they awoke. Among his
fortunate gains was the promise of the new Governor, W. Kerr Scott, to
back the substitute Bill. Three other staunch defenders of the "art fund
for art" were Senators W. H. S. Burgwyn, Jr., who declared that "this is
the greatest opportunity we have had to serve the future generations";
R. E. Little who hoped "we'll leave the fund right where it is"; and Paul E.
Jones of Pitt who felt that "this move is ill-timed and ill advised . . . it
would be destroying rather than creating."

Lennon's amendment was killed on April 11, and on April 15 the
House passed Rodman's bill, authorizing the State Art Society to accept
the Kress Foundation's gift of paintings and clearing the way for the million dollar appropriation of four years before to be used for the purchase
of art. But Attorney General Harry McMullan created still another hurdle

to be cleared before the paintings already selected by the State Art Commission and held by New York dealers could be claimed and paid for. Unsure of his judgment, and that of Humber and the State Art Commission in their selection of art for the State, McMullan added two amendments to the bill. One limited acquisitions to masterpieces of the American, British, French, Spanish, Flemish, and Dutch schools of art, and specified "no modern art." (The term "modern" was eventually dropped.) The other specified that every purchase be approved by, among others, the director or chief curator of the National Gallery of Art at Washington, D. C. The National Gallery declined the responsibility of passing on the acquisitions, and this, under the existing law, made any purchase impossible. Humber then brought a "friendly suit" against the Attorney General in order to establish a legal substitute authority to pass on art purchases.

By this time work from eight schools of painting, ranging over five centuries, had been selected by the Art Commission, and an authority with extensive knowledge of various fields was essential. Carl Hamilton suggested William R. Valentiner, former director of the Detroit and Los Angeles Museums, then in California, as the one person thus qualified. Humber persuaded Hamilton to fly to California with Kodachromes and transparencies of all the proposed paintings and to seek Valentiner's appraisal and approval. Time was precious! The New York dealers were becoming anxious over the various delays in finalizing the purchases of the works they were holding and had stipulated a final deadline of December 31, 1951. It was already December and Valentiner hesitated in committing himself to appraise adequately the 180 paintings in so short a time. When he saw the Kodachromes and transparencies, however, his fears dissolved; he knew from his long experience in Europe and with museums in this country the background and provenance of all but twelve of them.

In a last minute finish worthy of the screen, Hamilton flew back to Raleigh with Valentiner's reports. On December 31 Humber took them to the Attorney General's home, along with some thirty books written by Valentiner. The Attorney General agreed to appoint Valentiner as the substitute authority, and Humber telephoned the galleries that the deal was final, that their checks would be made out and sent right after the

New Year's holiday. But then the Attorney General wavered about the legality of his decision, and the case was taken to the County Superior Court, which upheld the substitute appointment. Appealed to the Superior Court, the case was also won there.

All legal entanglements were unsnarled by February, 1952, and State Auditor Henry Bridges, fortified with nearly $900,000.00 and the "blessings of the State Supreme Court," went to New York to honor the vouchers for the paintings already selected by the Art Commission.

Historically, the museum could not have found a more propitious time for buying art. Just as the Metropolitan Museum of Art found a favorable market in its beginning, created by wealthy Germans being expelled from Paris and having to sell their fine paintings, the North Carolina Museum of Art profited by a buyers' market created by the dispersions of European collections following World War II. The Art Commission had been searching the art market and hopefully reserving paintings since the 1947 appropriation of $1,000,000 was made. In a talk to the Faculty Club of the University of North Carolina in 1956, Humber told of the "breaking up of great collections in Europe and the United States," stressing that North Carolina had to get some of them "now or never." One acquisition he described was a celebrated painting by John Singleton Copley which had stayed in William Randolph Hearst's castle in Wales for four years after Hearst's death "and then came into North Carolina's possession, through legal complications and the whims of heirs, at a price far lower than had been thought possible."

With the aid of Carl Hamilton, whose earlier forays in behalf of the museum have been noted, the million dollars that North Carolina spent in the New York art market netted a collection worth well over two million dollars. Dealers listened to Hamilton's arguments that a fine collection in the South would help create a new market for their wares and sold many paintings and sculptures to the museum at incredible bargains; for instance, a painting for which J. P. Morgan had paid $150,000 in the twenties came to the museum for $15,000, and the "Joan of Arc" by Rubens for only $35,000. With this auspicious beginning, it is small wonder that the museum is often referred to as "the miracle of Morgan Street."

With this fabulous collection in hand, a building to house it in presented its share of difficulties. Obviously, as argued by Senator Charles Gold during the 1951 legislative debates, "the state would have to spend more millions to provide a place in which to keep the paintings purchased with the $1,000,000 and those the Kress Foundation would give." The General Assembly carried out this prediction by earmarking $200,000 from a bond issue for renovating the old Highway Building on Morgan Street into a Museum of Art. The total cost at the time was estimated to run around $234,000, but Humber utilized his persuasive powers to lop off a bit here and there. Contractors Davis & Safran, Stahl-Rider (air-conditioners), and Thompson & Company (electrical contractors), chipped in $1,000 each; Willie Lee, painter, $200; R. L. Dresser (flooring contractor) $500; United Terrazzo & Tile Corporation, $194; and Peden Steel Company, $50. The Board of Public Buildings and Grounds garnered $26,000 from other funds .

To maintain costs in proper perspective, the board of directors of the State Art Society on June 30, 1954, appointed an official building committee, "to make final decisions on revisions of plans and other matters requiring official action as the building gets underway." The building committee consisted of the executive committee of the board and of Edwin Gill, state treasurer. Appointed as official consultants to the building committee were Dean Henry L. Kamphoefner, architect; Carl W. Hamilton, art consultant and advisor; and Noah W. Sites, Jr., representing the Budget Bureau. Members of the executive committee were Robert Lee Humber, chairman, Clarence Poe, Clemens Sommer, Mrs. Isabelle Bowen Henderson, and Sylvester Green. The gallery director, Lucy Cherry Crisp, Ben F. Williams, Edgar Thorne, and others of her staff were ex-officio members of the building committee.

But costs mounted, due to numerous changes and delays, and so did tempers. Edward T. Waugh, architect for the renovations, and Carl Hamilton, consultant, had so many disagreements that Waugh informed Governor Luther Hodges that he would "be able to expedite the completion of this job" if Mr. Hamilton were removed from further participation in the project. Among the time-consuming changes, which ran the total bill up to around $400,000, were imported marble to replace plaster as facing around a dozen columns, changes in partitions, cork floors to replace plain asphalt tile, and the addition of an elevator. Budget Bureau Engineer Noah Sites considered the changes to be worthwhile "in producing a better art museum," and Edwin Gill, conscientious State Treasurer and a director of the State Art Society, insisted that "we have tried to do a really good job on an old building. I don't believe we have had undue delays considering the problems we encountered."

The goal for finishing the museum was set for December, 1955, to coincide with the Art Society's participation in "Culture Week" in Raleigh, but delays dictated postponement until April 6, 1956—just under two years from the date on which George B. Cherry, Superintendent of the Board of Public Buildings and Grounds, and Dave Coletrane, Assistant Director of the Budget, signed contracts clearing the way for the remodeling of the old Highway Building into a Museum of Art.

That same year Valentiner's catalogue of the museum's collections was published, with the assistance of Mrs. May Davis Hill and of Paul Wescher, who helped with the French and German sections. In the introduction Valentiner cites North Carolina as a possible example for other states:

> The creation of the North Carolina Museum of Art is a unique achievement not only in the history of American museums but in that of the whole museum world. As far as we know, this is the first time that so large a sum has been appropriated by a government body for the acquisition of a public collection of paintings prior to the construction of a new building to house them . . .
>
> In the past, the general tendency has always been to contribute first a fine museum building. Usually the funds were exhausted by the time the building was finished. The collection, then, had to be started with gifts from private collectors—a procedure which was rarely advantageous to the creation of an all round museum collection.
>
> But the realization of the plan could not have been accomplished if it were not for men who combined knowledge of art with an unselfish love for serving the public and who could devote their time to study of the art market with the idea of providing material for the future Raleigh Museum. These persons were found in Rob-

ert Lee Humber, well-known lawyer and advocate of World Federation, and Carl W. Hamilton, noted in the art world through his collecting of Italian masterpieces. They have been greatly aided by two other members of the Art Commission, Mr. Edwin Gill, State Treasurer, and Dr. Clemens Sommer of the University of North Carolina.

Publication of the elaborate catalogue in two volumes was made possible through the generosity of Mrs. Kenneth Mountcastle, Jr., of Winston-Salem, N. C.

Despite his love of the early Masters, Valentiner recognized the museum's gap in contemporary art in its early collections and the need to remedy it, and since no funds were available for this purpose, he generously donated late in 1956 various works from his own collection to inaugurate a contemporary collection in the museum. Included were works by Dias, William Congdon, C. S. Price, Richard Diebenkorn, Robert Motherwell, Emerson Woelffer, Ynez Johnston, Mark Tobey, Harry Bertoia, and Enrique Montenegro among other important contemporary artists.

Mindful of the museum's role in education, Valentiner appointed Charles W. Stanford, Jr., a native Tarheel, as curator of education soon after Miss Crisp resigned the post. Stanford graduated from the University of North Carolina with a major in English literature, attended the School of Education at Columbia University, and then worked on his doctorate in archaeology and the fine arts at Princeton University. His function, as stated by Valentiner "will be to act as liaison between the Museum and the public in the field of education . . . the development of a program involving the public school teachers . . . preparation and delivery of a series of free gallery talks on Sunday afternoons . . . enlargement of the free Sunday afternoon concert series . . . development of free Saturday programs at the Museum for both adults and children . . . preparing a television series on art . . . and developing a training program for volunteer guides at the Museum."

A foundation for these programs had been inaugurated by the staff of the old State Art Gallery and transferred to the museum. The Junior League of Raleigh, for instance, became involved as volunteers when the

State Art Gallery was in the Archives and History building; and long to be remembered among the early Sunday afternoon programs was "A Poets' Hour" on a November Sunday in 1954, planned by Richard Walser and Miss Crisp. Thirty poets read and discussed their poems. Walser recalls that he and Miss Crisp announced the program with some trepidation, but that "poets poured in from everywhere."

One of Stanford's first achievements was a two-volume study of forty masterpieces in the North Carolina Museum collection which he designed and wrote as a teaching aid "to be profitably and pleasurably used by clubs and other organizations or individuals," as well as by the public schools. Entitled *Masterpieces in the North Carolina Museum of Art—A Color-slide Tour*, one volume has been contrived as two plastic frames into which transparencies are fitted and may be removed for viewing through a projector; and the other volume contains ninety pages of text, illustrated with twenty-nine black-and-white reproductions and eleven color plates. The two volumes are keyed to each other and, in effect, are an art critique on the artists, their work, their styles, and the history of the period in which they lived. The Raleigh Junior League underwrote the project with a grant of $8,000. Stanford's televised "Art Tours—North Carolina Museum of Art" proved so popular that Channel 4, WUNC-TV did at least one re-run of the series. His museum tours for school children immediately lured thousands annually.

Many of the programs now flourishing in the museum were initiated by Ben F. Williams, curator. The only person of the old State Art Gallery group who has continued with the museum, Williams has been a quiet but cohesive influence throughout its entire history and has carried on his curatorial work without interruption throughout the turmoil of changing directors. He has been responsible for numerous gifts to the museum, among them the Arrington collection, and has written articles on the museum that have brought attention to its collections at home and abroad. *North Carolina's Capital, Raleigh*, published by the University of North Carolina Press, was assembled under his editorial chairmanship. He was one of nine Americans selected to represent the United States (North Carolina) at the International Summer Session of the Rijksbureau voor Kunsthistorische Documentatie, The Hague, Holland, and awarded first

place in competitive examination. Williams has received numerous citations from various North Carolina governors for his work on such committees as the Canova Statue and the Tercentenary Commission, and by
1970 he had designed and written over seventy catalogues, with the help
of his staff, and had staged well over two hundred exhibitions in the North
Carolina Museum of Art. In the words of Miss Lucy Cherry Crisp, former
director of the North Carolina State Art Gallery, "no one can hang an
exhibition so well." North Carolina lost one of its most important painters
when Williams became a museum man, but is fortunate in owning one of
his works, "Geanie," which won a purchase award in the North Carolina
Artists' Annual in 1947.

The Museum's First Director

William R. Valentiner, the first director of the North Carolina Museum of Art, came to America in 1909 as the first curator of the Department of Decorative Arts just installed at the Metropolitan Museum of Art
in New York City. He had received his doctorate from Heidelberg and
had been an assistant to Dr. Hofstede de Groote of The Hague. He also
had studied with and worked as assistant to Dr. Wilhelm von Bode,
director-general of the Kaiser Friedrich Museum in Berlin, who described
Valentiner to the Metropolitan Museum as "the most gifted and best
equipped young student of art that I have ever had in the museum." Even
that early Valentiner was regarded as an authority on Rembrandt and the
early Dutch and Flemish schools.

When World War I was declared, Valentiner returned to his home-
land and enlisted as a private in the German army, where he served with
distinction and was decorated for bravery. He returned to this country in
1921 to catalogue the Widener Collection and in 1939 was director-general
of the "Masterpieces of Art" exhibition assembled for the World's Fair
in New York City. After serving as director of the Detroit Institute of Art
and later going to the Los Angeles County Museum, where he had a great
influence on West Coast collectors, he retired to Italy to spend the remainder of his life writing. It was then that Hamilton and Humber persuaded him to become the first director of the North Carolina Museum of

Art, a challenge he felt he could not forego. As already related in the chapter on the State Art Society, he brought James Byrnes with him as assistant director. Byrnes had been his assistant at the Los Angeles County Museum.

In 1958 Valentiner went to Europe in search of material to be used in a revision of his earlier Rembrandt studies for the projected reissue of his *Klassiker der Kunst* series. This tour was against the advice of his physician and friends and was interrupted by enforced rests along the way. Nevertheless, his genius for discovering masterpieces lost through the centuries to art historians led him to a painting in the London art market which previously had been known to him only through photographs. After studying the original, he pronounced it a portrait of Marie van Uylenburg, painted about 1633 by Rembrandt. In an expression of faith, Valentiner sent the painting to the North Carolina Museum of Art, hoping to find some means of purchasing it. Alex Andrews, a prominent Raleigh citizen, fulfilled this hope by purchasing the painting and giving it to the museum.

Soon after leaving England for Germany, Valentiner realized his physical inadequacy for travel and hurried back to New York City and to the apartment of his friend, playwright Clifford Odets, just around the corner from the Metropolitan Museum where his career began a half-century earlier. There he died on September 6, 1958.

The third anniversary of the North Carolina Museum of Art was marked by the W. R. Valentiner Memorial Exhibition, "Masterpieces of Art," the state's tribute to the man whose long and illustrious career in American museum work was concluded in Raleigh. A similar exhibition had been planned to celebrate Valentiner's fiftieth anniversary in the American museum field and, fortunately, he learned of this intention a few days before he passed away.

The exhibition, which ran from April 6 to May 17, 1959, included works from all epochs, showing the breadth of Valentiner's interest and knowledge. In order to make the event a fitting testament to the extraordinary service rendered by Valentiner, Governor Luther Hodges and the Council of State acted upon a request presented by Edwin Gill and provided $8,000 to help defray the costs of transportation, insurance, and other exhibition expenses. To arrange "a single project which would attempt to survey the life of a man whose professional career spanned more than half a century—building the collections of four major museums—acting as consultant and advisor to a large number of art collectors—and publishing more than six hundred books, catalogues, and articles ranging over the entire history of art—appeared all but impossible. With the combined efforts of the museum staff, however, and the cooperation of numerous other museum directors and private collectors, the exhibition was assembled within the short space of eight months."

Divided into three sections, the exhibit was designed to demonstrate the extraordinary scope of Valentiner's knowledge and interest, his contribution as a creative museum director, his accomplishments as a scholar and art historian and, finally, his active role as a private collector. This exhibit drew the largest attendance of any special show held at the museum up to that time—25,410 according to one report and 28,000 according to another—nearly double the 15,000 recorded for the Rembrandt exhibit held in December of 1956.

In warm response to the announcement of the projected exhibition, friends and admirers of Valentiner presented to the museum memorial gifts of art works valued at more than a quarter of a million dollars. Armand Hammer of the Hammer Galleries of New York gave a Medicean sixteenth-century paneled room that originally came from the Medicis' San Donato Palace in Florence. At the time of the gift, Byrnes, acting director, said: "We are particularly pleased to have the room, because Dr. Valentiner initiated in America the idea of the 'period room' . . . in which both the fine and decorative arts of a given period are displayed." (It was at the Metropolitan Museum of Art that Dr. Valentiner applied this idea which had originated at the Swiss National Museum in Zurich in 1898, according to Calvin Tomkins in his *Merchants and Masterpieces* [New York, 1970].)

Another unique memorial to Valentiner was a painting partially purchased by the square inch. On his last trip to London he wrote that he had found "an extraordinary painting . . . a newly discovered work by Carel Fabritius, almost the rarest of the outstanding Dutch artists, the master of Jan Vermeer. He was killed at the age of thirty-two in an explosion in Delft and only seven or eight paintings are known by him." This painting,

"St. Matthew Writing the Gospel," was acquired by public subscription. Several thousand dollars toward its purchase came through a Memorial Fund. Then a scale drawing of the painting was divided into 1700 one-inch squares, each "selling" for ten dollars. The many friends of Valentiner who wanted to honor his work were free to contribute as many inches as they wished. The painting's significance to the museum collection is verified by Valentiner's own words: "I think a specialty of our Museum will be a representation of the masters around Rembrandt . . . If we acquire the present painting, (these paintings) will be better represented in Raleigh than anywhere else in the United States, and in Europe surpassed only by the Rijksmuseum at Amsterdam."

The immediate affection Valentiner developed toward his adopted state is materially expressed by his will in which he left the bulk of his estate, valued at $318,358.03, to the North Carolina Museum of Art. His divorced wife contested the will, but through a settlement out of court the museum received a great portion of the estate. Volume II, No. 1 (1958) of the museum's *Bulletin* carries a final article by Valentiner and a memorial page by Robert Lee Humber for the State Art Society, and Volume III, Special Edition (1959) is devoted to tributes and articles eulogizing the museum's first director. The catalogue, which contains Valentiner's own story of his "Emigration to America," excerpted from his unfinished autobiography, is a veritable history of art itself. A sentence by Humber best expresses the sentiments of the State: "William R. Valentiner symbolized an epoch, the greatest fifty years yet known in museum history, and North Carolina is proud and grateful to have had his services as the first director of its State Museum of Art."

The Kress Collection Arrives

On June 8, 1959, the State Art Commission accepted the Kress gift of seventy paintings and two sculptures—eight years after the Kress Foundation pledged to match with gifts of equal value a state appropriation of one million dollars for art purchases. But the eight-year lag had proved profitable: The collection had increased in value from the early promise of $1,000,000 to $2,500,000. Humber told the Art Commission that the

Kress Foundation "far exceeded the letter of its contract" in making the gift (even allowing for the increase in art prices since 1951). Actually, twelve years had been involved in the negotiations between the Kress Foundation and the State Art Commission, including, of course, selection of those paintings that best filled the museum's need, and an interim when they were in New York being cleaned, treated for preservation, and appropriately framed.

Mrs. R. H. Kress, sister-in-law of the late Samuel Kress, cut the ribbon on the evening of November 30, 1960, opening this long-awaited exhibition of the Kress gift. Governor Hodges accepted the collection for the North Carolina Museum of Art. Of the eight museums in the United States to which the variety store executive gave collections, North Carolina's is exceeded in size only by the collection given to the National Gallery in Washington. In fact, many of the paintings came to North Carolina from the National Gallery where they had been on loan. Paul Wescher, who had helped Valentiner catalogue the museum's collection, joined the museum's staff on a temporary basis as consultant to Acting Director Byrnes, and particularly to catalogue the Kress Collection.

An unusual exhibition, covering the history of tobacco, followed the Kress exhibition. Because of the vital role tobacco has played in North Carolina's economy as well as its early history, Byrnes felt that such an exhibition would have special significance. Entitled "Tobacco and Smoking in Art," and grouped in three sections, the exhibition included ancient smoking implements (some prehistoric); paintings related to tobacco and smoking from the seventeenth through the twentieth century; and folk art and amusing "oddments."

The Museum's Second Director

James Byrnes resigned from the museum a few months later, to be succeeded by Dr. Justus Bier. Much of the debate over the search for a man of more scholarly attainments than those of Acting Director Byrnes, is recorded in the chapter on the North Carolina State Art Society.

Justus Bier, a native of Germany, as was Valentiner, assumed his responsibilities as director of the North Carolina Museum of Art on January

1, 1961. He came to the museum from the University of Louisville, Kentucky, where he was dean of the Department of Fine Arts and director of the Allen R. Hite Art Institute which he established and expanded into an eminent teaching museum. During his twenty-three years at the University of Louisville, the Department of Fine Arts became one of the most important in the nation. His early training included studies at five different universities, including the Universities of Munich and Bonn, and the University of Zurich where he received his Ph.D. degree *magna cum laude*. He was founder and director of the Museum for Industrial Design in Hanover, Germany, from 1930 to 1936, and curator and director of the Kestner Society Art Institute in Hanover during the same period.

Justus Bier was no stranger to North Carolina. In 1951 he served with Lamar Dodd and Leslie Cheek on the jury for the Fourteenth North Carolina Artists' Annual. Little did he suspect that just ten years later he would be the director of the North Carolina Museum of Art and would also represent it in his native country. In October of 1961, with eight other American museum directors, Bier toured German museums as a guest of the Government of the Federal Republic of Germany and, as a Tarheel ambassador, presented letters from Governor Sanford to West German Chancellor Konrad Adenauer and to Berlin Mayor Willy Brandt.

A world-renowned specialist in late German Gothic sculpture, Bier's immediate reaction to the museum's collection was regret over its weakness in the area of sculpture. His special interest during much of his professional life had been research and study of the Tilmann Riemenschneider sculptures, on which he has authored several volumes in German. Through his many museum contacts, nineteen sculptures by this great Gothic German sculptor were brought together and shown in Raleigh in the fall of 1962. This was the first Riemenschneider exhibition ever held in the United States and the first major sculpture exhibition held at the North Carolina Museum of Art.

Several of the world's leading art museums honored Bier's invitation to participate in the exhibition, including the Louvre Museum, Paris; the Metropolitan Museum of Art, New York; and the Rijksmuseum, Amsterdam, Holland. Seldom had these treasured sculptures left their home museums, and never had the European ones journeyed to this country.

Dr. A. van Schendel, Rijksmuseum Director, wrote at the time: "Though we have certain hesitations in allowing a precious and fragile alabaster group to make such a very long trip, we think that the scope of the Riemenschneider exhibition is such that we are justified to lend our 'Annunciation' as a homage to your museum and to your scientific work on the matter."

Another unique event sponsored by the museum during the early phase of Bier's directorship was the statewide conference on "Responsibility for Aesthetic Quality," held in Raleigh October 18–20, 1962. Organized by Mrs. Charles B. Aycock of Kinston, chairman of the museum's Education Through Art Committee, and Gregory D. Ivy of Greensboro, program chairman, the conference was underwritten by the Richardson Foundation of North Carolina and New York. Other members of the committee were Dr. Charles B. Carroll, State Superintendent of Public Instruction, and Mrs. William Joslin, both of Raleigh. The conference drew 128 representatives from the state's museums, college and university art departments, communications media, civic clubs, cultural organizations, and elementary and secondary school art departments "to search for new standards in Education through Art." Speakers included James Johnson Sweeney, then director of the Guggenheim Museum in New York, Victor D'Amico, director of education at the Museum of Modern Art in New York, and Warren Ashby, head of the philosophy department at Woman's College of the University in Greensboro.

Announced as "a primary step by the rather recently created board of trustees of the North Carolina Museum of Art toward the development of a more comprehensive educational program within the structure and the function of the museum," the conference's goals, as stated by Ivy, were "to explore fully the range and the scope of present programs; to give special emphasis to the relationship of the various activities to the future educational program of the museum; to explore methods and means by which the museum program may be effectively coordinated with the many established programs; and to envision new programs which may be established in the future to the satisfaction and enjoyment of the people of this State."

The final report of the committee on the proceedings of the conference, and the recommendations included in it, created a tempest in a teapot. Some of the suggestions were interpreted as criticisms of the museum and its board. Briefly, the report recommended that the museum be more active in educational matters, that it pay more attention to North Carolina artists, and that its staff be enlarged to meet the needs of the growing interest in art in the state. Further suggestions had to do with the museum's acquisitions policy, additional traveling shows, educational programs, and the like. None of these recommendations were startling. Perhaps the most important recommendation was that an associate director be appointed at the earliest possible date. Gregory Ivy, co-chairman of the program, said the reports left him feeling more optimistic about art in North Carolina than he had ever hoped to be.

In January of 1965 the museum announced that "based on a pilot study undertaken by Curator of Education Charles W. Stanford and Mrs. William Sprunt of Raleigh, the NCMA has initiated a new project designed to teach blind persons to appreciate art through a sense of touch." Stanford had extended his educational activities at the museum to include lectures to sightless children from the North Carolina School for the Blind and found that through the use of sculpture they could be taught art appreciation. The success of Stanford's experiments led to the establishment of a special gallery for the blind, using sculpture already in the museum. The Mary Duke Biddle Foundation of New York City made a donation of $17,500 to underwrite initiation costs, and the gallery was named the Mary Duke Biddle Gallery, honoring Mrs. Biddle—a noted benefactor from Durham, North Carolina.

The gallery has been supplemented by several grants from the U. S. Department of Health, Education and Welfare through its Commission of Vocational Rehabilitation. Here sightless students, or other visitors, are introduced to original works of art from all periods and as many regions as possible through their exploration of the sculpture through touch. Since the gallery opened, around three hundred works of art have been donated by generous persons throughout the country. A major lender of art objects has been the Olsen Foundation of New Haven, Connecticut, but the gallery is gradually building its own collection through gifts from artists and friends, among them Marjorie Daingerfield Howlett's "Head of Julie," given by the artist herself, and a bronze swan sculptured and given by Countess Kurt Reventlow.

Special guide rails and Braille instructions enable sightless students to move safely through the gallery and study the objects which are displayed on a counter space two feet wide and three feet from floor level. On the inside of the rails are Braille labels describing the objects. The items are within easy reach and the blind visitor may examine them thoroughly by touching them. Professor Brian Shawcroft's fourth year design class at the School of Design at the State University of North Carolina at Raleigh provided plans for the special gallery. They were carried out by Jerry B. Jerome Woodcrafters, also of Raleigh.

Allen H. Eaton, director of the Department of Arts and Social Work of the Russell Sage Foundation, tried as early as 1956 to interest museums around the country in providing programs to meet the needs of the blind, of whom it is estimated there are at least 350,000 in our country. When Stanford sought help in the early planning of instruction for the blind, Miss Mary Switzer, who at that time was Commissioner of Vocational Rehabilitation of the U.S. Department of Health, Education and Welfare, arranged for Eaton, who meanwhile had authored *Beauty and the Blind*, "to come to our museum and present invaluable aid."

In May of 1968, Charles Stanford participated in a meeting of the Soviet Committee of the International Council of Museums held in Leningrad and Moscow by delivering a paper on the pilot project of the Mary Duke Biddle Gallery for the Blind and explaining the educational program at the North Carolina Museum of Art. His success in developing this program also won for him in 1969 the coveted North Carolina Award for Fine Arts.

Justus Bier resigned his directorship of the North Carolina Museum of Art at the December, 1969, meeting of the museum's board of trustees, to become effective April 1, 1970. Upon acceptance of the resignation, the board elected Bier director emeritus and named him curator of the new Department of Research. In his letter to the Board, Bier said: "Since I have reached the status of septuagenarian, I feel I should consider how best to use the coming years. I have been extremely happy in this position as director of a museum that has developed in so few years to an institution of national and even international renown . . . I would like to offer the Board, with the expression of my esteem, my resignation as director of this Museum to be effective on April 1 of the coming year in order that I might devote the active years left to me to research and scholarly production. I hope I can make a lasting contribution in this field which will reflect favorably also on the Museum with which I have been connected."

When the *Museum Calendar of Art Events* announced Bier's resignation in the January, 1970 issue, it also announced the appointment by Robert Lee Humber of a committee of five to search for a successor. The committee consisted of Egbert Davis of Winston-Salem, chairman; Joseph Sloane of Chapel Hill; Mrs. L. Y. Ballentine and Edwin Gill, both of Raleigh; and Mrs. James Semans of Durham. The committee worked quietly and fast, with little publicity and none of the fanfare that had accompanied the appointments of Valentiner and Bier. And, contrary to past efforts to find an internationally established scholar under whose halo the museum could gain prestige, the committee turned to its own museum, which meanwhile had developed its own prestigious staff. On Wednesday, March 18, 1970, the press announced the appointment of Charles W. Stanford, Jr., as Bier's successor.

Among the many problems facing the new director is that of a new building, which has been under debate during several sessions of the General Assembly. As early as 1959 it was foreseen that the old Highway Building would soon be "bursting at the seams," and, as the *Winston-Salem Journal* then pointed out: "Like any parent, the state can be pleased at its child's growth, but also, like any parent, the state can't overlook the fact that growth can be expensive." On Wednesday, February 19, 1964, the trustees of the museum got down to serious discussion of square feet needed and a suitable site. In July of 1967 Senator Thomas White introduced a bill to facilitate action and the State Art Museum Building Commission consisting of fifteen members was approved. The 1969 General Assembly appropriated $3,000,000 to be used toward building a new museum, and Senator White, chairman of the Building Commission, announced that the Commission unanimously accepted the recommended appointment of New York architect, Edward Durrell Stone and his Raleigh associates, Holloway-Reeves, as architects for the project.

Presumably the $3,000,000 is the "challenge gift to enhance the possibility of attracting donors," suggested to the General Assembly by Humber in 1968, for the 1967 bill carried no appropriation, and Representative R. D. McMillan of Robeson, House floor manager for the bill, said "the building funds are expected to come largely from foundations and other private sources 'although future State participation may be needed.' "

Robert Lee Humber died on November 10, 1970, in his home-town of Greenville, N. C. Concerned about a new building for the museum, he and members of the commission had just returned from a grueling inspection tour of museums around the country "to ascertain, if possible, what not to do as well as what to do—"deleting features that have limited value and incorporating those that have the promise of maximum rewards," he wrote to me on November 5, 1970. He further stated:

> We visited the Amon Carter Museum in Fort Worth and also conferred at great length with Dr. Richard Brown of the Kimbell Museum, which is now in the process of being built at a cost of $8,500,000.00 and which already possesses an outstanding Collection of Old Masters; the Anthropological Museum of Mexico City, a remarkable edifice that truly embellishes the cultural assets of the Western Hemisphere; the Los Angeles County Museum, with its various cosmopolitan activities; the Oakland Museum, with its inherited three museums: Science, History and Art, restricted uniquely to California subject matter; and finally the Legion of Honor and the de Young Museum of San Francisco.
>
> We returned with many interesting ideas and much valuable information. Last Spring we studied the administration, operation and maintenance of the National Gallery of Art in Washington as well as the Metropolitan Museum, the Frick, the Whitney, the Guggenheim and the Museum of Modern Art in New York. I do hope that we can erect in Raleigh a Museum that will embody the spirit of our people, serve their cultural needs and become a center of international influence in the appreciation of art.

Without the guiding hand of Humber, the Commission is now faced with heated controversy over a site for the future museum.

6. THE ACKLAND ART MUSEUM

The William Hayes Ackland Art Center dedication on September 20, 1958, on the campus of the University of North Carolina at Chapel Hill, marked the realization of a dream of a prosperous Tennessee native to have a memorial erected in his honor, and the reward of twenty years of litigation.

That such an event would someday occur on the University campus was predicted as early as October 12, 1907, when Francis Preston Venable, then president of the University, delivered an address on University Day. Projecting his hopes for adequate "though not luxurious" buildings for the campus, and qualifying his deprecation of "luxurious surroundings," he emphasized that "this does not mean that beauty must be banished. Rather is this taste for the beautiful to be cultivated in buildings and grounds and the gathering of the finer works of art. Some day many such treasures will be gathered in a museum here."

William Hayes Ackland, for whom the building was named, was born September 6, 1855, on the family plantation, "Belmont," near Nashville, Tennessee. His mother was first married on July 2, 1839, to Isaac Franklin of Gallatin, Tennessee, a wealthy southern planter who owned plantations in the Parish of West Feliciana, Louisiana, as well as Fairview Plantation in Sumner County, Tennessee. After Franklin's death, his widow, who before the Civil War owned over a thousand slaves, married Colonel Joseph Alexander Smith Acklen, and it was to them that William Hayes (who later changed his family name to Ackland) was born. His family's fortune dematerialized, but at the age of ten months Ackland inherited $110,000 from his half sister, Emma Franklin, who died on November 1, 1855. Presumably this inheritance was kept in trust until he was old enough to manage it. According to John E. Larson, counsel for the trustees of the Ackland bequest to the University, "through prudent investments and accumulations of income, the inheritance amounted to $1,350,000 at the time of Ackland's death on February 16, 1940." Larson also noted that Ackland's inheritance was greatly increased as the result of an opinion rendered by the Supreme Court of Louisiana which declared void a clause of Isaac Franklin's will that directed his trustees to use one-third of his large estate for the establishment of an academy. Franklin's plan to devote a large part of his "colossal fortune," to use the expression of the Louisiana Court, in perpetuity for the "higher and ornamental branches" of education would seem to have come to fruition indirectly through the provisions of Ackland's will.

Ackland studied at Nashville University and the Law School of Vanderbilt University, after which he practiced law in Washington, D. C. He traveled extensively in this country and abroad, visiting museums of art wherever he went. At what period in his life this successful bachelor began to envision a memorial museum in which his body would be interred and his manuscripts and art collection would be preserved is unrecorded. But on May 4, 1936, at age 81, he executed a will by which he devised and bequeathed his entire estate to Edson B. Olds and the American Security and Trust Company of Washington, D. C., as trustees, stipulating that the principal of the estate be kept intact and the income be accumulated in a separate fund; that his trustees cause to be erected a memorial building in the form of a gallery or museum upon the campus of Duke University, or, if permission could not be obtained, then upon the campus of the University of North Carolina, Chapel Hill, or if permission could not be obtained from either of those universities, then upon the campus of Rollins College, Winter Park, Florida.

In December of 1936 Ackland himself initiated action toward the fulfillment of his will by writing to all three universities "substantially in the following language":

> I am the owner of some valuable paintings and statuary and have thought of building and endowing a gallery in conection with a southern university. Before making my will, I should like to know whether such a gift would be acceptable and under what conditions the gift would be received? The style or architecture is to be in keeping with other buildings and the site I would expect the university to furnish. In regard to other particulars, which do not occur to me at the moment—I should be glad to be informed through the authorities.

William P. Few, president of Duke University, had just encouraged Louise Hall, Professor of Art at Duke, to make a survey of the arts in the Southeast for 1935 to 1936, with a view toward building an art museum on the Duke campus. In reminiscing about President Few's deep interest in art, Miss Hall wrote to me on December 21, 1965, saying: "At Harvard he had been exposed to the great pioneer in the teaching of art history, Charles Eliot Norton, and, as a man of letters he knew the place of the arts in the life of all cultivated men." Ackland's letter, therefore, must have appeared as manna from Heaven.

President Few immediately pursued the opportunity Ackland presented. He visited Ackland in Washington and he had Ackland visit Duke. President Few gave oral and written assurances that the building contemplated by Ackland would be constructed upon the Duke campus and furnished Ackland the services of the architect of Duke University, who drew plans for the proposed gallery, or museum.

Convinced that his museum of art would be built on the Duke campus, that it would be known as the William Hayes Ackland Memorial and would include an apse for the interrment of his body, Ackland executed a new will on November 10, 1938, wherein he revoked his previous one and in which he named only Duke University as the site for the museum.

Both Ackland and President Few died early in 1940. After a period of uncertainty and despite the efforts of many at Duke University to carry out Ackland's last will, the executive committee of Duke University declined the bequest at a meeting held on September 6, 1941, "based mainly upon sentimental reasons," according to one member. The press speculated as to other reasons, one of which was that the estate would be under management of the trustees named in the will. *Time Magazine* suggested that Duke University might not wish to add another body to those of the "tobacco-rich Dukes already in its Memorial Chapel." A more accurate summation from a more reliable source revealed that the acceptance of this gift, with its many provisions, could threaten Duke's continued support by the Washington Duke Foundation.

Ackland's nieces and nephews claimed their uncle's money when Duke rejected it. They had tried earlier to get the will declared invalid "on the usual grounds of undue influence and lack of testamentary capacity, based upon Ackland's age and ill health when he made his last will favoring Duke University." (Larson said in his account of events that "there never was any question in our minds that Dr. Few intended faithfully to carry out all the terms and provisions of the will.") But they still had to deal with the trustees of the estate, Rollins College, and the University of North Carolina. And from *Time Magazine's* summary of the subsequent frenetic actions of all, it appeared for a time that Rollins would win:

> Ackland's nieces and nephews rushed to court to seek the fortune they had given up as lost. The University of North Carolina (with the late Ambassador to Britain O. Max Gardner as lawyer) and Rollins (with ex-U. S. Attorney General Homer S. Cummings) followed. First to lose out, after five years' litigation, were the nieces and nephews. That left the two colleges to fight it out between themselves.
>
> Last week a District of Columbia Court ruled that in his last days Ackland had been definitely partial to Rollins and that Rollins, therefore, should get the money. Unless the decision is reversed on appeal, Rollins will have its Museum, and Ackland's bones a place to rest.

Strangely enough, while Duke University and Rollins College were wooing Ackland, entertaining him on their campuses, and drawing architectural plans for a museum to his specifications, the University of North Carolina sat silently by. It was the trustees of the Ackland Trust who, in their determination to carry out the spirit of Ackland's will, approached the Honorable O. Max Gardner of North Carolina to ascertain whether the University of North Carolina was interested in the trust. Governor Gardner was greatly interested and promptly talked to Frank Porter Graham, president of the University. A meeting was arranged in October, 1941, between President Graham, the trustees of the University, and the representatives of the Ackland trustees.

On February 25, 1949, the University of North Carolina's right to the trust fund was established finally and beyond legal revocation, in accordance with a mandate from the United States Court of Appeals, which on February 3 reversed an earlier ruling of the district court that gave the fund to Rollins College in Florida.

The University had been fortunate in having two powerful and brilliant allies—Governor Gardner who loved the University, and John Larson, counsel for the Ackland trust. Both believed that the actual beneficiaries of the Trust were intended to be students and other members of the public throughout the South interested in art; that the dominant idea in the mind of the Testator was "the cause of art in the South; and, that Mr. Ackland intended that the seat of his enterprise should be a University, with its well-known accompaniment of students, instructors, research and publication facilities, permanence of administration and of educational purposes." Both men also believed that the University of North Carolina more nearly met these qualifications than did Rollins College, and both were anxious to explore and apply the doctrine of *cy pres*, the only legal principle through which the Trust could be saved after Duke renounced it.

Governor Gardner died on February 6, 1947, but his partners, Fred Morrison, Nat Townsend, Ward Lattin, and Thomas Bedow, continued the fight. By the time the Ackland Center was built, the gift of $1,500,000 they won for the University had increased to $2,225,000. The Raleigh *News and Observer* on February 6, 1949, said: "During his lifetime, the late O. Max Gardner won many victories of which he was justly proud. But no victory ever gave him more satisfaction than he would have obtained from the victory won this week by his law firm." These men had been supported by a distinguished group appointed by President Graham to prepare the groundwork necessary to the acceptance of the legacy: Chancellor Robert Burton House, Claude Teague, R. J. M. Hobbs, John Allcott, Kenneth Ness, W. D. Carmichael, Jr., and Miss Lynette Warren, among others.

President Graham retired in March of 1949, to be followed by Gordon Gray, 1950–55 and William C. Friday in 1956. Interim Acting Presidents were William Carmichael 1949–1950, and Harris Perks from January, 1955 until November of that year. All played vital roles in the acquisition of the Ackland bequest.

After Federal estate and District of Columbia inheritance taxes, legacies and other obligations of the Ackland estate were paid, the executors turned over to the trustees an estate of around $955,000.00, approximately the cost of the Ackland building, but the accumulated income fund, available for the purchase of art objects, came to $285,000.00. At the time of the dedication the permanent endowment fund was valued at about $1,450,000.00 and was producing an annual income of about $65,000.00, which has continued to grow with economic advancement.

Then came the difficult search for a director of the Ackland Art Center. Such a man would have to fill the triple role of professor of art, director of the museum, and administrator of the Art Department to be included in the center. Following months of interviewing, evaluating the qualifications of various candidates, and vice versa, Joseph Curtis Sloane, head of the Art Department at Bryn Mawr, accepted the job in June of 1958. Sloane was unable to take up his duties in Chapel Hill then, but did attend the dedication of the Ackland Art Center. Kenneth Ness, acting director, continued in this capacity until Sloane's final arrival in Chapel Hill in January, 1959.

Already distinguished for his scholarly writings, Sloane soon finished his book, *Paul Chenavard, Painter of 1848*, which was published by the University of North Carolina Press in 1962. In 1963 he was elected Alumni Distinguished Professor by the University of North Carolina at Chapel Hill.

Sloane encountered his first challenge immediately. Ackland had left no art to hang in his museum. Burke Davis succinctly reported the situation in the *Greensboro Daily News* on September 9, 1958: "When at last, a few days ago, the Ackland will flowered into the handsome gallery here, there were some surprises for visitors. First, there was no Ackland collection to be seen; all paintings were on loan from other college galleries and must be returned by October 21." Edson B. Olds, one of the Ackland trustees, had early warned the University of the paucity of Ackland's art collection. "We were surprised by what we found. There really isn't anything to hang. Mr. Ackland wasn't much at home in the field of buying art. One fine painting that was thought to be a Sully turned out to be only a copy—a fine copy, but merely a copy. . . There is, however, a consolation: Some $40,000 a year is available for the purchase of art works . . .

though this is rather a pittance when works of acknowledged masters are being considered."

Ackland did leave a rather handsome portrait of himself in which Robert O. Skemp, the painter, captures some of the elegance of his surroundings. This portrait greets visitors entering the Ackland. Farther down the hall in a secluded niche is a marble sarcophagus which contains Ackland's remains. The architects finished off the tomb with a stiff, reclining figure of Ackland, sculptured from startlingly white marble, which was later chipped away and replaced in 1961 with a more fitting bronze tomb sculpture by New York artist Milton Hebald, a 1955–58 winner of the Prix de Rome.

Funds for increasing the museum's collections were soon available. When William A. Whitaker, an alumnus of the University of North Carolina, died in February, 1960, he left $1,750,000 to his Alma Mater. This trust is now known as the William A. Whitaker Foundation. Another bachelor, who, like Ackland, loved art and appreciated its great contribution to mankind, Whitaker specifically earmarked for the purchase of art a third of the income from this trust, but with these precepts incorporated in his will of February 20, 1957:

"One third of such income to be used for the acquisition of art such as sculptures, paintings, etchings, and prints, whose character and excellence would qualify them for inclusion in a university gallery of art. Not to be included are specimens of what is termed today as 'abstract art' or any type of art which may be termed 'faddist' or a departure from the accepted canons of art."

A native of Winston-Salem, Whitaker was the son of William A. and Anna Bitting Whitaker. He was graduated from the University of North Carolina in 1904 and later received the master's degree in chemistry at Columbia University. He taught at City College in New York for a time and later became professor of metallurgy at the University of Kansas. After World War I, at which time he served on the Naval Consultation Board, he forsook the academic life and worked in Greece and Turkey in the import-export business, at which time he also became an avid archaeological "digger." He became a founding partner of Francis I. Dupont & Company, New York dealers in securities. Upon retirement in 1940, he devoted his time and interest to art, scholarship, rare books, and the University of North Carolina.

As Olds pointed out in 1958 regarding the Ackland income, $40,000 a year was a pittance with which to search for a proper teaching collection. But the Whitaker trust, earmarked for the purchase of art, increased the Ackland's buying power considerably.

Two fine print collections were transferred from the University library to the Ackland soon after its opening: The well-known William Pickard Jacocks print collection and the Burton Emmett collection. Dr. Jacocks's collection includes works by Rembrandt, Dürer, Agostino Caracci, Fragonard, Cezanne, Matisse, Chagall, Miro, and Americans George Bellows, Thomas Hart Benton, Edward Hopper, and Grant, among others. The Burton Emmett collection is "a veritable gold mine," according to Sloane. It came to the University at Chapel Hill from the Institute of Graphic Arts when the Institute shifted its interests toward commercial printing and felt an obligation to find another recipient of the collection which had been willed to it. William Reydel, of the Graphics Arts Institute, remembered that William D. Carmichael, Jr., Comptroller of the University of North Carolina, had worked for the Newell-Emmett company and had been a good friend of Emmett's. So, with the blessings of Mrs. Emmett, who hoped the collection would materialize into a memorial to her husband, Reydel informed Carmichael of the availability of the collection. Intrigued with the prestige such a collection would bring to the University, Carmichael and Charles E. Rush, librarian of the Louis Round Wilson Library where all prints were kept, collaborated in buying Emmett's whole collection on October 31, 1951, for a mere $9,000. Carmichael paid half the cost and the Library managed the other half.

This collection contains some 4,900 books, around 3,000 prints spanning six centuries, and as of now an undetermined number of paintings and sculpture. On today's market some of the individual prints would sell for more than was paid for the entire collection. Upon completion of the Ackland building in 1958, all of the prints which had been housed at the library were transferred to the Ackland, where they are slowly being properly catalogued and receiving other special care.

When in 1965 the Kress Foundation made twelve five-year grants of $50,000 to departments of art history around the nation, the University of North Carolina Art Department received the only one given at that time to any Southeastern university. This was an expression of confidence in what could be done rather than recognition for achievement. The grant was renewed on the expiration of the first five years—for scholarships, books, slides, and photographs.

In September of 1968 the Ackland Center commemorated its tenth anniversary by an exhibition of many of its acquisitions entitled "The First Decade of Collecting." The catalogue for the exhibition listed sixty-eight donors (mostly couples) in addition to the collections described above. The basic policy of Sloane and his advisory committee is to acquire a teaching collection. Their acquisitions span the period from 3000 B.C. through all the major historical art forms. "Very often . . . we might buy a picture that would not do for a public gallery but would excellently serve our teaching purpose . . . a picture which involved a technical problem which our students could study. Or a work might not be a masterpiece but would cast much light on the era in which it was produced," Sloane has pointed out.

Even with what once was considered the Ackland's affluence, its needs as a research center as well as a teaching center grow by leaps and bounds. Finally, the Ackland continues to look to North Carolinians—the sons and daughters of the University—for enrichment of its collections. Now that the state has come of age in the Arts, a sophisticated research collection such as the Ackland's is of inestimable value.

The Art staff, in addition to those who moved over from Person Hall, includes such distinguished teachers as John Schnorrenberg, history of art; Robert Barnard, art education; Marvin Saltzman, studio; and Robert W. Schlageter, curator.

7. GALLERIES

Greensboro: The Weatherspoon Gallery

Soon after the establishment of the Art Department at Woman's College in 1934, it became necessary to find a gallery, not only to show the works of students but to bring in works by professional artists and exhibitions from museums, collectors, and dealers, as part of the teaching process.

A room in the McIver building was set aside for this purpose and was named in honor of Mrs. Elizabeth McIver Weatherspoon, the first art teacher on the campus and sister of Charles Duncan McIver, founder of Woman's College.

In 1942, during the celebration of the fiftieth anniversary of the founding of the college, "Friends of the Weatherspoon Gallery" was organized —the accomplishment of Mrs. Roger McDuffie, Mrs. B. C. Parker, Mrs. Frederick Ferguson, and Mrs. Charles Perry; four women who foresaw the cultural opportunities "of a fine art gallery and a strong art department in Greensboro at Woman's College." Many others helped in the promotion of this organization but none more faithfully than Chancellor Jackson. In 1946, the name of the organization was changed to Weatherspoon Gallery Association.

An important result of the work of the Weatherspoon Gallery Association has been the growth of a permanent collection of original works of art for the University. The Association has encouraged gifts from donors and has carried out successful auctions to raise money for the purchase of art works for the collection. Through the perspicacious selection and purchase of paintings, sculpture, and graphics, carried out by Gregory Ivy over a period of nearly thirty years, and later by his successor, Gilbert F. Carpenter, and Curator James Tucker, the University of North Carolina at Greensboro as of 1970 had a collection of more than a thousand art works with excellent instructional value plus a monetary value of roughly $650,-000. One of the finest collections of modern art in the Southeast, it adds immeasurably to the cultural resources of the state by complementing the historical collections at the North Carolina Museum of Art in Raleigh, the Ackland Art Center in Chapel Hill, the Mint Museum in Charlotte, and the Hickory Museum of Art in Hickory.

An exhilarating gain in importance for the Weatherspoon Gallery came in 1950 when the fabulous Cone sisters, Miss Etta and Dr. Claribel, of Baltimore and Greensboro, willed a portion of their immense collection of modern art to Woman's College. The two ladies were great admirers of Henry Matisse and other French artists of the time, and each had a portrait sketch done by Matisse himself. And when they visited Paris, they always returned to their Baltimore apartment with works by Picasso, Degas, Renoir, Gauguin, Corot, or some modern artist. The bulk of the

Cone collection, valued at $3,000,000 back in the fifties, was presented to the Baltimore Museum of Art, but Woman's College received six bronzes by Matisse and over one hundred lithographs and other graphic works by Picasso, Matisse, Laurencin, and other European and American artists.

Among the important acquisitions of contemporary American art, which have come to the gallery through astute purchases and gifts, are works by Willem de Kooning, Robert Mallary, Alexander Calder, William Ronald, John Marin, Lyonel Feininger, Robert Henri, and others. Among a growing list of Tarheels in the permanent collection are Mackey Jeffries, Mark Lynch, and Lynn Moody Deal Igoe.

When the Art Department moved to its new quarters in 1959, with its enlarged Weatherspoon Gallery, Gregory Ivy hired James Tucker as full-time curator. Under the guidance of Tucker and with the challenge of increased space, the exhibition program has been tremendously accelerated. A major exhibit, "Art on Paper," sponsored jointly by the Weatherspoon Guild (a women's group) and the Dillard Paper Company, has been an excellent source from which the gallery has added to its collection by purchase awards.

Soon after Gilbert Carpenter arrived as successor to Ivy, who resigned in May of 1960, he wrote of the Weatherspoon collection: "This collection today would cost between a quarter and a half million dollars. Only a small fraction of this amount was originally paid for the works. As an economic fact this is remarkable, but more important is the fortunate windfall benefiting this community that derives from the superb discrimination and boldness of the Cones and of the members of the Woman's College Art Department who selected, almost unerringly, wonderful examples out of the conglomerate of contemporary art."

The Weatherspoon Gallery Association is supported not only by the Dillard Paper Company, which by 1970 had contributed a total of $63,-500.00 to underwrite exhibitions and provide purchase funds, but by a number of other Greensboro firms and the Greensboro Junior League.

Greenville: The Greenville Art Center

A Fine Arts Festival sponsored by the Greenville Woman's Club in 1935 caught the attention of Gene Erwin of Durham, who was then director of the Federal Art Project in North Carolina. Impressed by the festival, he followed up this interest in 1939 by establishing a FAP Art Gallery in Greenville. At the termination of WPA and FAP, the sponsoring board of the gallery continued its operations but changed its name to the "Community Art Center."

Through the indefatigable leadership of Mrs. J. H. B. Moore, the unflagging support of Robert Lee Humber, John D. Messick (then president of East Carolina College), George A. Douglas, director of the Danforth Foundation Project of East Carolina College, and others, a strong interest in the fine arts spread throughout Eastern North Carolina, leading in 1956 to the organization of the East Carolina Art Society. Pitt, Lenoir, Edgecombe, Nash, Northampton, Onslow and Beaufort Counties were represented at the organizational meeting of artists and art-interested citizens.

The new society fell heir to the Community Art Center, its small library, and its collection of some 80 works of art. Small quarters in the Greenville library served for years as its headquarters and for exhibit space for North Carolina artists and others whose work was sought out, hauled, and hung by Mrs. Moore, who also brought outstanding speakers to the community.

From its beginning the East Carolina Art Society looked toward developing a museum in which to house the art it was acquiring, to provide space for the teaching of arts and crafts, and to exhibit the works of local artists. Expressing the potential of the area, W. H. Watson, president of the Society, wrote the following to its members through his "From the President" column in the fourth issue of its *Bulletin*, October, 1957: "With the college in Greenville, there is no reason why Greenville should not become the cultural center of Eastern North Carolina, and anything our Society can do to further this end will be beneficial to the community as a whole."

When space for art in the library diminished with the library's own growth, it became necessary for the Society to begin a serious search for that long-planned museum. A committee was appointed to the task and, on December 31, 1959, it acquired a large three-story brick house, with a "double garage, adequate for a ceramics center," which it considered a real bonus.

"Almost immediately, committees went to work to convert what had been a beautiful home into a suitable art gallery. . . . Merchants, painters, carpenters, architects, electricians, doctors, lawyers, housewives, Boy and Girl Scouts gave unstintingly of their time," converting the large residence into an art center and possibly the "cultural center" that Watson envisioned two years earlier, and for which Mrs. Moore had directed all her energies for more than thirty years.

About a thousand guests attended the Sunday afternoon opening of the new Greenville Art Center on May 1, 1960. Eleven art dealers in New York City lent paintings by Old Masters for the inaugural exhibit, including work by such notables as Lorenzo Lotto, Titian, Tintoretto, Frans Hals, Gainsborough, Joshua Reynolds, Nattier, Constable, and Magnasco.

In 1964 the Greenville Art Center announced the appointment of Miss Lucy Cherry Crisp as its director. Her wide experience as director of the North Carolina State Art Gallery, and later of the Florence Museum of Art in South Carolina, enabled her to expand the interests of the Center. After the death of Mrs. Moore in 1965, Miss Crisp inaugurated the Moore Memorial Gallery at the Art Center, where art works contributed by artist friends of both Miss Crisp and Mrs. Moore will remain on permanent view. The Moore Memorial Gallery was dedicated on February 5, 1967. An exhibition of works by Charles Baskerville marked the occasion.

Mrs. Moore provided in her will that her property be sold and the proceeds be invested in a foundation fund for the Greenville Art Center. Known as the Rachel Maxwell Moore Foundation, at this writing the fund is nearing $100,000, due to the quiet efforts of Robert Lee Humber who proposed to Mrs. Moore's brothers, Grover and Jeff Maxwell, a challenge pledge of $50,000.00, which later became a gift.

Chapel Hill: The Genevieve B. Morehead Memorial Gallery

The Morehead Memorial Art Gallery, which occupies a rotunda inside the main entrance to the Morehead Building in Chapel Hill, was dedicated May 10, 1949. It is a permanent gallery and honors the first Mrs. John Motley Morehead, whose portrait by Artur Lajos Halmi is centered on the far wall, facing the visitor entering the gallery.

Other portraits in the rotunda are "James Watt" by Sir William Beechey; "Martha Washington" by Rembrandt Peale; "The Scribe" by Aart de Gelder; "Portrait of a Lady" by Jan Anthonisz van Ravesteyn; "Portrait of Paulus van Beresteyn" by Michiel Jansz van Mierevelt; "Portrait of John Bigelow" by Charles Loring Elliott; "Rembrandt's Sister, Liesbeth van Rijn" by Rembrandt; "Portrait of John Andrew MacDonnel Bonar, Esq., of Kimmingham and Warriston" by Sir Henry Raeburn; and the fifteenth replica of the "Porthole Portrait of George Washington" by Peale. Additional portraits are displayed in the private dining room on the third floor.

The Memorial Gallery is flanked on either side by the north and south galleries. For several years both of these galleries were available to individual artists or art groups as exhibition space. After a time, however, the south gallery was paneled in elegant walnut and confined to private use by the Planetarium. The north gallery has continued to show changing exhibits, many of them by North Carolina artists. Usually a new exhibition is installed each month, unless interrupted by special events at the Morehead Planetarium which require exhibition space.

On permanent view in the north gallery is a Brussels tapestry from the studio of the master weaver Reydams, made about 1725. It is one of a famous series depicting the adventures of Telemachus and represents Venus appealing to Neptune to save Telemachus's ship. Five of the series have remained Austrian State property.

Changing art exhibits in the north gallery have ranged in value and prominence from the Parke-Davis "History of Pharmacy" originals, valued at over a million dollars, to works by the novice art student. By 1970 an estimated three hundred and fifty separate art exhibits had been viewed by over two million visitors since the opening of the Morehead building in 1949.

Raleigh: The Erdahl-Cloyd Union Gallery

When the architects designed the Erdahl-Cloyd Union building for student activities at what was then State College in Raleigh, they included a sizeable art gallery and designed the main walls to be used as exhibition space for a permanent collection. Other walls were designed for traveling exhibitions and one-man shows. For many years following its opening in September, 1954, there were annual student art competitions and annual art auctions of works by students and faculty members of the School of Design, the latter to raise money for the school student publication. Both of these affairs have been discontinued, but numerous opportunities are still provided for students and faculty to exhibit their work.

Traveling exhibits assembled by such institutions as the American Federation of Arts, the Smithsonian Institution, Pratt Institute, and George Eastman House have furnished a wide and sophisticated range of international and local contemporary artistic moods in printmaking, photography, sculpture, painting, etc., and have been of great educational value to art students in this area, Henry Bowers, Director of the Erdahl-Cloyd Union Division of Student Affairs in 1966, reported in a letter that year.

In the fall of 1959, the Union Gallery inaugurated a purchase plan whereby it could buy paintings for its permanent collection. Also, through a bequest left by Chancellor John W. Harrelson, a painting is purchased yearly as an award from the North Carolina Artists Annual Competition, held at the North Carolina Museum of Art in Raleigh, and added to the University's permanent collection. Many of these art works are displayed in the Union building. Since 1963, the following works by Tarheel artists have been purchased from the N. C. Artists' Annual by the Harrelson fund: "Stone and Wood" by Horace Farlowe (1963); "Colossus" by George Bireline (1964); "The Bomb at the End of the Road" by Anne C. Pollard (1965); "Blue over Black with Red" by Walter Thrift (1966); "Wyoming Landscape" by James L. Burton (1967); "Machine for Alignment with the Sun" by Frank Tolar, Jr. (1968); and "The Totem" by Mark Lynch (1969). Other outstanding North Carolina painters in the Erdahl-Cloyd collection are Joe Cox, Claude Howell, Lesley Laskey, Ed Rankin, and James Tucker, most of whom have had one-man shows at the Gallery, as have Ruth Clarke, Howard and Anne Wall Thomas, George Arnold, and Sarah Speight, among others.

Over fifty exhibitions held in the Erdahl Gallery have originated in North Carolina for North Carolina artists.

Winston-Salem: The Gallery of Contemporary Art

Incorporated first as the Winston-Salem Gallery of Fine Arts, May 8, 1956, the Gallery of Contemporary Art in Winston-Salem is the culmination of an idea presented to a group of art-interested people by two young Winston-Salem artists—Miss Ann Carter Pollard and Miss Sue Moore. As Winston-Salem was already deeply art-oriented, immediate action was taken to establish what "became virtually the first full-time non-profit sales gallery of fine arts in the South."

Chief purpose of the gallery has been to promote the works of artists residing in the southeastern states. Starting with an area including only five states, the gallery now serves eleven: North Carolina, South Carolina, Georgia, Virginia, Tennessee, Alabama, Mississippi, Louisiana, Florida, Kentucky, and West Virginia. The role of the gallery was clarified at the start by Mrs. R. Philip Hanes, Jr., who has remained a forceful patron and motivator of the project: "Although the gallery is aware of and deeply interested in its educational role in the community, its main function is to exhibit and to sell."

The gallery's first home was an old piano warehouse at 104 North Trade Street, renovated and modernized by over 700 man- and woman-hours of volunteer labor by carpenters, painters, decorators, and other professional people. Immediate response from artists and laymen in the area resulted in the sale of forty paintings by seventeen artists during the first three months of operation.

Competent management by part-time directors, dedicated volunteers, and the high standards sustained for both artists and juries have led to phenomenal success and the following praise from Ben F. Williams, curator of the North Carolina Museum of Art and ex-officio member of the board: "You are performing a unique and valuable service to the arts throughout North Carolina and the South and providing more stimulation and encouragement in the area of the visual arts than any other similar institution." Growth is reflected in mounting sales. The first year sales totalled $1,500.00 (at that time considered a generous amount for such a young gallery), but by 1970 sales climbed to $53,000.00. Early part-time directors were Mrs. Miriam V. Dubose, who served for four years in this capacity, Mrs. Dorothy Preslar, and Mrs. Peter T. Wilson, Jr.

The gallery emphatically supports the jury system, one of the advantages of which, it affirms, is the presentation of artists to top professional people throughout the country. This inspires a high quality of performance by the artist and consequent public confidence in the work offered by the gallery. The high caliber of work thus produced has attracted cosmopolitan decorators and interior designers to the gallery in search of art for their projects. Dan Cooper, a New York decorator, found the Winston-Salem gallery in 1961, purchased $1,000.00 worth of paintings on one visit, and gave a show of paintings from the gallery in his New York studio on East 54th Street.

Juries have included such distinguished people as John Hartell, chairman of the Art Department at Cornell University; Seymour Knox, president of the Albright Museum, Buffalo; Theodore Rousseau, Jr., curator of paintings at the Metropolitan Museum; Julius Fleischmann, private collector and trustee of the Cincinnati Museum, who bought several paintings for a traveling exhibit; Gordon Washburn, director of the Carnegie Institute (as a result of Washburn's visit, four artists were invited to submit slides of their work as possible candidates for a Carnegie International show); Dorothy Miller, curator of paintings at the Museum of Modern Art, New York; North Carolina's own Hobson Pittman, Bryn Mawr, Pa.; and others of equal stature.

On numerous occasions jurors have favorably compared the achievements of these southeastern artists with those in more cosmopolitan areas, their enthusiasm exemplified in the words of Jacob Kainen, curator of prints at the Smithsonian Institution: "Work of the artists of this area compares favorably with that by artists of any area in the country. There is a notable lack of the attempt to follow fashionable trends, and there is a clear effort to expand in original directions." Gerald Nordland, director of the Washington Gallery of Modern Art, earlier applauded the Winston-Salem Art Gallery for its "wholehearted devotion to American art and artists," and saluted the artists for their support.

For several years the Gallery of Contemporary Art received purchase award funds from the Winston-Salem Council of Architects, the Junior

League, and Thalhimer's, the two latter contributing with a view to accumulating a collection to be circulated as a unit among the public schools; Thalhimer's purchases were also exhibited at their store in Winston-Salem. The Lucy Hanes Chatham Fund winners were added to the permanent collection of the City-County Library. The North Carolina National Bank has been a generous client from the beginning, purchasing several thousand dollars worth of paintings annually to hang in its various banks around the state.

The original board of directors, many of whom still constitute the backbone of the gallery, were: Mr. and Mrs. Lamar Northup, Ralph Burgard, the late Mrs. Reby Lewis, D. L. Maddocks, Owen Lewis, Mrs. Leonard Jones, Mr. and Mrs. E. F. Shewmake, Miss Ann Pollard, Raiford Porter, Mrs. Mary M. LaPrelle, R. Philip Hanes, Jr., J. T. Diggs, Mrs. Agnew Bahnson, Jr., Brant Snavely, and Calder W. Womble. Among the many active leaders and patrons from the gallery's inception have been the Ira Julians, the Harold Voglers, Douglas Lewis, the Philip Haneses, Mrs. Paul Montague, Jr., Mrs. Albert Wilson, Mrs. Winfield Blackwell, Jr., William Carr, Mrs. O. J. Freund, Mrs. Carl Goslen, Weston Hatfield, Mrs. William Herring, Ariguo Randolph, William Ross, Ben Rousie, Mrs. Howard Shields, Mrs. Claude Strickland, James Tucker, Ed Wilson, Mr. and Mrs. Peter Hairston, and many Winston-Salem artists.

By 1960 the gallery was receiving from 500 to 1,000 entries to its juried competitions and was bulging at the seams. An imperative search for a more accessible and larger location led its leaders to explore historic Old Salem. There the Cape Fear Bank building captivated their imagination, and efforts to acquire it were set in motion and a temporary gallery established in the old Moravian village. On October 10, 1965, the trustees of Old Salem, Inc., and the directors of the Winston-Salem Gallery of Fine Arts, Inc., announced the acquisition of the bank building "through the generosity of Miss Katherine Hanes's heirs." A history of the building is contained in the Moravian historical records. The new gallery at Old Salem opened on May 13, 1966, with a special showing of work by Gallery Award Winners from its first ten-year period.

In 1967 the gallery changed its name from "The Winston-Salem Gallery of Fine Arts" to "The Gallery of Contemporary Art" to more nearly reflect the nature of its operation. That year it also employed its first full-time professional director—Ted Potter from San Francisco. Potter, an artist, had taught painting at the University of Kansas. Under his direction the program expanded to a full calendar of exhibitions involving one- and two-man shows, group exhibits, and regional invitational exhibitions. The gallery is actively involved in providing loan exhibits to other galleries, universities, and art guilds throughout the Southeast, its premise being that "the best way to support our fine artists is to make their work available for purchase, and to best serve the public is to present and exhibit the finest work being produced by our regional artists."

The gallery is financed through sales commissions, memberships, individual gifts, and the Arts Council.

Wilmington: St. John's Art Gallery

St. John's Art Gallery, opened on April 5, 1962, is housed in a famous old landmark of Wilmington and uniquely combines historic interest with exhibits of contemporary art. Situated at 114 Orange Street, the gallery draws its membership from some forty towns and cities in North Carolina and in eight other states.

St. John's Gallery has made definite contributions to art and has encouraged greater public interest. It provides a practical connection between Wilmington and the remainder of the world of art. It is a focal point for teaching and is active in the encouragement of art education in Southeastern North Carolina.

The building housing St. John's sets a fine and inspiring example for other communities whose historical buildings might be salvaged as cultural centers. Constructed of bricks brought from England as ballast on sailing vessels and laid in Flemish Bond, it was erected by the Masonic Lodge No. 1. A year book (1963–64) published by the gallery tells of how, prior to its present cultural role as an art center, the building served over the years as a Lodge, a residence, a tavern, and a target for vandals.

It was a great day for Wilmington when in March of 1962 Mr. Henry B. McKoy and his brother James placed the building in trust to the Art Gallery Corporation in the form of a 99-year lease, subject to transfer to the corporation at the end of five years. December 9, 1964 was an even greater day, for then Mr. and Mrs. Henry McKoy deeded the property outright to the gallery, following an earlier gift on October 10, which Mr. McKoy stated was "the beginning of a permanent endowment fund." He also said, "I want it particularly understood that this gift comes from my brother James H. McKoy (deceased) also. He was the one who first loved the historic St. John's Lodge property, and on his advice, I bought it. He was the one who worked on it and made it popular and famous."

Founded by members of the Wilmington Art Association, which was more or less absorbed by the gallery, St. John's had by 1970 presented 141 exhibitions of works by American and European artists and craftsmen. At this writing the sales gallery has a roster of fifty-one artists, and the educational program of the gallery includes films and lectures and a series of Sunday afternoon musicales. House tours and antique shows are sponsored by the gallery to raise needed funds.

Services offered by St. John's to surrounding areas consist of supplying exhibits, judges for art contests, art instruction, talks about the gallery, and art appreciation to schools and civic groups. The staff works closely with the North Carolina Museum of Art in Raleigh, sponsoring chartered bus trips to that city, and bringing speakers and exhibitions from the Raleigh Museum to Wilmington. A year book and a monthly bulletin keep members and the general public aware of St. John's various activities.

The lead editorial in the *Wilmington Star News* on January 5, 1964, summing up the success of St. John's is equally applicable today: "As one looks back, it is easy to conclude that one factor stands out above all others in the extraordinary success of St. John's Art Gallery. That factor is spirit— an unbounded willingness to face both challenge and opportunity and, through practical means, make the most of both in creation of a community asset which promises so much in a better life in the future."

Rocky Mount: The Rocky Mount Arts Center

An old water tank, abandoned by the Atlantic Coast Line railroad, now functions as the most unique art gallery in North Carolina. A part of the Rocky Mount Arts Center's teaching plant, and tagged "the little

Guggenheim" by a national magazine before it opened, the gallery offers striking arrangements of "Art in the Round."

When the new center opened on May 25, 1963, it appropriately featured the works of Francis Speight, a native painter who had returned to eastern North Carolina after winning distinction as an art teacher at the Pennsylvania Academy of Fine Arts. It was also the crowning achievement of three young businessmen who organized the Rocky Mount Arts Center, Inc., in October of 1957.

For some time William L. Thorp, Jr. (an attorney who paints), William A. Rawls, Jr. (secretary and treasurer of a business firm, with a degree in drama from the University of North Carolina and credit for study at the Parsons School of Design and the Dramatic Workshop of the New School for Social Research in New York), and Robert C. Perkins (organist and choirmaster of the Episcopal Church in Rocky Mount), had dreamed of a place where Rocky Mount people could meet to practice and share their creative interests. They also kept close watch on the pulse of the community for an indication of its desire for such a place. When it came, they confided their plans to a local patron who not only gave them financial aid but solicited other patrons. Soon there was an advisory board consisting of Betsy Brown Daughtridge, Elizabeth Kincheloe, Elizabeth Pearsall, Dottie Stolzenberg, Panky Broadfield, Charlotte Toler, Vivian McMillan, Ann Kornegay, Polly Spruill, Jim Trotter, Don Evans, Sunny Lea, Bob Wiley, Frank P. Meadows, Jr., and Elizabeth King—and the dream of an arts center was a reality!

A house was rented at 311 South Grace Street and adapted for use as an art center, and within a short time the Center gained wide attention through its first sidewalk art show (now a classic), described by the local newspaper as a "whing-ding Whang-doodle." Dramatic emphasis was furnished by costumed flower girls and "Left Bank artists" circulating among the crowd. The block-long Park Place in which it was held was festooned with colorful pylons, pennants, and gay balloons. A "sidewalk cafe" served refreshments, giving visitors an opportunity to enjoy art European style. The two local banks supported the project by exhibiting the winning paintings.

From the beginning sponsors of the Art Center have been amazed at its growth. At the end of the first year, the center reported to its members the completion of "more than 8,500 hours of creative activity and enjoyment." The board members attribute this success to the premise they adopted early that "the demand must come first; then an attempt is made to supply the demand; and when enough people express a desire for a specific activity and are interested enough to organize it, we get busy and provide a teacher."

Its founders feel strongly that small dedicated groups should not have to "sell" culture to the community. They agree, however, that when a community is ready for these things, provision should be made to meet the need.

So successfully did this approach pay off, the old house on Grace Street was soon outgrown, and new, larger quarters became imperative. During the search for new quarters someone thought of the old Atlantic Coast Line pumping station on Nashville Road, near the Tar River bridge, as a possible solution. To strengthen the idea, Mrs. Fairy Bandy, director of the Rocky Mount Recreation Department, suggested a merger of the Art Center and the Recreation Department—with city support—and adaptation of the abandoned pumping station as a center for both. This idea appealed to the city fathers and others concerned, and soon the merger of the two organizations was confirmed and repairs to the old pumping station were begun.

Almost immediately Hugh B. Hines, Jr., then city manager of Rocky Mount, began to envision the adjacent water tank as a miniature replica of the Guggenheim Museum of Art in New York City. Fifty-two feet in diameter and sixty feet high, this circular "tank" was also acquired and now has a handsome façade of glass and brick designed by Ryland Edwards, a local architect, and a foyer which forms a lobby and space for the stairway leading to the second and third floors. A central weight-bearing core could not be removed, so it is utilized to provide powder rooms, and heating and air-conditioning units. The peripheral walls, which are well lighted and covered with off-white peg board, constitute the circular gallery where one may walk 'round-and-'round to view art exhibits. The "Little Guggenheim" has been dedicated to the memory of Hugh Hines, who is honored by a bronze plaque on the entrance wall.

Since both buildings were on city property, the city not only gave them to the Arts Center but underwrote the entire original investment of $100,000.00 and set up a budget for the salary of a director and for utilities, supplies, and repairs.

The three founders of the Arts Center minimize their own contributions to Rocky Mount's cultural outburst, emphasizing the early groundwork laid by Virginia Kyser Noell, Mrs. George L. Parker, Mrs. L. W. Kornegay (a former opera singer), Mrs. W. Bruce Lea, Mrs. Archie W. McLean, Bob Perkins (a former director), Jim Trotter (formerly of Salisbury), and Bob Wiley from Charlotte, and by teachers imported from Woman's College in Greensboro, the University of North Carolina at Chapel Hill, the Department of Architecture and Design, Raleigh, and East Carolina College, Greenville.

Miss Ann Chipley, a native of Rocky Mount who served as the art center's first executive secretary, has given credit to the State Art Museum in Raleigh "as a guide in forming our tastes for better art," emphasizing its many resources available to any community groping toward the organization of an art center.

Now a member of the North Carolina Arts Council, the continued goals of the Rocky Mount Arts Center are "to provide nourishment for the creative spirit and to provide an enlightened atmosphere in which the children of the community may grow up."

8. ART ASSOCIATIONS

Durham: The Durham Creative Art Group,
Durham Art Guild, and Allied Arts

Allied Arts and the Durham Art Guild both stemmed from the Durham Creative Art Group, one of the oldest groups of working artists in the state. Organized in February of 1947, at the home of Mrs. Bingham Dai, the Creative Art Group has been a strong force from the beginning in making Durham art conscious, by exhibiting its own work and by bringing outstanding exhibits and art instructors to Durham prior to the organization of the Durham Art Guild.

Charter members of the Durham Creative Group, many of whom

still work together in 1970, are Mrs. Bingham Dai, Mrs. Robert Wilson, Mrs. Robert Lyon, Mrs. Elvin Latty, Mrs. Smith Whiteside—all of Durham—and Mrs. John Foushee of Chapel Hill. This group quickly added to its early membership Miss Mary Burgess, Mrs. Howard Gamble, Miss Helen Kendall, Mr. and Mrs. George C. Pyne, Jr., Mrs. Beverly Raney, Mrs. Robert S. Rogers, Miss Elsie Smith, Mrs. Barnes Woodhall, Mrs. W. W. Woodley, Mrs. Anne Basile, and Mrs. Charles Humphrey, among others. To ensure high standards in its own work, the group persuaded Gregory D. Ivy, then head of the Art Department at Woman's College, U. N. C., at Greensboro, to meet with them one night a week in Durham as a critic. This he did for eleven years. All true disciples of Professor Ivy, these artists have sometimes been tagged "the Ivy League."

Other outstanding critics and instructors have worked intermittently with the group, among them Professors Earl Mueller, W. K. Stars, and Charles Sibley, from Duke University; Professors George Kachergis, Emma Lou Davis, Robert Shannon, and Robert Barnard, University of North Carolina, Chapel Hill; and Professors Joe Cox, Duncan Stuart, George Bireline, Manuel Bromberg, and Roy Gussow, University of North Carolina, Raleigh.

The initial meeting of the Durham Art Guild, Inc., was held July 25, 1949, and although the bulk of its membership came from the Durham Creative Art Group, the new organization widened its scope to include commercial and professional artists and interested laymen.

The first permanent officers and board members of the Art Guild were: Mrs. Smith Whiteside, president; A. M. Tidd, vice president; Randy P. Jones, secretary; Mrs. B. D. Gaddy, treasurer; Mrs. Robert S. Rogers, George C. Pyne, Mrs. E. M. Manasse, James W. Hamm, Miss Billy Rivers, and Charles Sibley. Charter members who have remained strong forces in the organization and have held office at some time are essentially the same as those in the Creative Art Group.

Among the outstanding services of the Art Guild to the Durham community is its support of art education in the schools. For several years its members judged the Durham city and county school art exhibitions, sponsored annually by the Junior League and the Durham Creative Art Group.

For several years it also sponsored a Beaux Arts ball, the proceeds of which went for the promotion of art through exhibitions and art classes. Its annual sidewalk art shows have attracted as many as 750 entries and drawn an estimated 5,000 spectators. A sizeable number of its artist-members have exhibited and won prizes outside of North Carolina and spearheaded the organization of other art groups.

Almost from the start the Art Guild has sponsored art courses for adults and children, either free or at nominal rates, subsidizing its budget through its art auctions and membership fees.

By drawing on the art departments of Duke University and the University of North Carolina at Chapel Hill, Raleigh, and Greensboro for its teachers and lecturers, the Durham Art Guild has done much to raise the sights of art-interested people in Durham and surrounding areas.

In an effort to widen its public involvement, the Guild participated in a "Mile of Art" exhibition at Forty Oaks farm in Durham County in 1962 that launched a series of programs on "Art in Business." Artists from all over the state brought their works and displayed them on country fencing and barn walls. Twenty young business executives from Durham and Chapel Hill judged the show and selected paintings they felt suitable for business offices. Entitled "Executives Choice" these were then exhibited in both towns and later hung in the various offices of the jurors. Channel Two (W.F.M.Y.–TV) in Greensboro made a twenty-minute film strip of the "Mile of Art."

In 1963 the Guild began to feel that it was losing its identity as a participating member of Allied Arts of Durham, due to overlapping of various functions of the two organizations. Several meetings of the Guild's charter members were called and the organization was reincorporated. Directors of the new corporation were Mrs. Howard Gamble, G. C. Pyne, Jr., Miss Margaret Smith, and W. K. Stars, all of Durham. Incorporators of the Guild were Mrs. Ruth W. Latty, Mrs. Dorothy T. Rogers, and Mrs. Jeanne S. Whiteside, also of Durham.

With their various differences clarified and resolved, the Durham Art Guild and Allied Arts of Durham were reunited in April of 1964, the former retaining its position as a "participating" member of the greater organization.

Durham, like many other large cities, found its cultural efforts over-lapping and becoming burdensome. Consolidation appeared to be the answer; so in 1953, the Durham Art Guild, the Theatre Guild, the Camera Club, and the Durham chapter of the North Carolina Symphony united under the name of United Arts. The group membership soon grew to eight, and the name was changed to Allied Arts of Durham.

In January, 1954, Allied Arts moved into the elegant Watts Home on South Duke Street and remained there until 1961, when the mansion was sold and demolished. At this time the Foushee mansion at 810 Proctor Street became available, and a campaign to raise $69,310 was launched to buy and renovate this house as a permanent home for Allied Arts. Individual memberships had by now reached 750 and a full-time director was employed.

On Wednesday evening, March 1, 1961, the Junior League of Durham, which had contributed $12,000.00 to Allied Arts during its first few years, was host at a formal opening of the new center on Proctor Street, still the art hub of Durham and nearby areas.

Mrs. Watts Hill, Jr., a former president of Allied Arts, was instrumental in forming the Tri-States Arts Council and served one year as its president, during which time she expressed the benefits of uniting as "the best plan yet for combined fund-raising, alerting a community to its local talent, and preventing overlapping of scheduling," the prime function of the Arts Council idea. Allied Arts was a charter member of the Tri-States Arts Council.

Greensboro: Greensboro Artists League

A member of the United Arts Council, the Greensboro Artists' League was formed on November 14, 1956, with a temporary staff of officers appointed by Anthony Burrows of Bradenton, Florida. Burrows at the time was conducting a private art school in Greensboro. At the first regular meeting the following temporary officers were voted in, with Burrows as president: Mrs. C. B. Clegg, first vice president; Carl Coker, second vice president; E. L. Nelson, treasurer; Mrs. Frances Woodall, corresponding secretary; and Mrs. A. L. Masters, recording secretary.

The purpose of the organization, as set forth in its handbook, is "generally to develop and promote activities designed to advance art education and appreciation and specifically to sponsor classes to provide a creative stimulus and encourage all age groups to execute paintings, drawings, modeling and sculpture as well as the related arts and crafts; to sponsor and assemble local and traveling exhibitions; to program open meetings for showing films and engaging qualified lecturers by which works, techniques and historical development of art through the ages may be made known; to make donations and grant scholarships; to acquire a permanent collection of art works for Guilford County; to serve as a link to other arts groups, institutions and projects throughout the state."

An important gesture toward realization of these goals was the purchase of a painting by Jose Guerrero entitled "Red Sun," to be awarded annually to the first-place winner in the arts division of the Guilford County Fine Arts Festival. Commenting on this venture, Jack Wagstaff, president at the time, expressed the hope that this would be just a beginning and that the League would be able to make purchases each year to go into a nucleus collection for a future Greensboro Art Museum.

Among numerous panelists and speakers sponsored by the League have been Gregory D. Ivy, Joseph King, James McMillan, Ed Wilson, Ben Williams, Ola Maie Foushee, Raiford Porter, George Arnold, Robert Partin, Maude Gatewood, Phillip Moose, James Tucker, Phillip Couch, and Mrs. Egbert Davis.

Enthusiastic members have branched out into art promotion ventures of their own: Mrs. Merry John Fine started the popular but short-lived Merin Gallery situated at 825 Battleground Avenue. Failure of the Merin was tragic, as Mrs. Fine had hoped to help North Carolina artists by exhibiting and selling their work. The gallery also added a social dimension to Greensboro, through its gala "openings" which attracted artists and visitors from near and far. Another member, Mrs. Frances Scott, for several years has run the "Attic Gallery" in her own home, which serves as a sales gallery and a teaching center.

The Greensboro Artists' League has worked closely with the Greensboro Woman's Club and the Altrusa Club in their various art activities, such as a "Picture of the Month" exhibited on Main Street by Altrusa. In

October of 1959, Antoinette Lymas Masters of the League wrote: "We started with 25 paid members but our membership to date is more than one hundred." In 1962 the League was able to publish a 16-page handbook in which it listed as an honorary life member its founder, Anthony Burrows. The League lapsed for a short period, but reorganized in 1968.

Burlington: The Arts Association of Alamance County

A group of citizens interested in promoting art in Burlington and Alamance County gathered at a luncheon at the Alamance Hotel in November, 1956, and formed The Arts Association of Alamance County. Mrs. D. R. Fonville, Sr., a well known artist and art teacher, was elected president. Directors were representatives of industrial, cultural, and business interests of the county. Seven hundred letters were sent out by the officers in an appeal to the entire county for its support.

Mrs. Linwood Edwards, executive secretary of the Community Council, had earlier suggested a county festival to draw the entire Alamance area into the project and assisted the young organization in the promotion and arrangements of its first festival. The late Ross Churchill was chairman of the affair, held in the National Guard Armory the first week in May, 1957.

The usual pangs of finding an art center were finally assuaged when the residence of the late Erwin A. Holt, built in 1904, was offered to the Association by the city of Burlington in 1961. "You might call it 'The Center that Courage Built,'" one writer said of it. "Its former owner and occupant was a member of the Arts Association, and the mansion with its prismed chandeliers, heavy draperies, carpeted floors, curved stairways and library shelves were evidence that art and culture had been treasured topics within its walls for more than half a century."

Classes in painting, drawing, modeling, and mosaics; in ceramics, copper enameling, rug hooking and needlework; cooking, Scout craft, and caning all seemed at home in the place where famous artists, musicians, and writers had walked in earlier days. But the City of Burlington soon needed the property for the erection of a Municipal Building, and the old story of "looking for suitable quarters" again plagued the group. Finally the former fire station in Graham was secured and members and friends redecorated the stark building into attractive galleries, classrooms, and storage space. Mrs. Jeannette Mast, a former director, clarified its aims in these words:

"Our purpose is to enrich the lives of any Alamance County residents we can, to introduce them to a form of individual expression. The more people who can express themselves, the better off they are. For this reason, fees are moderate and graduated to the individuals, many being paid anonymously from county or donor funds, so that any child with talent can get lessons."

The Association holds yearly competitions in several areas of the arts, with awards varying from citations and cups for literary competition to one-, two-, or three-man shows of paintings by local artists. Periodically traveling exhibitions and one-man shows by prominent artists are presented at the center. Financing is currently by membership fees and by subsidy from the Alamance County Board of Commissioners.

9. COMMERCIAL GALLERIES

Small commercial art galleries in North Carolina have had hard sledding and usually have been short-lived. Greensboro has been unusually ill-fated in its public support of commercial art galleries. They are well supported by artists, and the public goes to look, but buying is inadequate. The Merin Gallery, started by Merry John Fine in September, 1958, with all the prospects of immediate and lasting success, failed within the year. Thirty artists exhibited during its life-time.

Design Associates of Greensboro started by John and Anne Bonitz and Walter Moran in February, 1961, had all the flair of a big city gallery. But despite its distinguished exhibitions and its talented owners, it was closed within a few months.

Other important but ill-fated galleries around the state have been the Brady-Lewis Galleries in Winston-Salem, organized with a flourish in March, 1962, and dissolved a few months later; the Downtown Gallery in Durham, also opened in 1962 by A. M. Tidd. This gallery showed work by leading artists in the state and contributed a lively period to the cultural life of Durham, but faded away for lack of public interest. The Garden Gallery on the Durham-Raleigh highway is now opened for the third time, but its closings have been due to construction problems rather than lack of interest.

Among the few surviving small galleries that seem to have established a permanency are the Attic Gallery, Greensboro; the Art Gallery of Chapel Hill; the Carolina Art Sales Gallery, Raleigh; the Fenner Fine Arts Gallery, Wilmington (shows only the works of Alice Cranston Fenner); and several galleries in public libraries, among them the Greensboro City library, the Winston-Salem library, and the Southern Pines library.

CHAPTER FIVE

Arts Councils

Arts councils gained their first popularity in this country when the council concept seeped in from England and Canada in 1949. North Carolina immediately gained leadership of the movement through the perceptive stewardship of R. Philip Hanes of Winston-Salem, North Carolina—a tenacious promoter of the idea. Through his leadership the Winston-Salem Arts Council was inaugurated in 1949, the Tri-States Arts Council in 1959, and the North Carolina Arts Council in 1964. His theories on what an arts council can do stress community responsibility toward the creative life of its people.

The ideal arts council is a federated group of cultural organizations whose artistic interests, meeting dates and places, volunteer workers, various boards and fund-raising efforts have been united within a parent organization. Each organization remains autonomous in its performing activities but without the frustrations of overlapped scheduling and duplications. To qualify as an arts council an organization should have at least three participating groups—all incorporated and tax-exempt and with necessary papers from the federal government. "Participating" means simply any group with a functioning program—a madrigal group, a theater group, a symphony, a visual arts organization, or the like. Of course, there are existing councils in the state which have been structured differently, according to the nature of the community and its needs.

1. TRI-STATES ARTS COUNCIL

The first organizational conference for a Tri-States Arts Council to include North Carolina, South Carolina, and Virginia was held at the Robert E.

Lee Hotel in Winston-Salem, September 18 and 19, 1959. R. Philip Hanes addressed the group on "Why Have a Tri-States and National Arts Council?" Moderator Reed Sarratt, then editor of the *Winston-Salem Journal*, encouraged a representative from each city to offer specific information about the arts in his community, as stimuli for a general discussion.

Out of this conference came a steering committee consisting of nine members: Hilda Ewing, Burlington; Gertrude Flippen, Richmond, Virginia; Erik Fris, Asheville; E. S. Gregg, Statesville; R. Philip Hanes, Jr., Winston-Salem; Katheryn Kortheuer, Charlotte; Tom Nichols, Greensboro; and William Rawls, Rocky Mount, North Carolina. According to the minutes of this steering committee, "it was agreed by all that the prime purpose of a Tri-State Arts Council should be to encourage the formation of individual arts councils throughout this area." It was further agreed that the area not be considered as three individual states, but as a large area comprised of many cities with considerable cultural endeavors—most of which could profit by forming local arts councils.

The group voted to hold the first board of directors meeting in Richmond, Virginia, on November 20, 1959. The first Tri-State Arts Council convention was held in Charlotte, May 13 and 14, 1960. By April, 1961, the steering committee completed a five-page cultural survey of community arts in all the major towns and cities in the two Carolinas and Virginia, noting those having Little Theatre, Summer Stock Theatre, Symphony, Opera, Ballet, and Museum Galleries.

Hanes from the beginning envisioned not only a Tri-States Arts Council but also an organization on the state level, consisting of a state board of directors of Arts Councils which could work together and possibly seek such things as legislation, newspaper coverage and the like on a statewide level. He discussed this possibility with Governor Terry Sanford at the annual conference of the American Symphony Orchestra League and the Community Arts Councils, Inc., in the summer of 1963.

2. THE NORTH CAROLINA ARTS COUNCIL

On December 3, 1964, the North Carolina Arts Council (actually a large committee) was established by executive order of Governor Sanford with

Philip Hanes as chairman. The Council's purpose was, in the words of the order, "to advance the interests of the arts, to survey the status and the needs of the arts of North Carolina, to develop the influence of art education, to encourage professional training and standards in the performing and fine arts in North Carolina. . . ."

Through 1965 and 1966 the Council's activity focused on the question of the feasibility of a permanent Council. Panels on the arts (theater, dance, creative writing, etc.) were formed and asked to report on the advisability of a permanent state arts council. All of the panels concluded that the North Carolina Arts Council should be made a permanent institution and could perform a variety of useful activities.

The Committee of Painting, Graphics, Sculpture, and Photography met on May 8, 1965, in the Art Department at Wilmington College, with the following present: Claude Howell, chairman; William C. Fields, ex-officio; Ogden Deal, Raiford Porter, Elizabeth Sommer, and Donald Sexauer. Absentees who sent in their written suggestions were: Lucy Hairston, Frank Colby, and Perry Kelly. While expressing views and recommendations on the general uplifting of art standards, they cautioned:

> With regard to the establishment of a North Carolina Arts Council, we would like to say that the addition of yet another organization to the present scene is a depressing thought, unless that organization is in a position to make a real contribution, and can help eliminate some of the present confusion, duplication, and inefficiency. However, an effectively functioning State Arts Council, properly staffed, and financed, could be extremely useful in raising standards, in the field of promotion, in acting as a central clearing house, and in eliminating much duplication in clerical work. . . .
>
> Much duplication of time and effort in clerical functions could be eliminated, and clerical work could be more efficient if handled by a central office staffed with permanent paid help rather than enthusiastic but often changing and inept volunteers.
>
> We agree with the Rockefeller report that as "vital to our cultural health as the amateurs are, the fact remains that it is (on) . . . the professional . . . artists and arts organizations that ultimate responsibility for the highest levels of creative output and quality rests."

The Council Committee reported to Governor Moore on March 26, 1966, recommending the establishment of a permanent state arts council, and having performed its functions under the terms of the original executive order, was dissolved.

On April 28, 1966, a new executive order by Governor Moore re-established the Council, again with Hanes as chairman, and placed it within the Department of Administration "to advise the Department of Administration of all matters concerning the arts." The following June, the Council engaged Robert Brickell as full-time executive director and, with a study grant of $24,820 from the National Endowment for the Arts and a matching grant of $12,053 from the National Endowment, launched a state-wide study of arts resources in North Carolina.

This study was finished and its results published in a 127-page report the summer of 1967. Divided into four sections, its purpose was "to develop a picture of where we are in the arts in North Carolina and where we ought to be; and to suggest ways in which we might move from where we are to where we ought to be."

Charter members of the North Carolina Arts Council include: R. Philip Hanes, Jr., Winston-Salem, chairman; Sam Ragan, Robert Gatling, Edwin Gill, A. J. Fletcher and Henry Bowers, Raleigh; James B. Rush, Winston-Salem; Mrs. Charles Cooke, Wilson; Mrs. J. Nathan McCarley, Jr., and Robert W. Gray, Asheville; Francis Speight, Greenville; Mrs. Leslie Boney, Jr., Wilmington; Mrs. J. Emmett Winslow, Hertford; Mrs. Harriet DuBose Kenan, Durham; and executive director Robert V. Brickell, Raleigh.

In the foreword of the report, Governor Dan K. Moore points out that North Carolina is committed to the total development of the state. "I believe that growth in the arts represents an essential part of that development." In his praise of the report he adds, "I believe that the study will prove to be a useful document. It clearly shows that while we have much to be proud of, there is yet, in Paul Green's words, 'hard and jubilant work to do.' "

On April 7, 1967 the General Assembly granted the Council statutory permanency and began annual appropriations for the partial support of the Council's activities. The board of the Arts Council is composed of twenty-four citizens appointed by the Governor for three-year terms. Eight members rotate annually on July 1. The chairman is also appointed after nomination by the council, which meets annually, or more frequently if called by the chairman.

During the first biennium, the North Carolina Arts Council sponsored well over three hundred and fifty art-related projects at a cost of $240,-617.57. And although most of these projects were related to the performing arts, the chief audiences were public school children and teachers, supporting the Council's concern for the youth of today and "their participation in tomorrow's world."

Allocations to the fine arts include subsidies to the North Carolina Museum of Art to finance the publication of an illustrated text entitled *British and American Painting and Sculpture*, December, 1967; and in May, 1968, funds to finance one thousand color slide books of forty slides each, to be used by schools and colleges in the teaching of art history and appreciation.

Other programs receiving considerable financial support have been workshops at the University of North Carolina, Greensboro; art tours to major museums in Washington, Philadelphia, and New York for public school art teachers; a Businessman-Artists conference on the arts; and an Art Teachers' Seminar in June, 1969, attended by approximately twenty-five educators "to propose new guidelines to the Board of Higher Education to improve the quality of college curricula for the preparation of public school art teachers." Associated Artists of North Carolina also has received subsidies to assist in preparing and circulating its two annual traveling exhibitions.

Art museum study tours sponsored by the Council have made it possible for a large number of public school art teachers to visit museums in Raleigh, Washington, D. C., Philadelphia, and New York City. Its TA (Technical Assistance) program "means help for individuals and groups involved in the arts in the State of North Carolina." Its basic service is professional advice—how to organize a community arts council; start a motion picture film series; tighten up the administration of art museums; obtain expert panelists for conferences; and advice in organizing arts festivals, etc. Unlike most organizations, it actually begs to help. *The State of the*

Arts, a quarterly newsletter, is published by the North Carolina Arts Council and carries up-to-date reports on the council's various activities, grants, officers, and board members.

To improve liaison between local arts councils and community art organizations across the state, the Council created in 1970 the position of "Community Associate," and appointed George F. Bailey of Raleigh to the job. Bailey spends his time in the field, assisting with projects and providing communication with the state office. To receive professional expertise in organizing a council, a community needs only defray costs of food and lodging for such consultants.

The North Carolina Arts Council is affiliated with the national Associated Council of the Arts, incorporated in Winston-Salem as a North Carolina corporation, under the guidance of Philip Hanes, and first known as the Arts Councils of America. The national organization publishes the sophisticated magazine *Cultural Affairs*, which "brings together the diverse views of individual contributors concerned with the arts and with their implications for the public realm . . . it represents no concensus or institutional policy but is sponsored in the interest of thoughtful discussion on matters of importance to cultural democracy." Publication grants for *Cultural Affairs* have come from the Mary Duke Biddle Foundation as well as other sponsors from North Carolina, including the Mary Reynolds Babcock Foundation, Burlington Industries, Hanes Corporation Foundation, Mr. and Mrs. R. Philip Hanes, Jr., and R. J. Reynolds Tobacco Company.

Of the future of the North Carolina Arts Council Edgar B. Marston, its present executive director says: "We shall continue to strive for participation in the arts by a greater percentage of the state's citizens, and a situation wherein more professional artists can make their living in North Carolina." By June of 1969 the number of art groups functioning as arts councils in North Carolina had grown to twenty-seven, and, of course, the number increases steadily.

3. THE WINSTON-SALEM ARTS COUNCIL

In 1949 Winston-Salem became the second city in the United States to form an arts council. (The first arts council in Corpus Christi soon disbanded, leaving Winston-Salem the oldest council in the country.) During its first year the Winston-Salem Arts Council was sustained by funds supplied by the local Junior League, which had foreseen the need for such an organization in 1946 and had allocated $7,200.00 to be held in trust "until the Council crystalized its plans and proved its readiness to handle the money." Well on its way by 1952, the Council sponsored its first annual revue, "The Arts Council's Follies," and with the proceeds began working toward independence.

Its history began with World War II, when the Piedmont Arts Festival evolved to fill a cultural and recreational need in Winston-Salem. The festivals were sponsored by the old Arts and Crafts Center, of which Mrs. Chester Marsh was the director. In an article about the Council, Frances Griffin stated, "It was not with any idea of making history that the little group of arts leaders met in the summer of 1949 and started talking about federating the arts; it was a matter of self-preservation."

The Council has made history, however, and its success has attracted national attention through articles in at least four magazines. In *Footlight*, published by the John F. Kennedy Center for the Performing Arts, the Council is credited with luring the School for the Performing Arts to Winston-Salem. Also, in a fund-raising pamphlet, the Council claims a major role in bringing the "All American City" award to Winston-Salem. It states that, "When our case was presented to the National Municipal League jury in Springfield, Mass., a great deal of emphasis was placed on the Arts Council. The jury responded with interest and many questions about our progressive pioneering cultural programs. They were enthusiastic about the idea and its success."

In 1964, Alvin Toffler in *Show: Magazine of the Arts* referred to the Winston-Salem Arts Council as "a remarkable institution . . . the city's cultural flywheel . . . So effective . . . that it has come to be looked upon nationally as a training ground for arts council executives. Ralph Burgard, an imaginative former advertising man who served as Arts Council director from 1955 to 1957, was plucked from Winston-Salem to become executive secretary of the Council of Arts and Sciences in St. Paul. [He later went on to head the national organization, Associated Council of the Arts.] He was followed by Charles Mark, who in 1961 left to assume a similar post in St. Louis. [William Herring who succeeded Mark was subsequently called to Atlanta, Georgia, to head the Atlanta Arts Alliance.] Under Winston's influence, several other communities in North Carolina have developed arts councils strong enough to employ full-time directors."

An expansive account of the Arts Council movement in the United States, with great emphasis on the Winston-Salem Council, appeared in the February 25, 1961, issue of the *Saturday Evening Post*. Entitled "We're Cultured Too," by R. Philip Hanes, Jr., as told to Joe Alex Morris, it states: "From the beginning the arts-council approach meant progress for all. The harmonizing of culture's small voices into an articulate chorus attracted attention all over the country, but, most importantly, it won for us strong support in the community."

Hanes firmly believes that the community, not government, should support its own art. "Initial strength must come from the people themselves and the government should be seen only as an after thought," he emphasized in a letter in 1959.

Musical America of September 1962, in an article entitled "Winston-Salem—Pioneer in the Arts," reiterates that "support for these agencies comes from private sources, and the control and ownership of the organization is vested in the community through its leaders. As one of the earliest and most successful examples of this type of operation, the Winston-Salem Arts Council has become a prototype for many communities."

Not only the oldest arts council in the United States, but the largest in North Carolina, the Winston-Salem Council is housed in the expansive James Gordon Hanes Community Center, for which it helped raise building funds. First visualized by James Gordon Hanes, for whom it is named, the center was to have been the home of the fast-growing Arts Council, the Chamber of Commerce, and the United Fund. In May, 1956, Clifford Perry of the Hanes Corporation and Philip Hanes of the Hanes Dye Works, undertook a two-week fund drive to raise $700,000 for the project. This sum was augmented by the sale of the Arts Council property on West Fifth Street and by a $200,000 donation by the Hanes Hosiery Mills Foundation. Charles H. Babcock donated the ten and one-half acres on which it is situated and by March, 1957, the architectural firm of Larson and Larson presented the plans, which were accepted. Cornerstones for the Arts Council and the Chamber of Commerce were laid in October of 1958. The total area in the James Gordon Hanes Community Center is

50,000 square feet, of which the Arts Council and its twenty-nine members occupy considerable space. Now past its second decade, it has met many challenges, and, as stated in a recent report, "slow evolution still takes place as new problems, ideas and opportunities arise. Change is the one factor which remains constant."

Winston-Salem's pride in its cultural activities may be traced back to March of 1927, when a caustic editorial entitled "Exhibit A," reviewed a current exhibit:

> Eighty works of art in the realm of literature, music and painting by Winston-Salem artists are on public exhibition this week in the windows of a store on Trade Street. They are the product of some forty persons who are living or have lived at some time in the city and taken together they constitute Exhibit A to prove that our "little nicotine village" produces some commodities which are not manufactured in carload lots and shipped to the uttermost parts of the world.
>
> As a whole, the exhibit is a concrete refutation of the statement made by Mr. Mencken, and other pharisaical cant to the effect that North Carolina is altogether barren of culture and is the exact geographical center of the Sahara of the Beaux Arts. In fact, we should be quite pleased to have Mr. Mencken and all of his school of cynical contemners, including several North Carolinians who are suffering with the same disease, come down and look us over. . . Like Mercutio's wound, it may not be "so deep as a well, nor so wide as a church-door; but 'tis enough, 'twill serve" as a beginning or as Exhibit A at least to refute a contemptible and undeserved calumny.

4. ASHEVILLE CIVIC ARTS COUNCIL

The Asheville Civic Arts Council, Inc., was formed in 1953 as the Civic Arts Center. Twelve farsighted citizens met and decided "to establish and maintain a center for the people of western North Carolina, for the promotion, encouragement and development of the arts and crafts, including music, drama, dance, painting, sculpture, handcrafts, literature, folklore, nature study and recreation for the youth of the foresaid communities and any other activities reasonably connected therewith or which may be considered to be within the field of arts, and perform all things reasonably necessary or incident thereto."

The board of directors (originally twenty-five persons) is composed of a representative from each of the thirty-five member organizations, twelve members-at-large and seven officers. The organizations include performing and exhibiting groups in the arts and crafts, as well as those which are deeply concerned with the cultural enrichment of the area. The Asheville Art Museum Association (a member group) makes possible lectures on varied art subjects, demonstrations on art techniques, and group panels for self-criticism.

In May of 1965 the Council presented to the Asheville City Council a well illustrated 28-page proposal and request for a Civic Arts Center, valued at $2,000,000 to house its various art groups. A city-wide bond referendum was held and passed successfully in December, 1967, a part of which was 1.3 million dollars to construct an arts center which would include a theatre, museums, meeting and class rooms. The second portion of the referendum, providing for a convention facility-sports arena (a city center), was also passed. When architectural plans were completed for the two projects, it was apparent that there was a deficit of building funds. A second bond referendum in the spring of 1970 for an additional two million dollars failed.

Substitute measures enabled the City to begin construction, but a citizens' suit was filed, which in essence claimed that the combined facility was not what the voters passed in the 1967 referendum. All work on the project stopped. The case finally was heard by the Supreme Court of the State of North Carolina, which ruled in favor of the City on April 14, 1971. At this writing construction is expected to start momentarily.

5. CHARLOTTE UNITED ARTS COUNCIL

In 1959 Thomas L. Robinson of the *Charlotte News* almost single-handedly attempted to organize an arts council in Charlotte. He worked toward a $100,000.00 fund campaign to set up such an organization. To some extent his campaign was successful, for the Charlotte Arts Council, as it was first called, was host to the Tri-States Arts Council convention in Charlotte in May of 1960. There were twenty-two sponsoring member organizations, eight of which received money from the Charlotte Arts fund. Martin Lee was the Council's first president.

The Charlotte Council was active at that time in the cultural survey of the major cities in the two Carolinas and Virginia. Due to various vicissitudes, the first years of the Council were inconclusive, but through the support of Mayor Stanford R. Brookshire and C. A. McKnight, editor of the *Charlotte Observer*, the Council was reorganized in October of 1962, under the new name United Arts Council, Inc. J. Herbert Bridges became the new president and William E. King, executive director.

The Charlotte Council follows the standard council pattern of fund raising and distribution of funds to its member organizations. It also publishes a schedule of cultural events in the Charlotte area.

6. UNITED ARTS COUNCIL OF GREENSBORO

The first attempt at organizing an arts council in Greensboro came through the Chamber of Commerce in 1958 under the name, "Greensboro Community Arts Council." Gordon Blackwell, Chancellor of the University of North Carolina at Greensboro, was its first president and Mrs. Harriet H. Zauber its executive director.

In 1960 the council was reorganized and incorporated as a non-profit organization with George Eichhorn as president. Mrs. Milton Zauber served as executive director until 1967 when Miles H. Wolff, former editor of the *Greensboro Daily News*, was appointed to the position.

What may be accomplished when a council employs a full-time director is acutely demonstrated in the progress of the Greensboro Council. Under the able and energetic direction of Wolff, who as a newspaper man is well aware of the importance of public relations, this council has published an entertaining yet informative booklet illustrating its many activities and future goals, entitled "The Arts Are Fun," and an up-to-date directory of all working officers of member-groups participating in the council.

Although started in 1960, the council did not have a united fund drive until 1967. It raised approximately $95,500 in 1969 and $101,000 in 1970, exceeding its goal in both years.

The United Council of Greensboro now owns its house on Elm Street, purchased by funds raised in a campaign for that purpose, a far cry from 1962 when it entertained the Tri-States Arts Council at its headquarters in the Chamber of Commerce.

Past presidents of the United Council are George C. Eichhorn, Sydney M. Cone, Jr., L. Richardson Preyer, L. I. Swindell and Charles W. Cheek. James R. Turner is its 1970 president.

7. KINSTON ARTS COUNCIL AND ART CENTER

When Mrs. James M. Tyler sparked the idea of an Arts Council in Kinston in 1964, the community lost no time in its feverish efforts to promote a wider appreciation of the arts in Kinston and the surrounding area. A firm foundation was laid for its quick growth by the election of an illustrious array of officers, led by Mrs. Tyler as president; Mrs. Laura Kirk, vice president; Mrs. Jack Hogarth, recording secretary; Mrs. Alden Hobbs, treasurer; Mrs. Warren S. Perry, parliamentarian; and Mrs. C. B. Aycock, Mrs. Leo Brody, William L. Fay, W. E. Gladding, W. W. Hines, Hoyt A. Minges, Dr. Vernon D. Offutt, and Dr. Rose Pully, directors. Other active promoters were Mrs. Sam A. Parker, Mrs. Carl Wooten, Mrs. H. Fleming Fuller, Mrs. John H. Kelley, Mrs. Harold Hemrick, Mrs. Thomas White, and Mrs. Hoyt Minges. By the time the initial membership meeting took place in January, 1965, membership had increased considerably. Robert Lee Humber of Greenville, then president of the North Carolina Art Society, spoke to the session on "The Cultural Challenge to the Citizens of Kinston."

On the heels of this challenge followed Mayor Simon Sitterson's declaration of "Arts Council Week," and no momentum was lost as the council began to plan its full year of activity. Mrs. Thomas White was "chairman of the day" for this inaugural meeting, and an outstanding panel was presented to describe the functions of an Arts Center. The widely experienced panel included Perry Kelly, state arts supervisor; Ben Williams, curator of the N. C. Museum of Art; Mrs. Margaret Hall, director of St. John's Gallery; Miss Lucy Crisp, past director of the Greenville Art Center; Mrs. James Ficklen, past president of the East Carolina Arts Society; Charles Stanford, Jr., curator of education at the North Carolina Museum of Art; Mr. and Mrs. W. L. Thorp, Jr., founders of the Rocky Mount Arts and Crafts Center, and special guests—Mr. and Mrs. Philip Hanes of Winston-Salem and Dr. and Mrs. Francis Speight of Greenville.

Mrs. Harold Hemrick outlined for the group the Council's plans for the Fine Arts Center to be opened on Caswell Street, and merchants gave window display space to promote examples of coming exhibitions.

The Art Center, focal point for all the Art Council's activities, was formally opened on April 11, 1965, with an exhibition of paintings by Mrs. Sarah Blakeslee Speight (wife of Francis Speight) and a preview reception highlighting the occasion. The first classes to be offered to the public had an enrollment of 178 persons in thirteen different categories.

Beginning with Mrs. Speight's exhibition, the Center has aimed high in the selection of artists whose works have been shown at the Caswell Street gallery and during the annual arts festivals. On one occasion they were able to exhibit the works of Henry Charles Pearson—a native of Kinston—who has achieved an international reputation in the art world and whose work is more fully covered in the chapter on Tarheel artists. Another early one-man show was by Jack Berkman, who retired from Washington, D. C., to Wilmington, N. C., "to just paint," and who has observed that "art in North Carolina has a freshness that is lacking in the North."

Chief money-raising projects have been house tours and the spectacular Azalea Arts Festival inaugurated in 1966 and held in the Hoyt Minges azalea gardens. Focal point of this festival was the Japanese teahouse, shaded by towering trees and surrounded by lacy dogwood trees and hundreds of varieties of azaleas. Throughout this natural setting paintings and sculpture, selected by a jury, were exhibited. That year one of the contemporary southern art collections owned by Sears, Roebuck was included in the outdoor exhibition. Attending the affair were such dignitaries as U. S. Congressman L. H. Fountain, State Representative Guy Elliott, Mayor Simon Sitterson, State Senator Thomas J. White, Mrs. Dan K. Moore, Dr. Rachel Davis, long-time State Representative who has also served as president of the Kinston Arts Council. Dr. Davis keynoted the community's cultural attitude in the following statement about its first festival:

"Having experienced this highly successful Azalea Arts Festival, we are conscious of the presence of a rising real desire for, and appreciation of, the performing arts in Kinston, Lenoir County, in the State of North Carolina and in the entire nation. . . . It pointedly crystalizes for us the needs and desires of this community in all areas of performing arts. Moreover, it challenges us to make more and more opportunities available to all peoples for the development of their talents and an opportunity to exercise their appreciation of the arts: the true adornments of life and living."

A handsome seventeen-page illustrated booklet entitled *A Salute: The Kinston Arts Council and Azalea Arts Festival* fully records the many facets of this community activity, where "thousands of North Carolinians viewed some 150 paintings and sculptured forms chosen from over 300 entries, toured the winding paths surrounding the teahouse and lake and, on a cloudless afternoon, watched a parade of lovely young ladies displaying the latest fashions."

Two noteworthy projects carried out by the Kinston Art Center have been the cataloguing of historical homes in Kinston and Lenoir County and the publishing of a calendar featuring some of these homes and a sale of the calendars by the Arts Council. An outstanding service project backed by this group was the painting and framing of seventy portraits of mentally retarded children for the girls at Caswell Center in 1970.

The Kinston Art Center is contributing toward art education in the schools by circulating works from its permanent collection to schools in Kinston and Lenoir County. Further emphasis on creative incentive for children has been through exhibitions of their work in art classes at the Center and the numerous plays presented by the Children's Theater of North Carolina.

CHAPTER SIX

Artists

Measured by any standards, a large percentage of the growing number of Tarheel artists could hold their own nationally and internationally, provided with the proper opportunity. Over 800 artists annually submit works to the North Carolina Artists Annual at the North Carolina Museum of Art in Raleigh. Several hundred of these are, of course, art students from the state's various colleges and universities, and some are adopted Tarheels, but that still leaves at least 200 or so practicing native artists in the state. Many have achieved distinction throughout this country and abroad.

New York City, unfortunately, is still considered the mecca of the art world, despite the West Coast's claim to this position, and to get an exhibition in Gotham, much less a permanent gallery, is a major feat. To show in its major museums such as the Metropolitan, the Whitney, or the Museum of Modern Art, is an envied goal, and one that is easier to attain for those living in the area. Actually, there are other distinctions just as great. To exhibit in or be purchased for inclusion in the North Carolina Museum of Art validates the competence of numerous Tarheel artists, and since space forbids biographical sketches, we are simply listing farther on the native North Carolina artists represented in the North Carolina Museum of Art collection through purchase awards.

1. ELLIOTT DAINGERFIELD

Elliott Daingerfield was not native to North Carolina, but he was Tarheel bred, having been brought to this state at the age of two. He was born at

Harper's Ferry (Virginia, at that time) in 1859—the year that John Brown led his armed band of some twenty men against the federal arsenal there. His father, Captain John Elliott Parker Daingerfield, who fought in the first Battle of Manassas, was sent to North Carolina by General Lee during the Civil War to command the arsenal at Fayetteville, bringing with him a large amount of currency which he administered as paymaster.

Realizing that he was permanently stationed in Fayetteville, the Captain sent for his family, and North Carolina gained a potential "Artist of Note." The young Daingerfield before he was twelve years old decided he wanted to be a painter. "Everyone except a Mrs. William McKay, in Fayetteville, told me that I could never paint, but she called me to her home each day and taught me all she knew," he was quoted as saying by a feature writer in the early nineteen-thirties.

At age twenty-one, with only thirty dollars in his pocket and an old brown umbrella, Elliott Daingerfield followed his Muse to New York City to become a serious student of art. There he lived next to George Inness, whom he always credited with teaching him the technical methods of color and illumination which became the outstanding qualities of his work. His success as a painter was meteoric, beginning with a knock at his door by Inness, who marveled at his work and purchased a picture. The following day, according to old records, Inness took three of his wealthy clients to see Daingerfield's work, and they bought eleven pictures and ordered three more—at prices Inness himself put on them. From this time on, "his works were being heard of from the Atlantic to the Pacific." The Santa Fe Railroad Company even gave him a private car in 1911 to go to the Grand Canyon to paint. Those pictures sold so fast he had none left for himself.

Although Daingerfield established himself in New York City, he kept his ties in North Carolina, having married Miss Roberta Strange, "the lovely daughter of Judge Robert French, of Wilmington." After her death and an illness which left him quite weak and somewhat depleted of funds, he found his way to Blowing Rock, "where he might obtain room and board for $15 a week." Five years later he met Miss Anna Grainger of Louisville, Kentucky, whom he married after her recovery from a serious illness. They had two daughters, Marjorie and Gwendoline, and built their mansion, "Westglow," near Blowing Rock. The view from this house was the subject of many of Daingerfield's paintings, including "Carolina Mountain Country" which he exhibited at the first show of the North Carolina Professional Artists in 1931.

For many years Daingerfield ran a nationally known summer school of art at Blowing Rock. In winter he taught at the Art Students' League in New York and at the Philadelphia School of Design. He was considered to be an authority on the works of Ryder and R. A. Blakelock and wrote monographs on them as well as on Inness. With the exception of a year of study in Europe in 1897, he passed all of his active life in this country.

North Carolina was made aware of Daingerfield's prominence in the art world in 1927, when in March of that year the Grand Central Galleries of New York City sent 102 paintings and forty bronzes "by America's foremost artists," to be exhibited in Charlotte, N. C. J. E. Holmes, associate manager of Grand Central Galleries and a friend of Daingerfield's, accompanied the shipment of art works, valued at over $300,000.00 to Charlotte. In a lecture on the exhibition he said of the forty-eight paintings actually hung, "the more interesting of the group are two by Elliott Daingerfield, a North Carolinian, both of which were done near his home at Blowing Rock."

Daingerfield's works hang in most of the great museums of the country: The Metropolitan Museum of Art, the Brooklyn Museum, the National Gallery, the Toledo Museum, and the St. Louis Museum among them. His "Grand Canyon" and "Evening Glow" are in the North Carolina Museum of Art, and the Mint Museum in Charlotte has his "Autumn Scene," a gift from Mrs. Charles Cannon of Concord who had several of his works in her own collection. The "Monk Smelling a Bottle of Wine" won him membership in the National Academy of Design. He was particularly noted for his ecclesiastical paintings. His great mural in the Lady Chapel of St. Mary the Virgin in New York City and his "St. Mary of the Hills" in the Episcopal Church in Blowing Rock, North Carolina, are among his more beloved works.

Death came to Daingerfield on October 22, 1932, at his home in New York City, at the age of seventy-three. He was buried in his boyhood hometown of Fayetteville, near his ancestral home, which has been restored by the Fayetteville Woman's Club as their meeting place. In April of 1934, two years after his death, the Grand Central Galleries held a

memorial exhibition of Daingerfield's work, gathered from all parts of
the country. The Mint Museum of Charlotte and the North Carolina
Museum of Art will honor him with a large retrospective exhibition of his
paintings in 1971.

2. MABEL PUGH

When the North Carolina Association of Professional Artists organized
in 1931 and included Miss Mabel Pugh as a charter member, this young
Tarheel artist was already established in New York City as a printmaker,
illustrator, and painter. A native of Morrisville, North Carolina, she had
the good fortune to study art under Mrs. Ruth Huntington Moore, head
of the Art Department at Peace Junior College in Raleigh. From there
she ventured to New York to study at the Art Students' League. She then
went to the Pennsylvania Academy of Fine Arts in Philadelphia, where
she studied for five years, and in 1919 won the Cresson Traveling Scholarship, enabling her to travel, study, and sketch for four months in Europe.

Upon her return from Europe, Miss Pugh began work in New York
City, a courageous decision for a young, rather shy Tarheel. As a feature
writer later pointed out, "New York City in the nineteen-twenties was an
esthetic bedlam which teemed with thousands of young artists trying to
make a go of it, but fully conscious of the difficult path ahead, Mabel Pugh
set out to accomplish by concentrated hard work what she could not possibly have achieved had she been a disciple of the School of Temperament.
Her block prints began to appear on the jackets of popular and widely sold
novels, her pen and ink illustrations appeared between the covers, and her
paintings received recognition at exhibitions."

Miss Pugh's first prints were made in 1924–25 in Morrisville from
sketches made while traveling in Europe. She exhibited them, on the advice of Frank Weitenkamph, then curator of prints of the New York
Public Library, in the 1926 International Print Makers' Exhibition at Los
Angeles. A print sent to the 1926 Southern States Art League Exhibition
was bought by the director of the Museum of Fine Arts of Houston, Texas.
Thirty-two of her prints were sold from a later exhibit of hers at that mu-

seum. Praise of her prints came from as far away as Sidney, Australia, through Camden Morresby, art connoisseur and radio lecturer.

Publishers were quick to recognize the ability of this young artist as an illustrator, among them Dutton, Century, Doran, Doubleday, Crowell, and others. Magazines using her illustrations included *McCall's, The Ladies' Home Journal, The Forum,* and *The Survey Graphic.* Her drawing of Leon Trotsky, the fiery Russian revolutionary exile, appeared on the front of the book review section of the *New York Times.* The prizes Miss Pugh has won are too numerous to list, but the Special Prize from the Pennsylvania Academy of Fine Arts (1920), and an Honorable Mention by the National Association of Women Painters and Sculptors (1934) undoubtedly distinguished her as the leading woman painter of that day. Miss Pugh's portrait "My Mother" was included in the first New York World's Fair by invitation, while at the same time the National Association of Women Painters and Sculptors in New York City displayed her painting "Three Sisters."

Following the death of Mrs. Ruth Huntington Moore, Miss Pugh returned to Raleigh to become head of the Art Department at Peace College. Her classes grew to such proportions that she used part of her salary to hire an assistant. She is well known in North Carolina for her many fine portraits; three of former North Carolina Congressmen hang in government buildings in Washington, D. C. She is also author of *Little Carolina Bluebonnet,* a book for children. Published by Crowell in 1933, it was reprinted several times. The cover is a reproduction of her painting by that title and the book contains 67 line and color illustrations by the author.

Miss Pugh retired from Peace College in 1960 "to allow full time for creative work." She writes verse, composes music, but remains faithful to her painting. In 1966 she received a citation from Peace College naming her a "Distinguished Alumna of Peace College."

3. FRANK LONDON

Frank London, a native of Pittsboro, North Carolina, went north to study art at the age of nineteen, following two years' attendance at the University of North Carolina at Chapel Hill. After two years of study at Pratt Institute and three years at the William M. Chase School of Art, where he studied art and design, he elected to remain in the North, because there was little opportunity in the South in those days for the professional artist.

According to his nephew, Lawrence London, of Chapel Hill, he loved New York and felt that it was the only place for an artist to live; but this fondness for the North never dimmed his devotion to his native Southland to which he returned annually to spend much of the summer with his parents in Pittsboro. Relatives proudly attest to the fact that "Uncle Frank's long years in the North failed to rob him of his Southern accent."

From 1904 to 1923 London worked for his own firm, Montegue Castle and London, in New York City, as a designer of stained glass and other objects of ecclesiastical art. The one example of his ecclesiastical design in North Carolina is the altar in the Episcopal Church of the Good Shepherd in Raleigh. In New York, his most memorable work is a magnificent stained glass window in one of the chapels in the Cathedral of St. John the Divine.

In 1923 Frank London abandoned the business world to devote the remainder of his life to painting. Drawn to Europe early in his painting career, his work soon received acclaim in Paris and in other parts of Europe. A one-man show of his work was held in Paris in 1927, and that same year he was awarded the Diplôme d'Honneur at the International Exposition of Beaux Arts at Bordeaux. During his lifetime his work was exhibited in most of the major museums in this country, and one-man shows were given his work at the N. E. Montrose Gallery in New York City in 1924, 1928, 1936, and 1939.

London has been honored twice by his native state. In 1942 he had an exhibition at the Person Hall Art Gallery in Chapel Hill and at the Mint Museum in Charlotte; and in 1948 the North Carolina Museum of Art held a memorial exhibition of his work. Bradley Walker Tomlin, a friend of London's, whose work also is represented in the permanent collection of the North Carolina Museum of Art, wrote the introduction to the catalogue for the memorial exhibition in which he said: "One feels that after a lifetime, largely detached from his background and origins, the civilization of the South still imposed an emotional motivation upon Frank London's painting. Quite clearly he would have denied this with the petulance and the spleen he was inclined at times to vent upon the professional Southerner."

But, as Tomlin continues, "there is beneath this odd collection of paradoxical elements, a view of life which is deeply reflective. . . . The wit which flashed about the man himself with such piercing spontaneity speaks out, brilliantly beribboned yet strangely tempered by a muted bird call."

London was married in 1908 to Miss Augusta Johnson of New York City, who became one of her husband's best critics, according to relatives. She held membership in several art organizations, including the Museum of Modern Art, and continued to live in New York City until her death in 1968.

Frank London was an active member of the Woodstock Art Association from 1925 until his death in March of 1945, and an early member of the original Whitney Studio Club and of the Federation of Modern Painters and Sculptors. In the fall of 1948 a retrospective exhibition of his paintings was held at the Woodstock Art Association Gallery and from there toured the more important museums and art schools in the South, among them the Morehead Gallery in Chapel Hill and, as mentioned earlier, the North Carolina Museum of Art in Raleigh. From this retrospective exhibition the London family selected "Song Silenced" as a gift to the North Carolina Museum of Art in honor of this distinguished Tarheel artist.

4. FRANCIS SPEIGHT

Born in Bertie County, North Carolina, September 11, 1896, Francis Speight developed an interest in drawing as a teenager and was first taught by his sister, Tulie. Then, during his two years at Wake Forest College he commuted once a week to Meredith College in Raleigh to get art instruction from Miss Ida Poteat. This was followed by study at the Corcoran Art Gallery in Washington and five years of study at the Pennsylvania Academy of Fine Arts, where he was to remain and teach for thirty-three years.

In 1936 Speight married Sarah Blakeslee, an artist who has won prizes equal to those of her husband. (While studying at the Pennsylvania Academy of Fine Arts she won two Cresson European Traveling Scholarships and other prizes.)

Recognition of the validity and scope of Francis Speight's work came early, leading to such honors as the Fellowship of the Pennsylvania Academy of Fine Arts; Gold Medal Award, 1926; Medal for Landscape, Society of Washington Artists, 1928; Fellowship Prize for a Fellowship member, Pennsylvania Academy Annual Exhibition, 1930; the first Hallgarten Prize, National Academy of Design, 1930; the Kohnstamm Prize, Art Institute of Chicago, 1930; the Landscape Prize, Connecticut Academy of Fine Arts, 1932; Medal, Philadelphia Sketch Club, 1938; First Prize, Regional Exhibition, Pennsylvania Academy, 1940. He was elected a member of the National Academy in 1940, and to membership in the National Institute of Arts and Letters in 1960 with numerous honors in between.

Although Speight lived in Pennsylvania and taught at the Pennsylvania Academy for thirty-three years, he often served his home state. In 1940 he returned to jury the Third Annual North Carolina Artists Competition, held in Person Hall Art Gallery. He had just been awarded first prize in the 135th annual exhibition of painting and sculpture at the Pennsylvania Academy of Art for a rural scene entitled "Straw for the Cities' Horses."

The year 1961 was a full one for Speight. He received the Owens Award, given each year to a distinguished Pennsylvania artist by the Fellowship of the Pennsylvania Academy; he and his family returned to Greenville, N. C., where he became artist-in-residence at East Carolina University; and the North Carolina Museum of Art honored this famous Tarheel with a retrospective exhibition of his work—the first North Carolina artist to be presented in a one-man show at this museum. Of the works corralled for the exhibition from other galleries and museums and private collections, Curator Ben Williams described its assemblage as a pleasure and a revelation as well: "Little did we know of the quality and scope of his particular genius; for one does not usually feel the full importance of his art at a momentary glance nor in the study of a single work."

Honors have continued to fall to this handsomely rugged, quiet man, described by columnist Jane Hall as "an East Carolinian with an easy old shoe manner, a keen sense of humor, and a deep feeling for the land." In 1962 he received the D.H.L. degree from Wake Forest College; and in 1964, along with President Lyndon B. Johnson, he was given an honorary degree by the College of the Holy Cross in Worcester, Massachusetts. Twice he has been appointed by the Governor of North Carolina to the board of the North Carolina Arts Council.

When the State of North Carolina held its first awards dinner in Raleigh on May 25, 1964, Francis Speight was a recipient—the first artist to be so honored. The accompanying citation and attendant publicity failed to recall, however, that he had been a charter member of the North Carolina Association of Professional Artists in 1931, and that his art class at the University at Chapel Hill in 1934 precipitated the inauguration of an Art Department at the University. Neither has this been recorded in any other of his biographical studies. Nevertheless, the citation does feelingly capture the spirit of this man and his work:

Francis Speight receives a North Carolina Award for fine arts not merely because his work as a painter has brought honor to the State, but because—through the genius of his art—he has given joy to thousands in the future. Although his work is based in realism touched with impressionism, Francis Speight is very much his own master. The spirit which permeates his pictures, the superb technique, are his alone. The sharp, hard brightness of an early spring day might belong to all the early spring days that ever were. The first faint excitement is there. The light and shadow, the earth itself, has an almost invisible pulse-beat that seemingly will beat faster. On the other hand, a winter scene, with no human figure in it, suggests all the loneliness a human being feels. The railroad tracks that thread the snow give an inkling of the magic and the glamour of far-off places. Almost, the viewer can hear the echo of the train whistle from across the land in the deeps of the night. Such paintings as these can be seen in most of the great museums of the continent.

Speight's paintings are in the collections of the Metropolitan Museum of Art; the Art Gallery of Toronto, Canada; the Butler Institute of American Art, Youngstown, Ohio; the Encyclopaedia Britannica, Chicago; the Gibbs Art Gallery, Charleston, S. C.; the Museum of Fine Arts, Boston; the Norton Gallery, West Palm Beach, Florida; the Pennsylvania Academy of the Fine Arts, Philadelphia; the Rochester Memorial Art Gallery, Rochester; The Wood Art Gallery, Montpelier, Vermont; the Woodmere Art Gallery, Philadelphia; and the North Carolina Museum of Art, Raleigh.

5. CHARLES BASKERVILLE

Although Charles Baskerville served as vice president of the North Carolina Association of Professional Artists and exhibited with them in 1931, he has spent little time on the North Carolina art scene. Continuing family tradition, he was born in Raleigh, North Carolina, in the ancestral home of his mother, although his parents lived in Chapel Hill where his father was a professor of chemistry.

The Baskervilles moved to New York City when Charles was eight. After graduation from Cornell University, study at the Art Student's League in New York City and the Academie Julien in Paris, he began to roam the world in search of interesting characters and exotic material for his paintings.

In 1949 he made a flight around the world, chiefly to record on canvas the likenesses of the King of Nepal, and hereditary Prime Minister–Maharaja, ruler of that forbidden kingdom lying between India and Tibet in the Himalaya Mountains. He climbed on foot and used a Tibetan pony to reach the remote capital city, Katmandu, where he painted colorful scenes of medieval pageantry at a royal wedding. During this stay in Asia he also painted a portrait of Prime Minister Nehru of India, which has been widely published and exhibited, but retained in his own collection.

Baskerville is internationally known as a portrait and mural painter and has been noted in *Art Digest* as "one of the leading portrait painters of the nation." His list of portrait subjects includes Winthrop W. Aldrich for the

New York Clearing House, Stanton Griffis for the Cornell-New York Medical College; K. T. Keller for the Chrysler Corporation; Glenn L. Martin for the Martin Corporation, Judge David Peck for the Appellate Division of the Supreme Court; Miss Helen Hayes; the Duchess of Windsor; Cornelius Vanderbilt Whitney; Bernard Baruch; the Maharaja of Cooch Behar; and numerous others.

His murals decorate the S. S. *America*; the Conference Room for the Joint Committee on Military Affairs of the Senate and House; the Wall Street Club; the Florida home of Douglas Dillon (president of the board of the Metropolitan Museum, past Ambassador to France, and Secretary to the Treasury); and in South Africa the Johannesburg house of Mr. and Mrs. Charles Engelhard. Baskerville has served the National Society of Mural Painters as president for several years.

His professional career was twice interrupted by service as an officer in World War I and World War II. In 1917 he was a lieutenant of infantry in the famous "Rainbow Division," during which period he received the Silver Star "for Gallantry in Action," the Purple Heart with oak leaf cluster, the Conspicuous Service Cross, and four battle clasps on the Victory Medal. In World War II he reached the rank of lieutenant-colonel as official portrait painter of the Army Air Forces and was decorated with the Legion of Merit. The seventy-two portraits of heroes and commanding generals whose portraits he painted during this tour of duty were shown in the great museums across the country for three years. They now hang in the Pentagon as a permanent memorial and as affirmation of this artist's keen insight into American heritage. In 1945 he selected the artists and assigned the subjects for the Chrysler Corporation collection of "Significant War Scenes." For two years the American Federation of Arts took this collection on tour of museums around the country before its final installation in the Chrysler Corporation gallery in Detroit.

Baskerville has had numerous one-man shows in New York City. The Palm Beach Galleries exhibited his work in 1961, 1963, 1965, 1967, and 1969; and in 1965 the Parrish Art Museum in Southampton devoted the month of July to a retrospective exhibition of his paintings. He was honored in his native state with a one-man show of 27 oils, watercolors and drawings at the formal opening of the Rachel Maxwell Moore Memorial

Gallery at the Greenville Art Center on Sunday, February 5, 1967. Baskerville's work has been exhibited at the National Gallery of Art and the Corcoran Gallery in Washington, D. C., the Metropolitan Museum of Art, the Whitney Museum, the Architectural League, the Salons of America, the National Society of Mural Painters in New York, the Carnegie Institute in Pittsburgh, the Chicago Art Institute, the Four Arts in Palm Beach, the Art Association at Newport, the White Art Museum at Cornell, and by private command at the Viceroy's Palace, New Delhi, India.

Permanent collections containing Baskerville works include the National Collection of Fine Arts, the National Portrait Collection, the Smithsonian Institution, Cornell Medical College, Princeton University, the Philadelphia Academy of Physicians, the National Museum of Racing, the Museum of the City of New York, and the Northern Trust Company of Chicago. That this artist is not well known in his native state is obviously due to his concentration on the national and international art scenes. Tarheel recognition is long overdue.

6. HOBSON PITTMAN

Hobson Pittman was born at Epworth, North Carolina, at the turn of the century. As a child he went to live in Tarboro, North Carolina, where he studied art at the Rouse private school of art from 1912–16. Later he moved to Pennsylvania and studied at the Pennsylvania State University from 1921–22. Further study was carried on at the Carnegie Institute of Technology, Columbia University, and, in the summers, at Woodstock, New York. Beginning in 1928, he made several trips abroad to study and paint, usually returning with a series of watercolors.

Upon his return from Europe in 1931, Pittman began the dual roles of director of art at the Friends' Central Country Day School at Overbrook, Pennsylvania, and summer teaching of painting at the Pennsylvania State University, positions he held for over thirty years. At this writing he is lecturer at the Philadelphia Museum of Art and at the Academy of Fine Arts. His career as an artist gained much impetus in 1933 when the Museum of Modern Art in New York included his work in "Painting and Sculpture from Sixteen American Cities." An array of exhibitions, prizes, and other honors too numerous to include followed.

Pittman's paintings have been shown in major museums throughout the world. More than forty museums in the United States own his paintings, among them the Metropolitan Museum of Art, the Whitney Museum of Art, and the Brooklyn Museum of Art in New York City; the Pennsylvania Academy, Philadelphia; the Phillips Memorial Museum, Washington; the Virginia Museum of Fine Arts; the Carnegie Institute, the Cleveland Museum of Art; the Philadelphia Museum of Art; the Brooks Memorial Gallery, Memphis; the John Heron Art Museum, Indianapolis; the Santa Barbara Museum. They are in the collections of the International Business Machines Corporation, the Encyclopaedia Britannica, and the Abbott Laboratories.

Among unusual commissions have been one by Gimbel Brothers in 1945 to participate in painting "Pennsylvania as Artists See It"; one by *Life Magazine* to paint interiors of well-known houses in Charleston, South Carolina; and one by Clare Boothe Luce to do landscapes of Mepkin Plantation in South Carolina.

Hobson Pittman and his work have been the subject of articles in *Art News, American Art Today, American Artist, Art Digest, Holiday Magazine, National Geographic,* the *New York Times,* student publications, and books. Among the books featuring his work is *Through the American Landscape* by Kaj Klitgaard, published by the University of North Carolina Press in 1941. Catalogues and booklets featuring his paintings have been published by the Museum of Modern Art, the Carnegie Institute and others, but none is more impressive and more sensitively constructed than the catalogue *Hobson Pittman, Retrospective Exhibition of His Work Since 1920,* edited by Ben F. Williams and published by the North Carolina Museum of Art when his retrospective exhibition was presented at the museum in Raleigh in February of 1963. This was the third in a series of exhibitions at the North Carolina Museum of Art of "Great North Carolina Artists," and elicited from Justus Bier, then director of the museum, praise of Pittman as "undoubtedly one of the most significant artists native to North Carolina."

North Carolina has appreciated the work of this native son since early in his career. Prior to the founding of the museum, the old State Art Gallery presented an exhibition of his works in October of 1950. The North Carolina Museum of Art now owns several pastels and drawings by Pittman as well as four oil paintings—one an anonymous gift, one a gift by the Samuel Clark family of Tarboro, and one a gift from the artist himself in 1967. In 1971 the museum acquired his painting "The Rehearsal," which had been shown in a one-man exhibition in the Babcock Galleries in New York City. His paintings are reminiscent of his childhood in Tarboro, where he was influenced by Victorian houses with high ceilings, tall windows, Victorian furnishings, *objets d'art*, and his memories of frail spinsters of the lavender-and-old-lace era.

7. HENRY JAY MacMILLAN

Henry Jay MacMillan attained exceptional success as a very young artist; first, when he exhibited with the North Carolina Association of Professional Artists in 1933, and later, in 1939, when he had a painting selected for the New York World's Fair exhibition. The Federal Arts Project arranged this exhibition, which became so controversial that the *New York Times* devoted a whole page to the story, accompanied by four large pictures of art works included. One of these was MacMillan's "Windy Morning."

In 1941 MacMillan had a one-man show at Gallery 10 in New York, and again the *New York Times* ran a picture of one of his paintings, "Liz." Howard Devree, the *New York Times* art critic, commenting on several recently opened shows in the New York galleries, devoted considerable space to the MacMillan show, of which he said:

"In his first one-man show Henry Jay MacMillan, at the No. 10 Gallery, makes a very good impression. This Carolinian has been experimenting with tempera underpainting and resin glazes and obtains luscious color effects without going pretty sentimental. Among the especially attractive paintings are the portrait of the girl in green velvet; the sprawling adolescent, 'Liz,' the simple dune scene and the handsome still-life 'With

Amarylis,' together with several of the guaches, notably the 'sea things' fantasies."

Although this was MacMillan's first one-man show in New York City, his work had previously been shown in at least two one-man shows in North Carolina; one at Duke University in 1936 and one in Wilmington in 1940.

MacMillan is a native of Wilmington, North Carolina, and first studied art with Miss Elizabeth Chant. He later graduated from the Paris branch of the New York School of Fine and Applied Arts and continued study at the Art Students' League, the Colorado Springs Fine Arts Centre, and the Woodstock School of Painting. From 1946 to 1956 he was instructor of painting at the Parsons School of Design in New York City.

Upon returning to Wilmington to live he has devoted himself mainly to portraiture (his creative portraits might more accurately be described as "paintings of people"). But, although he is known chiefly as a portraitist, "his paintings of the southern scene around him are equally distinguished and reveal a many-faceted talent marked by sound craftsmanship and consummate artistry," according to St. John's Art Gallery in Wilmington, where he was honored with a retrospective exhibition of twenty-nine paintings in June, 1970. He has taken a lively interest in the historic activities in Eastern North Carolina, and is a former president and a board member of the Lower Cape Fear Historical Society, chairman of the New Hanover Historical Commission, and a board member of St. John's Art Gallery.

8. WILLIAM C. FIELDS III

Although numerous references have already been made to William C. Fields, nothing of his profession as a portrait painter has been recorded. Fields was born in Fayetteville, September 27, 1917. By alphabetical coincidence, in 1938 he received the first A.B. degree in Fine Arts given by the University of North Carolina, Chapel Hill. He then studied two years at the School of the Boston Museum of Fine Arts on a full tuition scholarship.

Fields maintained a studio in New York City from 1945 until 1962 and spent most of 1950 to 1952 in Europe—chiefly Italy—where he painted portraits of such notables as the late Pope Pius XII, Prince Enrico Barberini, Prince Urbano Barberini, Princess Maria Barberini, Prince Ludovico Chigi-della Rovere-Albani (Grand Master of the Sovereign Military Order of Malto), Prince Raimondo Orsini, Princess Maria Silvia Boncompagni-Ludovisi, Princess Maria Elena Pignatelli, and Vittorio Orlando (Prime Minister of Italy during World War I).

In New York he painted Eleanor Steber in her costume from Mozart's opera, "Cosi Fan Tutte"; Miss Cary Latimer, number one debutante of the 1955 season; and Jerome Zerbe, society editor of *Town and Country* magazine, among others.

Among the many prominent North Carolinians he has painted are Mrs. Terry Sanford, Mrs. Inglis Fletcher, Charles A. Cannon, Jr., Archibald Henderson, D. D. Carroll, Hugh T. Lefler, and others on the campuses of the University of North Carolina. In May of 1965 Fields was elected a Life Fellow of the Royal Society of Arts, London, of which Her Majesty the Queen is patron and His Royal Highness Prince Philip, Duke of Edinburgh, is president.

Fields has participated widely in the cultural life of North Carolina, as founder and president of the North Carolina State Ballet Company; as a member of the board of trustees of the North Carolina Symphony Society, and as president of Associated Artists of North Carolina. In 1962 he was appointed by Governor Sanford to the Carolina Charter Tercentenary Commission, and in 1964 to the Advisory Committee of the North Carolina Recreation Commission, as a special advisor on the visual arts, and to the North Carolina Arts Council Advisory Board.

9. CLAUDE HOWELL

Claude Howell was much younger than the members of the North Carolina Association of Professional Artists, but he made his first mark as a Tarheel artist when he had a painting accepted in their first juried exhibition for all North Carolina artists, held in December of 1937. Three years later his "Winter Landscape" not only was accepted in the third North

Carolina Artists Annual, then sponsored by the Person Hall Art Gallery in Chapel Hill, but it won a $200 Purchase Award from the International Business Machines Corporation and became an early addition to its growing collection. In 1939, through the Federal Arts Project, he had a painting shown at the New York World's Fair. Later, he was one of the first Tarheels to have work shown at the Metropolitan Museum of Art. These early successes launched Howell on a winning streak that has lasted throughout his career.

Wilmington-born and ocean-bred, Claude Howell has spent most of his life studying the sea, fishermen, and trawlers, and the paraphernalia they employ in their professions. He began the study of art with Miss Elizabeth Augusta Chant while he was still in high school. As a young man he worked for the Atlantic Coast Line Railway and could paint only in his spare time. But he managed to spend several summers studying with Jon Corbino and Bernard Karfiol at Rockport, Maine, and with Charles Rosen and others at Woodstock, New York. These men had a profound influence upon his convictions as a painter and his search for a style of expression all his own. His almost three thousand numbered paintings and drawings reveal his deep interest in the North Carolina coast and the activities that take place there, and have established him as the art chronicler of the coastal way of life. They also have distinguished him as one prophet who has not been without honor in his own country, for when Wilmington needs a reputable work of art, she turns to this native son; and it has been said that to view his murals in Wilmington and Wrightsville Beach is worth a trip to the coast, even off-season.

One of these murals, commissioned by the Presbyterian Church on Wrightsville Beach, was inspired by the Biblical story of the "miraculous draught of fishes," which he painted as a tryptych. The two end panels portray the "casting" and "dragging in" of the nets, while in the larger center panel Jesus, Simon Peter, Thomas, Nathanael, the sons of Zebedee, and two other disciples are grouped around a table for the "blessing breakfast."

Mosaic murals in the Wilmington area which he has constructed, or designed, include one in the Brunswick Town Museum, commissioned by the North Carolina Department of Archives and History; a large one in the entrance to the North Carolina Maritime building in Wilmington, commissioned by the North Carolina State Ports Authority; and a smaller one in Rehder's florist shop in Wilmington. The Maritime mural he designed on paper which was then sent to Italian artists in New York who constructed the mural in sections. These were then shipped to Wilmington and mounted on the walls of the building according to the design.

Howell's influence on the arts in North Carolina has been widespread. It has been particularly significant in eastern North Carolina, going back to World War II, when Wilmington organized the first museum of art in the state. Later, he spearheaded the organization of the Wilmington Art Association which sponsors the Cottage Lane Art Show. For several years, while still working for the Railroad Company, he taught night classes at Wilmington College (now the University of North Carolina at Wilmington). These classes led to the inauguration of an Art Department by the University, with Howell as its director.

A philosophy he shares with his students is that "the artist has a great responsibility in determining the degree of civilization of a people . . . he must constantly search for universal truth and not be misled by fashions," and these ideals are reflected in the constant refinement of his own disciplined and inimitable style, his exacting design, and his "personalized" use of azalea-pinks, ocean-blues, and atmospheric-grays and greens—colors so much a part of the area in which he has spent his life.

Throughout the years Howell has managed his work so as to visit foreign countries in the summers. Each foreign jaunt has generated a vast production of paintings and drawings. He undoubtedly is the most prolific painter and award-winner in North Carolina and often is characterized as the "Dean of North Carolina Painters."

One-man shows of Howell's work have been presented at the North Carolina Museum of Art, Raleigh; the University of North Carolina at Greensboro; Agnes Scott College; the Mint Museum of Art, Charlotte; Mercer University, Macon, Georgia; the Copain Gallery, New York; Salem College, Winston-Salem; the Georgia Museum of Art, Athens; the John Brady Gallery, Blowing Rock, North Carolina; the Artists' Gallery, Wilmington; the Morehead Planetarium Gallery, Chapel Hill; Queens College, Charlotte; and many others.

Among regional and national museums which have included his work in group exhibitions are the Baltimore Museum, the Norfolk Museum, the Pasadena Art Institute, the Corcoran Gallery, the Gibbs Art Gallery, and the Metropolitan Museum of Art.

His paintings are in numerous collections, including Charles Laughton's.

Listed in *Who's Who in American Art* and *Who's Who in the South and Southwest*, he is a charter member of Associated Artists of North Carolina and has served on its board from its beginning. In recent years he has joined the ranks of Tarheel illustrators.

10. TARHEEL ARTISTS IN NEW YORK

Warren Brandt, a Greensboro native, who is now one of the most prominent artists in New York City, says, "The day I graduated from high school in Greensboro, in 1935, I headed for New York City and started the art career I had planned ever since I could remember." But there were years of travel and study in New York and Europe before he returned to Greensboro and earned his M.F.A. at the University of North Carolina at Greensboro. Now living in New York City, he averages at least one exhibition a year, and the *New York Times*, *Art News*, and *Art International* frequently carry stories on his work. He is married to Grace Borgenicht, owner of the Borgenicht Gallery.

Edward A. Bryant, a native of Lenoir, North Carolina received his A.B. degree at the University of North Carolina, after which he taught arts and crafts in the Blind Center at Butner, the State Hospital at Raleigh, and the Psychiatric Department at Memorial Hospital in Chapel Hill. A Fulbright scholarship provided study in Europe and again at Chapel Hill where he received the M.A. in art history. In 1957 he won the Brooklyn Museum Fellowship for museum training, which led to a curatorship at the Whitney Museum of Art.

Henry C. Pearson was born in Kinston in 1914. He received his B.A. at the University of North Carolina and his M.F.A. at Yale University. The circuitous route to becoming an artist of note at age thirty-four followed an interest in theatre design and eleven years in the army. He re-enlisted in the army in 1946 and requested far-eastern duty, during which time he spent two years in Japan. During World War II Pearson was assigned to interpret topographic maps. His fascination with forms created by converging and diverging lines of the landscape, and the influence of Japanese art, led to experimentation with optical effects that landed him in the middle of the Optical Movement, and thence into the Museum of Modern Art's exhibition, "The Responsive Eye." The North Carolina Museum of Art honored Pearson with a Retrospective Exhibition in 1969.

Kenneth Noland was born in Asheville and is a product of Black Mountain College, where he worked under Josef Albers. He later studied with Ossip Zadkine in Paris. His works have won awards at the International Di Tella, Buenos Aires, and the Venice Biennale (U.S. Pavilion) in 1964; he was also the only Tarheel artist represented at Exposition 67 in Canada. He returned to North Carolina in 1965 to co-jury the North Carolina Artists' Annual. Noland lives and works in a luxurious loft studio-apartment in the new SoHo section of New York, where he sometimes uses three assistants in preparing his large paintings for New York showings.

James Bumgardner, a native of Winston-Salem, North Carolina, reached the New York mecca in 1960 with a one-man show at the Fleishman Gallery. He is represented in the North Carolina Museum of Art by several purchase awards, and was one of the few Tarheel artists to have work accepted in the New York "U.S.A. Art, 1959" exhibition.

Charlotte-born black artist Romare Bearden has fared well on the New York scene. Not only has his work been shown at and collected by the Museum of Modern Art, but that museum has prepared and sponsored a traveling retrospective exhibition of his works. Here again, the artist has been in the Metropolitan area at the right time. He grew up in New York City and graduated from New York University, with further study at the Art Students League.

Bearden has worked in the medium of collage for many years and is represented in the North Carolina Museum of Art collection by "Carolina Blue." The Museum of Modern Art acquired his "He is Risen" in 1945. His work has been included in many group exhibitions in America and Europe during the past thirty years. Bearden has worked diligently to improve the position of the Negro artist. He was one of the founders in 1963 of The Spiral Group, primarily concerned with the problems of Negro artists; he has been art director of the Harlem Cultural Council; and in 1970 he received a grant from the Guggenheim Foundation to write a history of Afro-American Art.

Lloyd Oxendine, a native of Wilmington, North Carolina, is probably the youngest Tarheel artist in New York City. He studied art at the University of North Carolina at Wilmington, with Claude Howell, and later at the Art Students League in New York. While working toward his M.A. in Fine Arts at Columbia University School of the Arts, he had work exhibited at several northern galleries including the Sermonetta Gallery in New York City, Columbia University, and the National Academy of Design. He was included in a poster exhibition in Ulm, Germany in 1970. He is the founder and director of the Native North American Artists and prepared an exhibition of contemporary American Indian Art for a major New York museum.

Thomas Sills, born in Castalia, North Carolina, in August of 1914, won a Copley Foundation Award in 1957. By the early sixties his work was being shown at the Museum of Modern Art, the Whitney Museum of Art, the New School for Social Research, and the Betty Parsons Gallery in New York City; at Brandeis University, and the Los Angeles Museum of Art. He had a one-man show at the Betty Parsons Gallery as early as 1955.

A growing list of Tarheels have exhibited in New York, among them Ruth Clarke, Greensboro; Maude Gatewood, Charlotte; Doris Leeper, Charlotte; Susan Moore, Williamston; and Victor Huggins, Chapel Hill.

11. TARHEEL ARTISTS AS ILLUSTRATORS

A large group of Tarheel artists have achieved distinction in the field of illustration. Regrettably, not much is generally known about their contributions in this field, as they are better known as painters, sculptors, and printmakers. The North Carolina Collection in the Louis R. Wilson Library at the University of North Carolina contains a wide selection of books illustrated by Tarheel artists, many of them also written by North Carolinians.

As far back as 1933, *The News and Observer*, in reporting on the Third Annual Exhibition of the North Carolina Association of Professional Artists, noted that "William Pfohl of Winston-Salem has on exhibition a series of etchings on his native city, many of which have been used for book illustrations," and that "Many of Miss Pugh's woodcuts have adorned the pages of modern books." Pfohl's "minute etchings" and some of his linoprints referred to in the article illustrated Ernest Eller's *Houses of Peace*, a book about the Old Salem community. A long list of books illustrated by Miss Pugh and more on Pfohl is given in another chapter.

John F. Blair, a Winston-Salem publisher, relies heavily on Tarheel artists as illustrators for his books. Some of those he has commissioned and the books they have illustrated include: Ann Carter Pollard, Winston-Salem, *Nematodes in My Garden of Verse*, a little book of Tarheel poems selected by Richard Walser of Raleigh; Primrose Paschal, Durham, *Ocracoke* by Carl Goerch (first published by Goerch); Claude Howell, Wilmington, *The Hatterasman* by Ben Dixon MacNeill, and *The Beachcomber's Handbook of Seafood Cookery* by Hugh Zachary; Raiford Porter, Winston-Salem, *A Night Out*, by Edward Peple; Mrs. Betty Spencer, originally of Winston-Salem, *Drought* and *El Tigre*, both by Edith H. Smith; Anne Kesler Shields, *Legends of the Outer Banks* by Charles Harry Whedbee; Mitzi Shewmake, *The Wild Queen* by George B. Saul; Virginia Ingram, Winston-Salem, *Ghost Tales of the Uwharries* by Fred T. Morgan; and Bruce Tucker, *Bugles at the Border* by Mary Lina Gillett.

Some of the "juveniles" Blair has published and their Tarheel illustrators are: *Kirsty's Secrets*, a sort of Scottish cookbook, by Marguerite Alexander, illustrated by Mitzi Shewmake; *The Misfortunes of Ogier the Dane*, by Marie Butts, (translated by Professor Robert Linker, formerly of Chapel Hill), illustrated by Mitzi Shewmake; *Smoke on Old Thunderhead* by Gene Harris, illustrated by Don Harris, then of High Point; *Taffy of Torpedo Junction* by Nell Wise Wechter, illustrated by Mary Walker Sparks, formerly of Greensboro; *Lord Ham* by Beth Hamilton Bell, illustrated by Ann Carter Pollard; and *Inky Puss* by Harrison and Mathilda

Reed, with line drawings by Eleanor Amis, at that time of Winston-Salem.

Volumes in a series of classics published by World Publishing Company have been illustrated by Nell Battle Booker, a Chapel Hill native who migrated to Washington, D.C. Her imaginative and sensitive watercolor illustrations of *Jane Eyre* and *Wuthering Heights* and her black-and-white sketches for *The Scarlet Letter* might well tempt the collector for the beauty of the art works alone.

Jeff Hill, of Raleigh, has strikingly illustrated a large number of books for the Peter Pauper Press, and his woodcuts for these classics vary from line drawings on the block to semi-abstract patterns. In a more sophisticated series illustrated by Hill are Baudelaire's *Flowers of Evil*, translated by Jacques Leclercq, which gains distinction through the stronger prints in black, white, and brown. *India Love Poems*—selected, and with an essay on "Women in India" by Tambimuttu—comes alive through the writhing, sensuous female torso Hill depicts in varying attitudes. Some of his prints were exhibited as far back as 1952 in two national shows simultaneously—the Audubon exhibition at the National Academy in New York and the Florida International.

Due to a twist of fate, a stack of illustrations by a former Chapel Hill water-colorist repose in the Smithsonian Institution in Washington, D.C. It all began when the late C. D. Beadel, superintendent of the Biltmore Estate in Asheville, became convinced that he was discovering more varieties of azaleas than botanists Coker and Totten of the University at Chapel Hill had found. To prove his point he commissioned Lucia Johnson, the late wife of Professor Cecil Johnson, to do watercolor sketches of the various azaleas he had "discovered" over the years—with a future book in mind. Due to Beadel's death, the book unfortunately was never published, but in some mysterious way the group of illustrations wound up at the Smithsonian. Since her death in 1970 these sketches have been in a traveling exhibition arranged by the Smithsonian.

Mrs. Johnson also did the delicate drawings depicting various aspects of ante-bellum life that embellish the end papers in *Woman's Life and Work in the Southern Colonies*, written in 1935 by Mrs. Julia Spruill of Chapel Hill, a University of North Carolina Press publication. Mrs. Johnson also illustrated, by maps, two of her husband's books: *British West*

Florida (Yale Press) and *Autobiographical Notes of John Lipscomb John-son*, grandfather of the author, which was privately printed.

Two widely different books were written in 1950 by Chapel Hillians and illustrated by Chapel Hillians. Professor John V. Allcott, of the University Art Department, by his lively illustrations made even more intriguing *The Pianist's Problems* by William S. Newman—a non-technical and modern approach to efficient practice and musicianly performance, published by Harper and Brothers. The other book will be a long and lasting memorial to its author and illustrator—William Meade Prince. *The Southern Part of Heaven*, his only book, was written soon after he returned to Chapel Hill, following a brilliant career as illustrator for such magazines as *The Saturday Evening Post* and *Colliers*. Published by Rhinehart & Company, the book is illustrated with Bill's own nostalgic drawings depicting episodes of his childhood in Chapel Hill.

Other books written by North Carolinians and illustrated by Tarheel artists not well known in the fine arts field include the Viking juvenile series, written by Thelma Harrington Bell of Sapphire, North Carolina, and illustrated by her husband Corydon Bell. *Snow, Mountain Boy,* and *Thunderstorm,* also by the Bells, have adult appeal, too, evoking as they do a nostalgia for childhood experiences. A barrage of "Outer Banks" books have brought fame to the North Carolina coastline, two of which were written by David Stick and illustrated by his father, Frank: *The Outer Banks* and *Graveyard of the Atlantic,* published by the University of North Carolina Press.

Richard Walser's *North Carolina Miscellany*, also a University of North Carolina Press publication, was illustrated by Paul Gray of Raleigh. Mrs. Joyce Kachergis, who joined the staff of the University of North Carolina Press in 1963 as book designer, did the drawings for *The Light That Shines* by Chancellor Emeritus Robert B. House. Each chapter is introduced by a sketch of a campus or town scene or by a portrait sketch of a former University scholar.

Newer additions to the North Carolina Collection include *The Year of the Swan* by Lewis W. Green (printed by Crowder's Printing Press, Route 3, Weaverville), with original woodcuts and cover design by Gene Bunker, then at Asheville-Biltmore College; and *North Carolina Parade* by Richard Walser and Julia Montgomery Street, illustrated by Didie Burrus Browning of Winston-Salem and published by the University of North Carolina Press. Mrs. Jean Fonville, Burlington, worked as assistant designer for J. B. Lippincott from 1942–44, where she designed several Munro Leaf books and the adult book *Earth and High Heaven*.

12. TARHEEL PORTRAIT PAINTERS

Most artists, even abstract painters, paint portraits now and then. Recognizing this, the State Art Gallery, which preceded the North Carolina Museum of Art, in March of 1954 invited forty-six artists residing in North Carolina to exhibit one portrait each, to partially answer the question of "Who is painting portraits today in North Carolina?" The catalogue for the exhibition pointed out that "of the forty-six artists represented, a number are chiefly known as portrait painters interested in doing commissioned portraits. Some are artists who do only occasional portraits. All are contemporary North Carolina artists."

Of this group, those known chiefly as portraitists were Dayrell Kortheuer, Charlotte; William C. Fields, Fayetteville; Joseph Wallace King, Winston-Salem; Henry Jay MacMillan, Wilmington; Henry Rood, Jr., Greensboro; and, until the last few years, Edmund Strudwick, III, Hillsborough. Those known to accept occasional commissions were Miss Mabel Pugh, Raleigh; Mrs. Mildred McMullan Rumley, Little Washington; Mrs. John M. Foushee, Chapel Hill; Mrs. Cantey Venable Sutton, Raleigh; Gerard Tempest, Chapel Hill, Boston, and Rome; and, until her death in 1969, Mrs. Isabelle Bowen Henderson. (The State Art Society dedicated its catalogue of the Thirty-Second North Carolina Artists Annual to Mrs. Henderson as one of the founders of the Artists' annual competition.)

Because portraiture over the years has become categorized as commercial art, it is rare that a portrait is accepted in art competitions. Occasionally an exception turns up. Mrs. Winn E. Hughes of New Bern, for instance, won honorable mention in the Fifth Annual "Painting of the Year" contest in Atlanta, Georgia, for her portrait of "Mary Katherine," and Primrose Paschal is represented in the North Carolina Museum of Art by "Beulah's Baby," which was lent by the museum to Winnipeg, Canada, for its exhibition on the theme "Mother and Child," celebrating the Winnipeg Centennial in 1967. William C. Fields's "Girl before a Mirror" and others by him have been chosen by such judges as Andrew Ritchie of Yale and H. H. Arnason of the Guggenheim Museum, for exhibition at the North Carolina Museum of Art, the Winston-Salem Gallery of Fine Arts, and in Associated Artists of North Carolina exhibitions.

Few Tarheel artists have been commissioned by the State for official portraits, a fact that has engendered hard feelings and considerable criticism by native artists, particularly since some of them have received signal honors nationally and internationally. They feel that when art commissions go out of the state, they not only lose the commissions but, through their taxes, vicariously contribute to the out-of-state painter. A three column invective by William C. Fields ran in several North Carolina newspapers, circa 1959, on the portrait of Governor Luther Hodges and, entitled "Wallpaper at $571 a Foot," not only criticized the state for using tax money for the project but pointed out in minute detail what he considered the portrait's flaws.

Chief objections by artists have included the method of selection. A Board of Selection is created by statute. Fields's solution is to repeal the Act providing funds for official portraits. In that way "the prerogative of commissioning these portraits will revert to the private individuals involved and perhaps from time to time an enlightened individual or family will achieve a distinguished portrait," he says. (The portrait of the late W. Kerr Scott, painted by Howard Chandler Christy, a New York artist of note, was paid for by funds raised by Governor Scott's friends.)

Another valid protest is that even good out-of-state portraitists fail to give North Carolina their "best." An excellent example of this is the portrait of Dr. Frank Porter Graham at the University of North Carolina that could be of any aging gentleman, sitting serenely in a chair in a large vacuum of nondescript color. An artist who knew Frank Graham personally might have provided a more symbolic painting, portraying him walking on the campus with the wind in his hair and the jovial bearing so well remembered by students and faculty who knew him as teacher and president of the University. The same is true of former Governor Terry Sanford's portrait, painted by John Koch of New York City, which completely fails to represent the vigor of Sanford or the artist's skill. One would never recognize it as a "Koch."

Occasionally a museum feels an obligation toward portrait painters and will have an exhibition similar to the one at the State Art Gallery sixteen years ago. The Mint Museum of Art in Charlotte held an exhibition of "Contemporary Portraiture" in June of 1959. Among the Charlotte portraitists whose work was shown were Paul Bartlett, Dayrell Kortheuer, Alice Steadman, Sarah Toy, and Charles Tucker.

Native North Carolina Artists in the North Carolina
Museum of Art Collection to 1970

Russell Arnold, Harriett Bozart, James Bumgardner, Margaret Crawford, Peggy Jewell Canipe, Going Back Chiltoskey, Lena Bullock Davis, Edward T. Draper-Savage, Jean Lane Fonville, Jeff Hill, Claude Howell, Virginia Ingram, Mary Anne Keel Jenkins, Helen Lockie Jones, Rachel Katzin, Frank London, Philip Moose, Susan Moore, Sarah Jane Moser, Primrose Paschal, Henry Pearson, Hobson Pittman, Anne Carter Pollard, Grove Robinson, Edwin Shewmake, Anne Mercer Shields, Francis Speight, Walter B. Stephen, Anne Wall Thomas, Helen Thrush, Walter Thrift, and Ben F. Williams.

13. ASSOCIATED ARTISTS OF NORTH CAROLINA

About sixty North Carolina artists and art-interested people met on Sunday, December 13, 1959, at the Merin Gallery in Greensboro, North Carolina, to discuss and try to remedy what they considered a serious situation developing in the arts on the state level. Actually, three events concerning art in North Carolina, more fully discussed in other chapters, drew the irate group together. First, Gregory D. Ivy, head of the Art Department at the University of North Carolina at Greensboro and the only artist on the board of directors of the North Carolina State Art Society, had not been re-elected to the sixteen-member board of that organization, which also served as a guiding force to the North Carolina Museum of Art. Secondly, a rift had developed in the Art Society board over the selection of a new director for the North Carolina Museum of Art. Finally, the group felt that practicing artists should have some say-so on these issues, plus better representation in the museum.

Well represented, the press reported that John Brady, an artist from Hickory; Gregory D. Ivy; and Mrs. John Foushee, Chapel Hill painter and writer, called the meeting. Brady actually initiated the meeting and brought the group together. The press variously labeled the gathering as a "pressure group," a "protest group," and "disgruntled artists." Brady was called a "rebel leader." Burke Davis, *Greensboro Daily News* staff writer, began his report with, "A muffled explosion signaled a palace revolution in Tar Heel art circles here yesterday," and Beverly Wolter, of the *Winston-Salem Journal*, wrote: "North Carolina artists, after taking pot shots at several figures connected with the North Carolina Museum of Art, took tentative steps yesterday toward forming a 'pressure' group of their own."

The rift in the State Art Society had started in September, preceding its December, 1959, meeting, when Robert Lee Humber, president of the Society, named a five-member committee to seek candidates for the museum's directorship left vacant by the death of W. R. Valentiner in September, 1958. James Byrnes, acting director, was favored by Edwin Gill and other board members as permanent director of the museum. Humber and the Greensboro group wanted a more scholarly director.

Determined to hang together and to wield some influence over these matters, the sixty or so who gathered in Greensboro tentatively organized that day as Associated Artists of North Carolina. They met again on January 10, 1960, at Woman's College, Greensboro, and formally adopted Associated Artists of North Carolina as a permanent name and began serious efforts to improve the status of art in the state. Again the press was well represented and one reporter, Alfred McCormack, Jr., representing the United Press, wrote:

"Note to Tarheel politicians: That lobbyist you see with brush and easel really may be an artist, and vice versa. . . . The group won't have to depend on pamphlets printed in members' basements or a weekly home-grown 'newsletter' to make itself heard when necessary. Mrs. Ola Maie Foushee of Chapel Hill, one of the directors, writes a weekly column on Tarheel artists and their doings which is distributed from the mountains to the Outer Banks. And keeping an eye on artists and politicians alike will be Owen Lewis, a Winston-Salem newspaper executive. He is president of the Associated Artists.

"Mrs. Foushee, a firm believer in lobbying, has made it crystal clear she intends to carry the good fight on behalf of her fellow artists from one chamber of the Legislature to another and back and forth into committee, as required." One editorial said, "The State Art Society can hardly ignore protests of the Associated Artists of North Carolina that the former organization's board of directors now contains no representation from Tar Heel artists.

"Prior to the blowup in Raleigh during Culture Week last month, there was artist representation on the board. Now that State Treasurer Edwin Gill's faction has triumphed over Robert Lee Humber's, the board's only artist representative, Gregory Ivy of Greensboro, has been kicked out."

Associated Artists of North Carolina inexorably allied itself with the Humber faction around March 28, 1960, when it permitted anonymous parties to use their private funds in the name of Associated Artists to fly Clemens Sommer, a member of the State Art Society's board, from Europe and back twice so he could vote on the election of a museum director. In further support, a letter dated November 15, 1960, from Owen Lewis, president, to all members of the organization, urged everyone not already a member of the State Art Society to join by October 20, in order to vote for the nominating committee's slate to be presented at the Society's November 30 meeting. The State Art Society slate, consisting of Gregory D. Ivy, Clemens Sommer, Egbert L. Davis, Jr., and Mrs. J. M. Broughton, Lewis pointed out, would maintain harmony in the Society and insure the hiring of Justus Bier as museum director.

With the museum controversy finally resolved by the selection in 1961 of Justus Bier as director, and Gregory Ivy back on the State Art Society board, Associated Artists of North Carolina bent its efforts toward goals emphasized in its by-laws: the advancement of the fine arts in North Carolina through programs, education, exhibits, and publicity; active participation in the affairs of the North Carolina State Art Society; cooperation with the educational institutions of the state, various museums, galleries, etc.; and to be truly representative of all of the professional artists of the state. It also immediately joined forces with other organizations in pressuring the State Department of Public Instruction to hire a State Art Supervisor, and began lobbying to get the Legislature to allocate funds for such a person.

Associated Artists of North Carolina established high standards for membership and leadership and has striven to keep representation statewide, as indicated by the names of its first officers and directors, many of whom have continued to serve in some capacity through 1970: Owen D. Lewis, Winston-Salem, president; John Brady, Hickory, vice president; Mrs. R. Philip Hanes, Winston-Salem, secretary; and Mrs. Ruth Clarke, Raleigh, treasurer. The Executive Committee was composed of Gregory Ivy, Greensboro, and Claude Howell, Wilmington, in addition to the officers. Board members were Erik Fris, Asheville; Robert Howard, Mrs. John M. Foushee, Miss Mary Ravenel Burgess, Chapel Hill; Miss Kathryn Ridgely and Mrs. Elizabeth Mack, Charlotte; John Kehoe, Miss Louise Smith, and Allen S. Wilkinson, Greensboro; Bruce Carter, Greenville; Duncan Stuart, Raleigh; Mrs. Philip Link, Reidsville; Mrs. Peter Hairston, Advance; Mrs. J. P. Huskins and E. S. Gregg, Statesville.

At this writing the organization has had five presidents: Owen Lewis, Winston-Salem, 1960–1961; William C. Fields, Fayetteville, 1961–1964; Mrs. Peter Hairston, Advance, 1964–1966; Leonard White, Chapel Hill, 1966–1968; Jim Moon, Winston-Salem, 1968–1969; and Perry Kelly, Cullowhee, 1970.

Other distinguished officers and board members who have served the Association are Joseph Sloane of the Ackland Museum; Curator James C. Tucker, University of North Carolina, Greensboro; J. T. Diggs, Art Educator, Winston-Salem; Peter Hairston, attorney, Advance; Edward N. Wilson, sculptor, North Carolina Central University, Durham; and Mrs. Clemens Sommer, to name a few.

The Association annually sponsors several traveling exhibitions of paintings, prints, and drawings. It has an annual "open" show for artists of any caliber who wish to become candidates for "exhibiting" membership. To insure the quality of exhibiting members, distinguished jurors of national standing are engaged for these exhibitions.

The organization has worked consistently toward raising the aesthetic standards of art used in public buildings, or exhibits organized by non-member groups. It was a major influence in getting a state art supervisor for the public schools. It has been supported by a number of business firms through purchase awards, among them, the North Carolina National Bank, the Foushee Realty and Insurance Co., Thalheimers-Ellis Stone, and the *Greensboro News-Record*.

To add to the festivities of Culture Week in Raleigh, Associated Artists in 1961 began the sponsorship of a subscription dinner and reception, held in the Elizabeth Room at the Sir Walter Hotel, to which members of all Societies were invited on the evening of the opening of the North Carolina Artists' Annual Exhibition at the North Carolina Museum of Art.

CHAPTER SEVEN

Corporate Support of the Arts

Corporations first became aware of the value of original art as a promotional image builder, as well as an altruistic medium, in the mid 'thirties. Container Corporation of America blazed the trail in 1942 with several series of advertisements based on various themes and illustrated with original paintings by such artists as Ben Shawn, Philip Guston, Leonard Baskin, Henry Moore, A. M. Cassandre, Fernand Leger, Gyorgy Kepes, and others of national and international stature. Their series on "Great Ideas of Western Man," will perhaps be recalled as the most popular group. At least one North Carolina painter was used in their series on states. Herbert McClure illustrated a full page advertisement on North Carolina. Over the caption "North Carolina—Annual Purchases: $2 Billion—Mostly Packaged," the composition includes a tobacco barn, a piece of furniture, a large factory smokestack, an over-size cone of yarn, and a strip of North Carolina's mountain peaks.

The Container Corporation collection, "Modern Art in Advertising," was shown at the Person Hall Art Gallery in Chapel Hill in 1947. Containing more than 100 original paintings and drawings by fifty contemporary artists, all commissioned by the Corporation in its national advertising program, it was lauded as "one of the most progressive art projects ever evolved in this country." Fifteen years later, another Container Corporation collection was shown in the Winston-Salem Public Library and accompanied by Ralph Eckerstrom, director of public relations and advertising for the Container Corporation.

International Business Machines also pioneered in bringing art and

business together. In 1940 it brought to North Carolina for several showings its "Contemporary Art of 79 Countries," assembled first to be shown
at the New York World's Fair and the Golden Gate Exposition at San
Francisco, where 3,000,000 people viewed it while visiting I.B.M.'s building. In appraising the exhibition while it hung in the Mint Museum of
Art in Charlotte, the *Charlotte Observer* quoted Thomas J. Watson,
young president of the company, as saying: "Three great patrons have
fostered painting throughout the long history of civilization: Priests have
adorned temples, rulers their palaces and public buildings, private individuals their homes and museums. In the last group, businessmen of many
countries became more and more important after the Renaissance . . . If
business men, why not business itself?" Watson, an early collector of contemporary art, was also a director on the boards of the Metropolitan Museum of Art and the Grand Central Art Galleries in New York at that
time. The *Charlotte Observer* also noted that "this year the International
Business Machine Corporation is asking the Jury of the Third Annual
North Carolina Artists exhibition to select two paintings representative of
the art and character of North Carolina, by artists who are citizens of
North Carolina, to be part of a collection made up of two paintings from
each state to be exhibited in the Corporation's building at the New York
World's Fair."

Soon other national corporations realized that if the arts were to sur-
vive, corporate support was a necessity, and for numerous reasons chose
original paintings as the sophisticated bridge between the consumer and
the manufacturer, or the client and the corporation.

Sears, Roebuck and Company furthered the idea in the early 'fifties
when it popularized art by making it available on the installment plan.
Movie actor Vincent Price, himself an avid collector and an authority on
contemporary art, was commissioned by Sears to purchase a collection for
the company that could travel to selected cities across the country—with
particular emphasis on cities without the benefit of major galleries or exhibition facilities. Usually they sponsored a local art competition from which
the winning works were purchased and added to the major collection, thus
helping the local artist to sell his product. In Greensboro in 1964, the
Artists' League and Sears jointly sponsored a "Festival of Art," and the

catalogue noted that "this group of works, circulating throughout the South, will be augmented by the three prize-winning paintings taken from the Greensboro show. All of the works in this traveling collection will be put on display at the end of the year in the Atlanta Art Museum where one painting will be awarded a $2,000 prize."

Sears's theory, as expressed by Vincent Price, was: "Urge every family to put an original painting on their shopping list, even if they have to pay for it on time. They buy stoves, refrigerators, and other necessities on time. Why not the ultimate necessity—Art?" At one point the Sears collection totaled 15,000 pieces purchased by Price, ranging in prices from $25 to $10,000, "which can be bought on a Sears' charge and with a money-back guarantee," one newspaper reported.

St. John's Art Gallery in Wilmington was a recipient of a pen and ink drawing, "R. F. D." by Robert G. Redden of Rome, Georgia, donated during the eleventh year of Sears's art sponsorship.

The Ford Motor Company, through its Foundation for the Arts, has reached into North Carolina several times with its benefaction to Tarheel painters. One of its most effective programs, announced in 1958, enabled artists of mature years to devote full time to their creative arts. Thirty-eight artists were chosen from the 482 nominated by several hundred persons in the visual arts. Six painters and four sculptors were awarded grants of $10,000 each to enable them to devote themselves solely to their creative work for periods of one to three years. Twenty-one painters, sculptors, and printmakers were awarded purchase prizes totaling $16,525, and their purchased works were donated by the artists to museums of their choice. North Carolina profited greatly from this venture. Two artists from the School of Design in Raleigh received purchase awards—George Bireline, painter, and Roy Gussow, sculptor. The North Carolina Museum of Art in Raleigh received two paintings as gifts from out-of-state award winners: "Blue Walls" by Robert F. Gates of Washington, D. C., and "Broken Trail" by J. Bardin of Columbia, South Carolina, and, already represented in the North Carolina Museum of Art, Bireline donated his "Painting W59" to the Mint Museum of Art, Charlotte.

Ford further supported artists by commissioning them for paintings to illustrate its magazine *Ford Times*. Every issue carried from thirty to fifty color reproductions. Philip Moose of Charlotte and Blowing Rock was commissioned to do a number of paintings for this project. In 1959 *Ford Times* ran a story by William Patrick Wootten of Statesville entitled "North Carolina's Autumn Show." Illustrated by Moose, those of Grandfather Mountain are as lush in color and as rugged in character as the old man himself—a far cry from Moose's more subtle abstracts which may be seen in the North Carolina Museum of Art.

When the Chase Manhattan Bank in New York City opened in June of 1961, as the biggest commercial structure completed in more than twenty-five years, it was decided that "the decorative element which would best complement the stark simplicity of its modern architecture was fine art." Accordingly, the bank recruited the services of a committee of art experts to select works which would contribute to a warm and stimulating environment in which the employees would work and at the same time express the bank's concern with those things man holds dear." The original selection committee consisted of David Rockefeller, president of the bank, and already a collector of note; Alfred H. Barr, Jr., and Mrs. Dorothy Miller of the Museum of Modern Art; Robert B. Hale of the Metropolitan Museum of Art; James J. Sweeney of the Museum of Fine Arts of Houston; Perry Rathbone of the Museum of Fine Arts, Boston; and Gordon Bunshaft of Skidmore, Owings & Merrill. In keeping with the entire dynamic concept of this art program, the Chase Manhattan Bank's collection has been frequently renewed and strengthened by a system of donations and acquisitions, and items from time to time are donated by them to museums and educational institutions.

North Carolina is vicariously represented in the Chase Manhattan Bank collection of Who's Who among painters and sculptors by a handsome sculpture by Edward Higgins, who studied art at the University of North Carolina at Chapel Hill and was considered by Professor Robert Howard as "probably the most outstanding student of sculpture we have ever had." When Higgins had a one-man show at the Leo Castelli Gallery in New York City, and the Museum of Modern Art purchased one of his sculptures, Chase Manhattan was one of the collectors that made the exhibition a "sell-out."

Nearly every bank in North Carolina has contributed in some way to the welfare of art in North Carolina, either through contributions, the use of their walls for local exhibitions, or through collecting by purchase awards. More and more they are following the Chase Manhattan Bank's philosophy that "a program of this kind will vivify the image of the Bank in the minds of the customers, the employees, and the public, by dramatizing the breadth and scope of the Bank's activities, and will emphasize the Bank's awareness of human values as exemplified by the emotional impact of the works shown."

The North Carolina National Bank is a giant in this field. For several years it has given purchase awards to the Piedmont Painting and Sculpture Annual sponsored by the Mint Museum of Art; the University of North Carolina School of Public Health annual art competition at Chapel Hill; the Gallery of Contemporary Art Competition in Winston-Salem; the North Carolina Artists Annual sponsored by the State Art Society; and the Associated Artists of North Carolina Annual. Of late it has widened its interests and is collecting on a global scale. It has placed a $30,000 seascape, "L'Entree du Port de Trouville" by Eugene Boudin on long-term loan with the North Carolina Museum of Art, and for its Charlotte branch has added an 88-foot-long construction by Richard Lippold. The art piece contains eight miles of gold wire supported by silver rods, and is entitled "Homage to North Carolina."

In a recent note to stockholders Addison H. Reese, Chairman of the Board, wrote: "We all share responsibility in the search for man's understanding of his nature. Each individual can contribute, but business with its resources and influence can contribute more. By becoming a patron of the arts, business can make available to all the image of man as reflected by his creative works. For this reason NCNB has taken a strong position of leadership in its commitment to support the arts."

In March of 1970 Mrs. Rebecca Des Mais, coordinator of NCNB's collection, reported it as including more than 150 original paintings, drawings, graphics, watercolors, constructions, and sculptures. In addition to embellishing the walls of the various branches of this bank, the collection is sometimes broken into small exhibitions available to museums, libraries and other institutions. Later in the year, when Robert L. Cheek followed Mrs. Des Mais, who resigned, Ken Clark, vice president and public relations director for the bank, said: "We feel that NCNB has come of age as a collector and patron of the arts, and our program has reached a level of genuine distinction." NCNB has acquired more than 500 works of art—the majority by North Carolina and Southeastern artists. The bank envisions newer ways of serving the public through educational programs, a consultation service on the arts, art conferences, and an anthology of North Carolina artists.

Central Carolina Bank is collecting on a smaller scale and possibly was the first bank in North Carolina to sponsor an art exhibition of significance. In April of 1958, when the Chapel Hill branch was the University National Bank of Chapel Hill, the writer arranged for an exhibition of seventeen North Carolina women painters which hung in the bank for a month and later traveled to Raleigh and other towns. Its popularity drew a caravan of artists from Greensboro one rainy night, and at their request the bank opened up for their viewing. Exhibitors were Mrs. Ruth Clarke, Miss Mackey Jeffries, Greensboro; Mrs. Margaret Click Williams, Raleigh; Mrs. Elizabeth Mack, Charlotte; Mrs. Anne Basile, Mrs. Edith London, Mrs. Ruth Latty, Mrs. Dorothy Rogers, Miss Helen Kendall, Mrs. Eleanor Griswell Reuer, and Miss Jane Bolmier, Durham; Miss Susan Moore and Miss Anne Mercer Kessler, Winston-Salem; Mrs. Jean Fonville, Burlington; Mrs. Frances Calhoun, Mrs. Harry Martin, and Mrs. John Foushee, Chapel Hill.

Through the influence and financial subsidy of George Watts Hill, Sr., a director of Central Carolina Bank, the bank continues to sponsor local exhibitions from which it purchases original art for its various branches. High standards are maintained for the selection of purchases through the jury system and outstanding art galleries. For example, when the Chapel Hill branch moved to its quarters in University Square in July, 1967, a member of the University art staff was asked to invite several local artists to submit works for an exhibition from which the bank would purchase paintings for the new bank. Works purchased from this exhibit were by Anne Wall Thomas, Irene Reichert, Robert Berket, Ione White, George Kachergis, and John Muench. Four cash prizes were awarded to Russell Kordas, Lynn Igoe, Mary Lasley, and Anne Wall Thomas.

Hill leans more toward support of art students and art professors for the major works purchased, although he also favors local exhibitions to seek out unknown artists. In the Durham branch, where Hill has his own office, Herb Jackson of Raleigh, now teaching at Davidson College, is represented by a painting; and sculpture, paintings, and pottery selected through the Garden Gallery are to be found in the "just right" places. Hill commissioned Joe Cox to design the bank's psychedelic ceiling, made up of aluminum strips and colored lights with a potential of over a million combinations of color.

Bankers Trust Company, based in New York City, focused international attention on North Carolina through the distribution of reproductions of paintings by North Carolina's primitive painter, Lem Nolan. In its global campaign of selling the United States as well as its bank, it tells the story of L. N. Nolan who at the age of seventy-eight retired from barbering and "picked up a paint brush and began to paint, purely for personal enjoyment. Soon his charming primitives were 'discovered' by a remarkable art patron: the people of Winston-Salem." The promotional material adds a glowing account of the Winston-Salem Gallery of Fine Arts and of the people of Winston-Salem as patrons of fine art.

Besides banks and large corporations, restaurants and shopping centers have become patrons of the arts. Beverly Wolter, a columnist for the *Winston-Salem Journal*, wrote in 1963: "Restaurants don't dare open without it, motels shout their acquaintance with it, even grocery stores are filled with it . . . 'It' is Art." These avenues have been used by local artists and art groups in North Carolina to exhibit their works for thirty years or more. Some restaurants and motels have incorporated special walls and niches for changing exhibitions. Early in 1960 this became quite a fad. When the Friendly Shopping Center opened in Greensboro, Edward B. Benjamin, art patron who developed the whole Starmount area, commissioned Gregory D. Ivy, head of the Art Department at Woman's College, to select art exhibitions for the specially-designed walls of the Mayflower Restaurant. In Raleigh, at about the same time, Ballentine's commissioned Roy Gussow of the School of Design in Raleigh to provide sculpture for its restaurant, and several restaurants around Charlotte and Blowing Rock featured John Brady's work regularly. The Howard Johnson restaurants and motels, and the Holiday Inns, as well as many private motels and restaurants throughout the state, regularly make their walls available to local artists.

Shopping centers are finding sculptural forms a captivating element in their landscaping. Watts Hill, Sr., was one of the first to incorporate sculpture in this manner when he built the Forest Hills Shopping Center in Durham about 1950 and added a wire construction by Roy Gussow. In a number of instances the sculpture is incorporated as part of a fountain, and is designed by the architects for the centers. Architects Hakan-Best and Associates of Chapel Hill have worked for two years to get just the right piece for the Crabtree Valley Mall near Raleigh, resulting in a thirty-foot high fiberglass tree, the branches of which carry water to hundreds of cupped leaves. From the leaves, which shelter tiny light bulbs, the water drips into a surrounding pool.

The City of Greensboro through its City Parks Department is placing commissioned sculpture in small selected park areas throughout the city. Ogden Deal is well represented by several: "Anthem" installed in 1968 in a traffic triangle; "Strong Song," (a figure 15 feet tall containing over 200 pounds of bronze, 5 sheets of copper, and 600 feet of quarter steel bars, all donated by General Metal, Inc.); "Metaphor," in the Youth Plaza, the concrete foundation for which is composed of a mosaic of hand prints actually printed by the hands of the Greensboro youth who worked on the project; and "Fishing Man," made of Corten Weathering Steel furnished by the Carolina Steel Corporation, and placed in the new Municipal Marina.

William Mangum's sculpture of Prometheus was unveiled in downtown Greensboro during the week that the University of North Carolina at Greensboro commemorated its seventy-fifth anniversary. His "Lamp of Learning" was done in 1968 as part of a series of outdoor art pieces leading up to the 100th Anniversary of the Chamber of Commerce. The Albert Pick Motor Inn and the Chamber of Commerce jointly commissioned his sculpture of Dolly Madison, which is placed at the Motor Inn.

Tarheel business participation in art increased enormously in 1961, due to several areas of promotion. Owen Lewis opened the Brady-Lewis Galleries in Winston-Salem and centered his promotion on business and art in the Piedmont area. "I particularly want to bring art and business together," he said. "I feel that art is important in office and plant decoration, and by buying and using original art Big Business has a wonderful opportunity to come to the aid of the artist." A number of furniture manufacturers have succumbed to this idea and used original art, on consignment, in their displays at the Southern Furniture Market.

That same year, as mentioned elsewhere, Allied Arts in Durham emphasized "Art in Business" throughout the whole year, beginning with a "Mile of Art" on the pasture fences of an old plantation from which young businessmen from Durham and Chapel Hill were invited to select exhibitions entitled "Executives' Choice." Some 500 visitors viewed paintings by top-notch painters from all over the state. The programs that followed at Allied Arts featured panel discussions by leading young executives. Watts Hill, Jr., of Durham, George Pine, Durham architect, Ray Staples, gift shop owner in Chapel Hill, and Edward Loewenstein, Greensboro architect, participated on some of the panel discussions that drew a state-wide audience.

Among the giants of industry collecting art in North Carolina are H. L. Dalton, textile manufacturer; the Hanes Mills in Winston-Salem; and the Dillon Paper Company, which finances the "Art on Paper" annual exhibition at the Weatherspoon Gallery in Greensboro. From the "Art on Paper" collection of over a hundred works, small exhibitions are selected for traveling throughout the South.

More and more architects are encouraging builders to incorporate art as an integral part of their architecture. They have also tried to get legislation toward having the state allocate a percentage of building costs for the inclusion of art in its buildings.

A. G. Odell, Jr., and Associates, a Charlotte architectural firm, has been a leading proponent along this line. Through its influence the Ovens Auditorium in Charlotte commissioned Mrs. Elizabeth Mack, supervisor of art in the Charlotte schools, to paint a harlequin design 15 feet by 34 feet long on the mezzanine ceiling. They also commissioned her to do a mural in Venetian glass tiles for the Geigy Chemical Company—an outside mural lighted at night for the pleasure of passers-by.

On the façade of the McIver Building on the University of North Carolina campus at Greensboro is a 35 x 20 foot mural by Joseph Cox, commissioned by Architect J. N. Pease, designer of the building. (A teacher of Visual Communications, Painting, and Graphics at the School of Design in Raleigh, Cox has murals in Indiana, Michigan, and Tennessee, as well as North Carolina.) The Branch Banking and Trust Company in Raleigh is embellished with an exterior panel of stained glass and anodized aluminum, designed by Cox, and in Lumberton the Southern National Bank is decorated with a Cox sculptural aluminum mural.

In 1960, architect Charles Boney commissioned Roy Gussow to design a sculpture for the Cooperative Savings and Loan Association at Wilmington, North Carolina. Entitled "Flight," this bird-like slash of stainless steel mounted on a black granite base handsomely marks the entrance to this building.

Many buildings in North Carolina are following the international trend of incorporating articulate walls, designed and precast prior to installation. The Greensboro Public Library is an example of the textural quality that may be achieved in this manner. Every outside panel is made up of different size stones embedded into concrete, and the hieroglyphics on the entrance panels were drawn into the wet concrete by Gregory D. Ivy while it was being cast.

Realtors for some time have used original art, usually by local artists, in their "houses on parade." Fred Herndon, who first sponsored the "Parade of Homes" in Durham, North Carolina, used paintings by Anne T. Basile and Betty Bell of Durham and Irene Reichert of Chapel Hill in a featured house. Among realtors collecting art is the John Foushee Realty and Insurance Company of Chapel Hill, which has donated several purchase awards to Associated Artists of North Carolina. The decor of the main office was designed around a large watercolor-collage by the late Walter Thrift. In the collection are works by internationally known Sylvia Carewe of New York City, a portrait by an artist of Florence, Italy; a striking painting by a Burlington high school student signed "Cissy"; sculpture by John Kehoe, formerly of the Art Staff of the University of North Carolina at Greensboro, and paintings and a mural by the writer.

Business Committee for the Arts, Inc.

In 1965 *Esquire Magazine* and the Business Committee for the Arts initiated a noteworthy corporate program of awards to corporations supporting the arts. The Business Committee for the Arts, Inc., is a private, tax-exempt, national organization created to encourage business and industry to assume a greater share of responsibility for the support, growth, and vitality of the arts. Patterned on the Council for Financial Aid to Education, the idea was first proposed by David Rockefeller, president of The Chase Manhattan Bank, in a speech before the National Industrial Conference Board's Fiftieth Anniversary dinner. Businessmen in every part of the country responded enthusiastically and groundwork for the organization developed into its formation on October 15, 1967.

A major premise of the Business Committee for the Arts, as stated by its first chairman, C. Douglas Dillon, is that "The arts are a major and effective weapon in any effort to improve the human condition."

To qualify for an Esquire-B.C.A. award a company must have actively participated in or conducted one or more projects fostering appreciation of the fine or the performing arts. Among North Carolina industries winning the awards have been Hanes Dye and Finishing Company in 1966 and 1968, North Carolina National Bank in 1967, and Burlington Industries for the second time in 1969. R. Philip Hanes, Jr., of Hanes Dye and Finishing Company, served on the 1970 prestigious panel of seventeen judges.

Thus encouraged, corporate support of the arts in North Carolina is increasing steadily. Greensboro firms supporting the Weatherspoon Gallery include the Carolina Steel Corporation, Jefferson Standard Life Insurance Company, North Carolina National Bank, Pilot Life Insurance Company, Burlington Industries, Inc., and Cone Mills, Inc., enabling the Gallery to add to its permanent collection roughly valued at $650,000 and to bring to the campus significant exhibitions.

The list of Corporate Members of the State Art Society has increased to include Harris & Covington Hosiery Mills, Jamestown; Leon L. Rice, Attorney, Winston-Salem; Glen Raven Mills, Inc., Glen Raven; Wood & Sons, Inc., High Point; Sapona Manufacturing Co., Inc., Asheboro; Nello T. Teer Co., Durham; Chatham Foundation, Inc., Elkin; Barrus Construction Co., Kinston; American & Efird Mills, Mount Holly; Broyhill Furniture Industries, Lenoir; and Bahnson Company, Winston-Salem.

In Wilmington, St. John's Gallery lists sixty-eight industries as patrons and members—ranging in scope from a mortuary to a super-market. The Gallery of Contemporary Art in Winston-Salem lists the following as using original art in their offices: The Hanes Corporation, Hanes Dye & Finishing Company, Wachovia Bank & Trust Company, Westinghouse Electric Corporation, and North Carolina National Bank.

As of December, 1970, the Business Committee for the Arts, Inc., listed over a hundred members, representing every state in the Union. Publications by the Committee available to business organizations cover such subjects as "Business a Growing Constituency for the Arts," "The Arts—The Challenge to Business," "Business Committee for the Arts," "Approaching Business for Support of the Arts," "Business and the Arts—A Question of Support," the latter suggesting corporate policy on contributions.

But, with all the support now available to art, Robert O. Anderson, member of the B.C.A. Committee, warns:

"The Arts simply cannot be left to the market place . . . Each community—and the businesses which prosper there—must be concerned for the quality of cultural life available to its citizens and their children."

Addison H. Reese, Chairman of the Board of the North Carolina National Bank, says that "business can become, through its widespread influence, a patron of art and culture . . . this half of the 20th century is clearly the Renaissance for our American society in art and culture . . . the enlightened corporation can make an invaluable contribution to the society from which it derives its income and existence."

Communication Media

The *Star* and the *Raleigh Register and North Carolina Gazette* carried art news as far back as the early nineteenth century, which is natural as most of the art activity of that time was centered in Raleigh. There were long lapses, however, when there was no art news at all, except for items of local interest as other newspapers developed around the state.

Since 1935 until today there have been efforts to get the art news out of the "petticoat" sections of the newspapers. At a meeting of the State Art Society at the Sir Walter in Raleigh on December 6, 1935, the *News and*

Observer reported: "An effort to extend further the sponsorship of art beyond the realm of tea-and-book-club 'society'—to take art news off the society pages of North Carolina newspapers—was endorsed by members of the State Art Society at their business meeting yesterday . . . Even while the members of the society were adopting their resolutions there was, in the adjacent ballroom of the Hotel Sir Walter, a convincing illustration of the truth of their position that interest in art in North Carolina no longer is limited to women's clubs and ancestral organizations." Yet, as late as November 25, 1962, the writer's column "Art in North Carolina," featuring internationally known sculptor Ibram Lassaw, ran in the Woman's Section of a Sunday newspaper near an ad for lingerie.

The year 1958 began to witness a change in the attitude of newspapers, and the writer was able to establish a weekly column, "Art in North Carolina," mentioned above, which ran in a number of Sunday papers, including the *Greensboro Daily News*, the *Durham Morning Herald*, the *Rocky Mount Telegram*, the *Wilmington Star*, and periodically in the *Charlotte Observer*, the *Winston-Salem Journal & Sentinel*, and the *High Point Enterprise*. That same year, when Jane Hall of Raleigh returned from a year's study in Europe on a Reid Fellowship, she resumed her column "Hall Marks" in the *News and Observer*, begun in May of 1955, and began to devote it to art. In a letter to me in September of 1964 she stated that: "at that time 'Hall Marks' was concerned largely with television shows and the theater . . . shortly after my return in 1958, I simply changed the column into an art column." At about the same time, a few newspapers began to employ Art Editors. The first two were Beverly Wolter on the *Winston-Salem Journal*, and Dick Banks on the *Charlotte Observer*, to be followed by Harriet Doar.

Except for W.F.M.Y., T.V., Channel 2, in Greensboro, which for years has sponsored the National Scholastic Art Awards and film-stripped unusual art events, television coverage of the arts has been confined more or less to Educational Television on Channel 4. A typical reaction to efforts to invade this field of communication is contained in W.R.A.L.'s reply to the North Carolina Arts Council's request to introduce a program on entertainment and the arts in the area: "Because of the limited appeal of a program such as you outline, it is my judgment that the station would not be justified in giving a program devoted solely to the subject discussed in your letter. The station will, when occasion arises, make special announcement on its 6:00 P.M. newscast and again on its 11:00 P.M. newscast, where the importance of the entertainment event justifies such recognition." It was further suggested that if the Raleigh Arts Council would solicit sponsors for a 3-minute or 4½-minute program, it might be arranged, "the price for which could be ascertained by calling the Sales Department of the station."

Art Education

The future of art in North Carolina depends greatly upon art education in the public schools. Until this decade school art programs have ranged from extraordinary to bleak, due to inadequate leadership on the state level. Dr. Charles Carroll, Superintendent of Public Instruction, for years sought funds for a state art director. It was 1962 before the Legislature appropriated funds for this purpose, despite Dr. Carroll's support from numerous individuals, organizations, and art teachers.

Dr. Antony Swider became North Carolina's first State Art Director August 13, 1962, but remained only a year because of the traveling involved. He traveled over 15,000 miles that year, conducting workshops attended by over 7,000 teachers. Swider was followed by Perry Kelly who traveled even more and increased the number of workshops. On November 3, 1965, Kelly wrote: "The teachers are most eager to improve the art instruction they offer and to better appreciate art themselves. They continually encourage employment of art specialists whenever possible."

North Carolina colleges and universities have provided excellent training for art specialists since 1909 when Miss Kate Lewis, head of the Department of Art at East Carolina Teachers College at Greenville, N. C., stressed this area of instruction. Then, when Gregory D. Ivy joined the Art Department of Woman's College, Greensboro, in 1934, that college developed an Art Education program that produced some of the most dynamic art teachers and supervisors in the United States. Among them were the late Callie Braswell, Mary Mason, and Mary Leath Thomas Howard. Others are Elizabeth Mack, Director of Art in the Charlotte

220

and Mecklenburg schools; Elsie Smith, Director of Art in the Durham City Schools; Margaret Click Williams, St. Mary's in Raleigh; and Mary Burgess, Director of Art in the Durham County schools. The 1970 Directory of North Carolina Art Personnel lists the following supervisors in addition to the above: Gabriel McNair, Highlands; Michael Davis, Asheville; Antony Swider, Winston-Salem/Forsyth County; Frances Crimm, and Clarence Phillips, Greensboro; Gwendolyn Doggett, High Point; Laura Boice, Rocky Mount; and Rose Melvin, Raleigh.

Although elementary teachers carry the major burden of art instruction in the schools, often their programs are implemented by scholarships, exhibitions, and competitions sponsored by organizations such as the North Carolina Federation of Women's Clubs, Altrusa, the North Carolina Symphony, the American Association of University Women, the Junior League, the North Carolina Museum of Art, Associated Artists of North Carolina, the Durham Art Guild, and the Chapel Hill-Carrboro School Art Guild.

Despite the absence of a state art director in the past, the State Department of Public Instruction made every effort possible to stimulate creativity through art appreciation contests, and in 1942 it issued a manual for classroom teachers entitled *Art in the Public Schools, Years 1–12*. By 1937 Woman's College at Greensboro and the University at Chapel Hill were sponsoring traveling school art exhibitions, in cooperation with the State Federation of Women's Clubs and the A. A. U. W. Many of these were shown at the State Art Gallery, from which Mrs. Isabel Bowen Henderson began a collection of children's work.

In 1944 the junior and senior high schools were put under the sponsorship of *Scholastic Magazine*, with Morrison-Neese Furniture Company, Greensboro, co-sponsor for North Carolina. This enabled the high school division to compete in the National High School Art exhibition held annually at the Fine Arts Galleries of Carnegie Institute, under the auspices of *Scholastic Magazine*—the American high school weekly. Gregory Ivy and Elizabeth Hammerick Mack were co-chairmen of the Regional Advisory Committee for Morrison-Neese. Governor J. Melville Broughton headed the honorary advisory committee, and Miss Julia Wetherington headed the active members committee.

The *Winston-Salem Journal and Sentinel*, in cooperation with the Winston-Salem Arts Council, sponsored the Scholastic Awards in 1955.

In 1956 *Scholastic Magazine* proposed that WFMY-TV, Greensboro, become regional sponsor for the Piedmont area. Manager Gaines Kelly accepted and appointed Miss Jeta Pace coordinator of the project. Increased interest soon necessitated limitation of works submitted. As the program has grown, North Carolina National Bank and the *Charlotte Observer* have become joint sponsors for the Mecklenburg County area, and Belk's in Asheville sponsors that area. Belk's and the Junior Chamber of Commerce in Raleigh sponsor eastern North Carolina. WFMY-TV accepts thousands of entries annually, and uses every television medium possible to bring recognition, incentive, and inspiration to teenagers in the public schools.

Many events and developments indicate a bright future in art education for the school children of North Carolina. The North Carolina Museum of Art continually expands its programs for school children; the art teachers themselves organized in 1964 as the North Carolina Art Education Association; and in 1970 the State Department of Public Instruction inaugurated the Division of Cultural Arts. James R. Hall heads this newly created division which brings together Music, Art, Drama, and Dance. Walter Hathaway heads the visual arts. The North Carolina Arts Council has initiated, and is financing, art study tours for art personnel in the North Carolina public schools, introducing them to the great museums from Washington, D. C. to New York City. Truly the seeds for a great harvest in art are being sown.

INDEX

223